ACCOUNTABLE

The TRUE STORY
of a RACIST SOCIAL
MEDIA ACCOUNT
and the TEENAGERS
WHOSE LIVES
IT CHANGED

PRAISE FOR **THE 57 BUS**

A *New York Times* Bestseller • Stonewall Book Award—Mike Morgan & Larry Romans Children's & Young Adult Literature Award Winner • YALSA Award for Excellence in Nonfiction for Young Adults Finalist • A *Boston Globe–Horn Book* Nonfiction Honor Book Winner

"A sensitive study of an incident wrapped up in so many modern conundrums."—*The Financial Times*

★ "The text shifts from straightforward reporting to lyrical meditations, never veering into oversentimentality or simple platitudes. Readers are bound to come away with deep empathy for both Sasha and Richard. VERDICT Slater artfully unfolds a complex and layered tale about two teens whose lives intersect with painful consequences. This work will spark discussions about identity, community, and what it means to achieve justice."
—*School Library Journal*, **starred review**

★ "With a journalist's eye for overlooked details, Slater does a masterful job debunking the myths of the hate-crime monster and the African-American thug, probing the line between adolescent stupidity and irredeemable depravity. Few readers will traverse this exploration of gender identity, adolescent crime, and penal racism without having a few assumptions challenged. An outstanding book that links the diversity of creed and the impact of impulsive actions to themes of tolerance and forgiveness."
—*Kirkus Reviews*, **starred review**

★ "Using details gleaned from interviews, social media, surveillance video, public records, and other sources, Slater skillfully conveys the complexities of both young people's lives and the courage and compassion of their families, friends, and advocates, while exploring the challenges and moral ambiguities of the criminal justice system. This painful story illuminates, cautions, and inspires."
—*Publishers Weekly*, **starred review**

"It is likely that this account will spark conversations, debates, and contemplation, perhaps leading readers to define for themselves what justice means."—*VOYA*

★ "[A] multi-layered lesson on the healing power of humanity."—*Shelf Awareness*, **starred review**

". . . a powerful story of class and race (Sasha is white), gender and identity, justice and mercy, love and hate. Slater has crafted a compelling true-crime story with ramifications for our most vulnerable youth."—*The Horn Book*

"This book challenged my views and it started a conversation in my house that I thought I'd never have. We all changed, at least in my house, because of this book."
—Kate Terbush, *The LA Times*

"Slater approaches both students' perspectives with nuance and complexity, and while there are no easy answers in this narrative, her compassionate writing shows that there's often more to the story than we see."
—Cady Lang, *TIME* magazine,
selected as one of the Best YA Books of All Time

ACCOUNTABLE

DASHKA SLATER

FARRAR STRAUS GIROUX
NEW YORK

Farrar Straus Giroux Books for Young Readers
An imprint of Macmillan Publishing Group, LLC
120 Broadway, New York, NY 10271 • fiercereads.com

Our books may be purchased in bulk for promotional, educational, or business use. Please contact your local bookseller or the Macmillan Corporate and Premium Sales Department at (800) 221-7945 ext. 5442 or by email at MacmillanSpecialMarkets@macmillan.com.

Library of Congress Cataloging-in-Publication Data
Names: Slater, Dashka, author.
Title: Accountable : the true story of a racist social media account and the teenagers whose lives it changed / Dashka Slater.
Description: First edition. | New York, NY : Farrar Straus Giroux Books for Young Readers, 2023. | Includes bibliographical references. | Audience: Ages 12 and up | Audience: Grades 10–12 | Summary: "A young adult nonfiction book on how Albany High School handles a racist social media incident that incurs lasting and devastating consequences"—Provided by publisher.
Identifiers: LCCN 2022043063 | ISBN 9780374314347 (hardcover)
Subjects: LCSH: Racism in education—California—Juvenile literature. | Educational accountability—California—Juvenile literature. | Social media—Influence—California—Juvenile literature. | Albany High School (Albany, Calif.)—Juvenile literature. | African American students—Social conditions—California—Juvenile literature. | Minority high school students—Social conditions—California—Juvenile literature. | Discrimination in education—California—Juvenile literature.
Classification: LCC LC212.422.C2 S53 2023 | DDC 371.829/009794—dc23/eng/20221011
LC record available at https://lccn.loc.gov/2022043063

First edition, 2023
Book design by Elizabeth H. Clark and Michelle Gengaro-Kokmen
Printed in the United States of America

ISBN 978-0-374-31434-7

5 7 9 10 8 6

To Denny, Felicity, Simon, Gordon,
Milo, Giuseppe, and Dexter

Being called all manner of things
from the Dictionary of Shame—
not English, not words, not heard,
but worn, borne, carried, never spent—
we feel now a largeness coming on,
something passing into us...

—TRACY K. SMITH

How do we hold people accountable for
wrongdoing and yet at the same time remain
in touch with their humanity enough to
believe in their capacity to be transformed?

—BELL HOOKS

ACCOUNTABLE

The TRUE STORY of a RACIST SOCIAL MEDIA ACCOUNT and the TEENAGERS WHOSE LIVES IT CHANGED

AUTHOR'S NOTE AND CONTENT WARNING

I was at a March 2017 Northern California booksellers event, signing advance copies of my first nonfiction narrative, *The 57 Bus*, when someone asked me if I had heard about the racist social media account that had just been discovered at Albany High School. That question ended up launching the four-year reporting journey that produced this book.

At the time, I had no plans to write another book about teenagers and hate. Far from it. Researching and writing my last book had been harrowing. I was hoping to find a sunnier topic for my next one. But what had happened in Albany wasn't an isolated occurrence. When I looked into it, I saw that there had been a dramatic uptick in bias-related incidents since 2016, particularly at schools. A report by the Southern Poverty Law Center documented 3,265 such incidents at K–12 schools nationwide in the fall of 2018 alone.

My three decades as a criminal justice reporter and my five years in the restorative justice community have persuaded me that, as a society, we can't prevent what we don't understand. True justice requires *listening*, with curiosity and compassion, to the human stories behind the headlines. Only then can we begin to repair what's gone wrong and reach for what's right.

This is a true story, about real people. While reporting it, I generated hundreds of hours of interviews, read thousands of pages of legal documents, and investigated every aspect of a story that had dozens of participants and just as many perspectives. The people who agreed to be interviewed did so in the hope that something good would come out of something terrible. They have given you their story in the hope that you will treat it with care. (Not everyone involved with these events wanted their stories told, of course, and I abided by the wishes of those who didn't.)

Most of the people in this book were teenagers when the events occurred. For that reason, both they and their parents are identified by pseudonyms and some identifying details have been omitted or changed. All other adults are identified by their real names. The story was reconstructed from a variety of sources, including interviews with the participants, public records, police reports, emails, texts, direct messages, videos, photographs, diaries, and social media posts, as well as my own firsthand observations. To report key events while including as many perspectives as possible, I relied upon court records, proceedings, and decisions. Quotes from all sources are verbatim except where the names or other identifying details have been replaced or in a few instances where a clarifying word or phrase has been added at the speaker's request. More information about sourcing is at the back of this book.

Content Warning: This book contains descriptions of racist, sexist, antisemitic, and ableist memes, images, language, and incidents, as well as references to suicide and disordered eating.

If you or someone you know are having thoughts of suicide or self-harm, please call or text 988 to reach the National Suicide Prevention Lifeline. You can also dial 1-800-273-TALK (8255) or text HOME to 741741.

CONTENTS

PROLOGUE

LOOKING BACK, IT'S HARD NOT TO WONDER HOW THE WHOLE THING could have been prevented. All the sorrow, all the fear, all the rage. All the lives derailed, all the milestones missed, all the plans upended. The hearings. The lawsuits. The brokenness that settled over everyone involved. The undefinable and uncountable losses: the friendships wrecked, the optimism withered, the joy stolen. Somebody could have spoken up before it went that far, before the entire town was shattered. But who?

The people closest to it were caught up in the group's centripetal force, the whirl of jokes and banter that kept them all together. To speak up would have meant risking being thrown out of orbit. At the time, that was the worst thing any of them could imagine. Being mocked by the group. Being exiled. Being alone.

But just because it *felt* impossible to say something doesn't mean it was. Any of the top dogs in the group could have done it, or even someone on the periphery who couldn't have been shamed into shutting up. It wouldn't have required any long speeches or dramatic pronouncements. Just one phrase would have done the trick:

Dude, this is really fucked up.

PART 1

BEFORE

FRIEND GROUPS

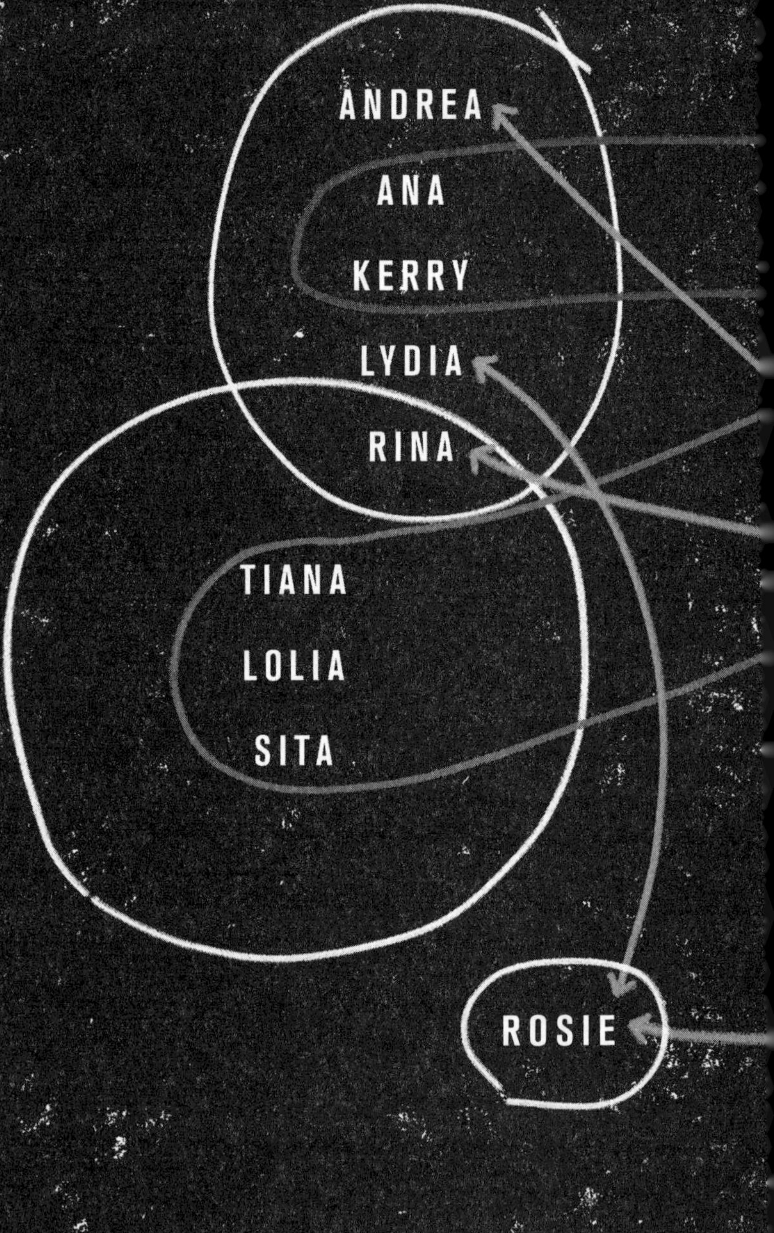

ANDREA

ANA

KERRY

LYDIA

RINA

TIANA

LOLIA

SITA

ROSIE

CHARLES

MURPHY

PATRICK

STEVEN

JON

GREG

OTIS

WYATT

EREN

GABRIEL

LUCY

BILLIE

SMALLBANY

PEOPLE IN TOWN CALLED IT SMALLBANY. IT WAS JUST UNDER TWO square miles, bordered by the city of Berkeley to the south and east, by the gray-blue waters of the Bay on the west, and by the town of El Cerrito on the north. In 2017, Albany had just under twenty thousand residents, residents who counted themselves lucky to live in a place that seemed to offer the sophistication of the metropolitan Bay Area combined with the intimacy of a small town.

Of course it was exclusive, when you considered the cost of housing, but it wasn't one of those fancy suburbs with gated subdivisions and sprawling McMansions. Albany felt like a funky little backwater. The town had two main thoroughfares: Solano Avenue, a pedestrian boulevard peppered with small boutiques and restaurants, and San Pablo Avenue, a charmless state highway lined with car dealerships and insurance offices and dive bars. The homes were mostly stucco bungalows and wood-shingled houses, and in 2017, the first year of Donald Trump's presidency, many were beginning to plant IN THIS HOUSE WE BELIEVE signs in their yards to signify that they were part of what was then being called "The Resistance" and thought that BLACK LIVES MATTER, WOMEN'S RIGHTS ARE HUMAN RIGHTS, and KINDNESS IS EVERYTHING. The town had a horse racing track, and a bowling alley, and a

310-foot hill that humped abruptly from the flatlands like the back of a dinosaur. It had a tiny bayfront beach and an odd thirty-three-acre open space called the Albany Bulb, a former dump for construction debris that had functioned at various times as a homeless encampment, a makeshift museum for graffiti art and scrap-metal sculptures, a marshland habitat, and a dog-walking trail.

Almost half the residents were white and more than a quarter were Asian. Thirteen percent were Latinx. You could call it "diverse," and probably did if you were white, but it didn't feel diverse to its Black residents, who made up just over 4 percent of the population and whose numbers were shrinking all the time. It wasn't that diverse economically either—regardless of race, most of the residents were professionals with college degrees. Still, there was something comforting about living in a like-minded community at a time when so much of America seemed to be embracing bigotry and prejudice. And even if you didn't love Albany, even if you missed being in a bigger or busier pond, you would stay until your children graduated from high school. Because the schools were Albany's crown jewel.

Three elementary schools. One middle school. One high school.

Forty-one percent of the town's 7,661 household units contained at least one kid, a kid whose parents had shoehorned themselves into whatever dwelling they could afford so that their child could snag a seat at one of the district's desks. Small schools, where your kid wouldn't get lost. Challenging schools, where your kid would get the best education.

If you were one of Albany's 1,129 high school students,

you knew you were lucky to be there. In 2017, your role was spelled out in a page-length poem in the high school yearbook that offered a breathless torrent of instructions for incoming students:

Work hard.

Make your parents proud.

Families rent Albany homes just so their kids can go to school here.

The prize at the end: college. And not just any college. A *good* college.

"Subconsciously your self-worth is partly defined by where you go to college," one white girl remembers. "Everyone was competitive and wanted to stand out. Our whole grade was fierce with college and academics."

If you were Black, the pressure was even more intense. While the percentage of white and Black students nationwide who got their education from community colleges is about equal, Black students were about one third less likely to graduate from a public four-year university, a discrepancy fed by differences in both income and access.

"I always told myself, I can't leave here going to a community college. Albany is the top—everyone leaving here is going to a four-year. I need to be going to a four-year just like everybody else," a Black girl recalls. "I had that in my head: I can't be one of those Black girls who doesn't graduate, doesn't go straight to a four-year. I need to get my SAT scores high, my ACT scores high. I always felt like I was competing against everybody else."

SLEEPOVERS

CHARLES WAS A KID WHO FLOATED, DRIFTING FROM ROOM TO ROOM like a half-filled balloon, neither soaring nor sinking. He was hard to pigeonhole because he was so often contradictory. At seventeen he was still more boy than man, tall but not yet filled out, good-looking but not yet handsome. He was smart enough to take advanced classes like AP Computer Science and AP Physics but not motivated enough to get better than Bs and Cs. Intensely social but also kind of shy. Obnoxious but also sweet. Naturally athletic but more interested in playing League of Legends than in playing basketball.

His core friends were a tight-knit group of a half dozen or so boys, most of whom he'd been close to since middle school or even earlier. They were the class clowns and the envelope pushers, the ones who said stuff at school that made people laugh but was also out of pocket. The ones who couldn't stop talking in class, far more focused on cracking each other up than they were on whatever they were supposed to be learning. Most of his friends would rather play video games than go to a party, but Charles sometimes went to parties too.

In middle school he'd dated a mixed South and East Asian girl named Sita, a relationship that mainly consisted of sending each other texts and Facebook messages and occasionally going to the movies together. In a Facebook post, she listed the reasons that she liked him: He was cute, nice, smart, funny, and Korean. (Both of Charles's parents were born in Korea; his mom had moved to the U.S. as an adult, while his dad came as a baby.) By high school, the two were just friends, but they still hung out a lot, and Charles had gotten close with Sita's friend group, particularly two Black girls named Lolia and Tiana, who were also tight with Charles's friend Murphy, who was biracial: Mexican and white. On weekends, they often slept over at Charles's house.

The house was the perfect party spot because Charles's mother and stepfather made themselves scarce, although they did try to enforce a no-drinking rule, without much success. The kids could close the sliding doors that separated the living room from the rest of the house and play Beer Pong and Truth or Dare, screaming with laughter at the stupid things they could make each other do: chug a mixture of everybody's leftover drinks, snort ground-up Sour Patch candy, swallow shots of ketchup straight from the bottle. There was a firepit in the backyard, at the top of a steep hillside, and sometimes they'd hang out there, drinking raspberry-flavored Smirnoff.

When Charles was drunk, his friends occasionally glimpsed signs that things weren't okay with him. Sometimes he'd sit and talk earnestly with one of the girls, his eyes filling with tears as he confessed how angry he felt most of the time. Other times he was reckless and goofy, filled with frenetic energy, as if daring himself to cross some invisible line.

Once, when the fire in the backyard pit was at full blaze, Charles decided to jump over it. Somehow, he managed to sail over the flames and land on the other side unscarred. But it just as easily could have gone the other way.

FREEFALL

"MY MOM WOULD SAY IT MADE ME BITTER," ANDREA SAYS ABOUT growing up in Albany. "And she's not necessarily wrong." She remembers feeling out of place as far back as the third grade, and that feeling intensified when she went to high school. She was biracial, with a Black father and a white mother, and she wasn't the kind of girl that Albany boys seemed to like. Those girls wore Lululemon leggings, tossed their long, straight hair over their shoulders, laughed when boys teased them or put them down. Those girls were smart enough to get into a good college, but not so smart they made people uncomfortable.

If Andrea didn't fit the mold, it wasn't for lack of trying. She even bought a pair of Lululemon leggings, explaining to anyone who asked why they were worth the money. But she was never going to be one of those girls. It wasn't just her curly hair and light brown skin, her low voice. It was something in the way she held herself, like a train carrying a dangerous cargo.

Still, she seemed to have it all together. When asked to describe her, her friends used words like *strong*, *sarcastic*, *funny*, *straightforward*. She was competitive on the soccer team, probably a little more aggressive than was called for at times, but it felt good to send another girl tumbling to the ground. Yet when her coaches barked instructions, pushing her to be faster or better, she would vanish inward, closing the door behind her. Because no matter how strong and self-sufficient she looked, she wasn't actually okay. She was falling, had been falling since the summer before high school, and what she looked forward to most of all each day was the moment she got home from school.

That was when she could change out of her clothes and into a bathrobe. Make herself an elaborate snack. Climb up to the loft bed in her room with her laptop and stay there, her face close to the wall, the ceiling inches above her, a fox huddled in her den. That was when she could watch Netflix for eight hours straight, sinking into whatever storyline presented itself: *Lost*, *Orange Is the New Black*, *Vampire Diaries*, *Friends*, *Grey's Anatomy*, *New Girl*, *The Hundred*. The particulars of the show didn't matter, as long as it was someone else's life, someone else's drama, someone else completely.

HOME/LIFE

CHARLES WAS AROUND TEN WHEN HE NOTICED THAT HIS PARENTS weren't getting along. There were frequent arguments, loud ones. His dad had lost his job in the 2008 recession and now he spiraled into a deep depression; eventually, he was diagnosed with bipolar disorder. He became verbally abusive, mostly toward Charles's older sister, Eliza. At some point his parents began sleeping in separate rooms. They were barely speaking to each other, relying on Eliza as an intermediary.

Eliza was five years older than Charles and she did what she could to keep her brother from seeing how bad things had gotten, caring for him as if she were his parent, ushering him out of the house to get a treat on Solano Avenue whenever things got too intense. Their mother was working full-time as a nurse now, trying to support the family. His parents sold their house and moved the family into a smaller rental. But nothing between them got better—if anything, things got worse.

As Charles remembers it, his mother finally sat him down and asked him a question. Did he want his parents to be together or did he want them to be happy? That's when he understood that they were getting divorced.

One Wednesday afternoon when Charles was twelve, he walked out of school to find his mom waiting for him. A judge had just awarded her full custody. That day she and Charles would be moving in with Alexander, an old family friend who was also recently divorced.

Charles had grown up going to Alexander's house. On the walk over, his father would carry him on his shoulders and then the kids would play video games in the living room while the adults played poker in the dining room. On the walk home, Charles would drift into sleep on his father's back. But now Alexander was his mother's boyfriend and the house that Charles used to visit was going to be his home.

Charles was furious. He sobbed in the car, talking to his father on his mother's cell phone, telling him he wanted to see him, demanding to know what was going on. From then on he refused to speak to Alexander beyond the most basic interactions.

Over the next few years, Alexander, who was white, tried to reach out to him in different ways. Observing that his stepson seemed depressed, he sent him emails brimming with spiritual advice and information on far-ranging topics like the creation of the universe and near-death experiences.

"Depression is one bad habit you cannot afford," he wrote in one such email. "To get out of it, you must fight every negative thought or feeling with something positive. You may have every reason to be depressed but accepting those reasons will only deepen your depression. Do not give in to the dark side . . . Choose not to be depressed!"

Meanwhile, Charles and his mother argued constantly. She was frustrated with his passivity, his lack of drive. Both of his parents tended to compare him to Eliza, who had been a model student, a star athlete, and a winner of accolades of every kind. Charles's mother had been similar—she'd emigrated from Korea to Japan, taught herself Japanese, gotten a degree in fashion and made a career for herself in the fashion industry, moved to the United States, taught herself English, and eventually gone back to school to become a nurse so that she could support the family after her husband lost his job.

Video games came to symbolize all that Charles wasn't achieving. His mother hated seeing him sitting in a dark room staring at a screen—she was sure it kept him isolated and depressed. Since Alexander was a software engineer, she enlisted his help in blocking Charles's access to the Internet. An elaborate game of cat and mouse unfolded as Charles figured out how to evade each method, whether it was by breaking into a locked closet to get the router password or figuring out how to disguise the MAC identifier for his computer. That part was fun, like solving a puzzle. But the arguments weren't. Charles took them harder than he let on. Every few weeks he'd call Eliza at college, crying because of an argument with their mom. But aside from listening to him vent, she couldn't get much information about what was going on.

"He didn't really open up about a lot of things," she recalls. "He wasn't the type of person who could just talk on the phone." Charles's friends also tried to get him to confide in them, without much luck.

"He was so emotionally closed off," one recalls. "I could ask him pretty often, kind of like trying to prod him to open up, but he would just kind of brush it off, like 'Oh yeah, everything's fine. I'm good.'"

But he wasn't good. He wasn't good at all.

HAIR STORY (1)

ANDREA STOOD IN HER BEST FRIEND LYDIA'S TINY BATHROOM HOLDING a pair of scissors she'd found in a drawer. It was August 2016, the summer before junior year.

"Are you sure you want to do this?" asked Lydia, who was also biracial—white and Asian. "Your hair is going to be *really* short."

It was always like this with the two of them. Lydia was more logical, Andrea more emotionally explosive.

Andrea examined her reflection in the mirror. The line of demarcation was so clear. Healthy, curly natural hair close to her scalp, giving way to damaged, straightened hair below her ears.

She started cutting from the bottom.

Snip.

Cutting off the shame she'd felt in elementary school when another girl told her, "Your hair's so frizzy!"

Snip.

Cutting off the decision to start straightening it in third grade.

Snip.

Cutting off those mornings in middle school when she'd woken up at 4 A.M. to get her hair ready for school.

Snip.

Wash it, blow it dry, flat-iron it in sections. So much hair to go through.

Snip.

Going back over the places she'd missed, making sure it was all stick straight.

Snip.

Opening the bathroom door when she was finished. The cloud of burnt-hair fumes setting off the smoke alarm.

Snip.

The compliments she used to get when she walked into school. "Your hair looks so nice!" Thinking it was worth the four hours it had taken to get there.

Lydia sat on the bathroom floor, watching Andrea as she cut. Periodically she stood up to get a better look. "Oh my god! *Girl!*" she said, half squealing, before sitting back down again. "You're cutting so *much*!"

Snip.

All the definitions of what being pretty was. What being girly was.

Snip.

The Coraline bob she'd had in sixth grade.

Snip.

The long hair she'd had in eighth grade.

Snip.

That day at the end of middle school, gathering with the popular kids. A boy named Greg playing an anime video on his phone.

Snip.

How grown-up she'd felt, hanging out with a mix of boys and girls. How nervous.

Snip.

Leaning forward to see the screen and hearing Greg say, "Get your nappy hair out of my face."

Snip.

That blank moment when she couldn't even remember where she was.

Snip.

Saying nothing. Not wanting to be the Angry Black Girl. Not wanting to be an outcast.

Snip.

Her exhausted hair, breaking apart in her fingers.

Snip.

The decision to stop straightening it after middle-school graduation.

Snip.

Two years of growing it out.

Snip.

The damage falling away now as her scissors sliced.

Snip.

Her hair, springing back to its own shape.

Then she was done. Her hair lay scattered on the bathroom floor. She stared at her reflection in the mirror.

This is me being healthy, she thought. *This is me looking how I want to look.*

SOME THINGS THAT HAPPEN WHEN YOU'RE BLACK IN A MOSTLY WHITE SCHOOL

1. Class discussion of slavery. Everyone looks over at you. Teacher asks you—the only Black kid in the class—if you have any thoughts.
2. Class assignment: Dress up like someone from history. Assignments are supposed to be random. You get Harriet Tubman. Maybe it's a coincidence. But you doubt it.
3. Your favorite teacher asks you to tell the class what your hair does when you go underwater and when you tell him the question makes you feel uncomfortable, he apologizes and then changes the subject by saying to the class, "Did you know that Black people don't get lice?" which isn't even true.
4. Your English class is reading a Maya Angelou poem aloud. Suddenly everyone's eyes are on you. You're thinking, *Why are you looking at me? I don't know anything about Maya Angelou. I didn't even do the homework.*
5. Teacher asks you if everything's okay at home. It is. So why is she asking?
6. You're watching *Pitch Perfect* in your eighth-grade class and someone comments that you're like Cynthia-Rose Adams, the only Black character, and everyone laughs.

You feel like you have no choice but to laugh along, even though the only thing you and Cynthia-Rose have in common is that you're both Black.

7. You're a pretty and popular Black girl, but at the school dance no guys will dance with you or your Black friends.
8. You complain about the fact that your World History class only spends a week covering the African continent. As a solution, your teacher suggests that you, the only Black kid, develop a lesson about Africa and teach it to the class.
9. When you mention that you're in an AP class or did well on a test, people say things like, "I didn't know you were smart."
10. People keep joking that you're an Oreo, or a burnt cracker, or a black-and-white cow, or some other two-toned thing because somehow your way of being Black doesn't fit their definition.

GRILLED CHEESE

(March 11, 2017)

THAT SATURDAY WAS ONLY MEMORABLE IN RETROSPECT. CHARLES, Ana, and Kerry had gathered at Kerry's house, the way they'd been doing since eighth grade. The Three Musketeers, Kerry had called them once. It was hard to say what made the three of them click, but they did. They'd been inseparable through freshman year of high school, but then, when they were in tenth grade, Ana moved to Ireland, where her mother was from.

When you coming back ho? Charles texted that fall.

Awhhhh Charles misses me 😊🖤, Ana texted back.

Bitch answer the question or I will nuke ireland

awhhhh 😂 Ana wrote. *End of July or June*

Goddamnit that's too late, Charles replied. *Come back sooner*

But by the time Ana returned, it wasn't exactly like it had been. It was junior year and they each had other friends they spent more time with. But even if they weren't the Three Musketeers anymore, they still had a special kind of ease together—like family.

Of all his friends, Ana was the one Charles felt he could talk to the most freely—even about the stuff he mostly kept to himself, like the video game battles with his mother and Alexander.

"She was very, very empathetic," he recalls. "If there was ever any type of issue, problem, it was really easy to talk to her about it because she didn't judge at all."

Standing just five-three, Ana had a childlike quality to her, with her soft voice and large eyes, her cloud of black curls. She was biracial, Black on her father's side and white on her mother's. Despite her small stature, she was a beast on the varsity soccer team, where she played forward. That Saturday in March, she was in shorts and a tie-dyed T-shirt, her hair pulled back to reveal her big hoop earrings.

Kerry had a round face, long black hair, and owlish glasses. Unlike Ana, she didn't party much. Her parents were immigrants from Thailand and she often had to work at the family's restaurant after school, waiting tables, packing to-go boxes, answering the phone. She had a tendency to act dumb, even though she wasn't, and she was such a good sport that her friends teased her constantly, particularly about her refusal to say anything bad about anyone. Still, she had a sharp sense of humor. Charles loved hanging out at her house, watching corny movies like *Frozen* and *The Notebook* just so they could make fun of them.

That Saturday was the last time things would ever be normal between them, but of course they didn't know that then. They made grilled cheese sandwiches. They FaceTimed with a friend and talked about prom, because a few of their friends were going together. They listened to an Ed Sheeran song, "Galway Girl," that Ana particularly loved. They danced. They took some photos: Ana and Charles resting their heads on one of Kerry's shoulders. Charles and Kerry flashing two fingers as they cuddled on the couch. Charles and Ana holding up a Trader Joe's chocolate bar. Probably there were in-jokes attached to every photo, because in those days they had tons of them, but nobody remembers them now. Actually, Ana remembers some of them, but she doesn't like to say, because in retrospect maybe she shouldn't have put up with certain things.

The race jokes, for example. Charles was always making them. Jokes about fried chicken or Ana being a slave. At the time it didn't seem that big a deal to her—he might even have asked her permission before he said the N-word in front of her the first time. She'd lob Asian slurs back to him and they'd go back and forth that way.

"I didn't care," she says. "At the time, I didn't really make any big deal because it was just, I don't know, it was just him being stupid as fuck."

It was a struggle, sometimes, to figure out how to behave around race in Albany. People would ask her things like "If you're Black, why is your mom white?" and she'd find herself tongue-tied, unable to answer.

"I would be confused," she remembers. "Because I don't *know*. I don't know either. It's really hard trying to find a place to be. I'm white but I'm also Black. I'm *not* white."

She suspected that for white kids, she was an acceptable level of Black—midrange on the school's Black-o-meter. "I feel like it might be different if I was dark-skinned or something, like a lot of people at my school might see me a little bit differently maybe," she says. "There's a certain limit for white people at Albany, at least white students—I feel like there's only so much Blackness they can take. But for the Black people, sometimes I felt like they thought, *Oh, she's hella white-washed*. I don't know. I'm trying to just *be*."

And so she'd let a lot of stuff go by. Stuff that when she thought about it later, maybe she shouldn't have. Charles was her friend; she was confident he didn't mean anything by the things he said.

"I didn't think—" she says, and breaks off. "I thought it was something he would say just to me."

HIERARCHIES

ANDREA WASN'T REALLY FRIENDS WITH CHARLES, BUT SHE WAS friends with Ana and Kerry, so she was kind of in his orbit. She had another friend who was in Charles's circle: Wyatt. Andrea and Wyatt had dated for six months in middle school, and then the summer before junior year they had both taken classes at Berkeley City College and ended up hanging out together. Her friends said it was obvious he was attracted to her, but she didn't really know whether to believe them.

Wyatt, who was white, was sweet but awkward. His guy friends seemed to pick on him, egging him on to do stupid things just because he was that kind of person, the kid in elementary school who'd make milk come out of his nose just to get a laugh. But it was hard to tell sometimes whether his friends were laughing *with* him or *at* him. Andrea suspected the latter. There was a definite hierarchy to his group of friends, all of whom were either white or Asian. At the top were the boys with the big mouths: Charles, his longtime friends Murphy and Patrick, and a boy named Greg, who was a basketball player and one of the more popular kids at school. Somewhere in the middle were quieter kids like Steven and Otis. Wyatt was at the bottom of the pile along with Jon, a pale, nervous white boy who always wore the exact same outfit: a blue sweater from Costco and a pair of sweatpants. They were the punching bags.

The Taco Bell four blocks from campus was their favorite lunch spot. They'd each buy a Baja Blast Freeze and on the walk back to campus, they'd try to catch each other by surprise by dumping the icy remnants over someone's head. Charles and Murphy remember it as a game. Jon remembers it as a "means of terrorizing people." That's because he and Wyatt were the ones most likely to arrive back at school soaking wet.

"They were kind of the butt of the joke almost every time," Murphy remembers. "And when people would make the butt of the joke be me or Greg or Charles, we'd instantly flip it around back on them to be like, 'Ha, gotcha. You can't really get us. We're alpha males. You guys are beta. You're not good enough.'"

If you'd asked any of them at the time, they would have said it was just normal guy stuff. They were friends; a little teasing wasn't anything to make a big deal about. But Andrea hated seeing how they treated Wyatt, how they seemed to pounce on every one of his insecurities, clowning him about his curly hair and his bad haircuts. One day she got tired of it and told them to shut the fuck up.

As she and Wyatt walked away, one of them, she can't remember who, said to her, "That's why your hair's like broccoli."

The insult was so weak, she was more amused than offended.

You guys need to get better at being racist, she thought, and kept walking.

GET OUT

(March 18, 2017)

MURPHY HAD SPENT THE AFTERNOON WITH LOLIA AND SITA ON Saturday, March 18. They'd gone to see *Get Out*, the comedy-horror film about a Black guy who discovers the racist secret being kept by his white girlfriend's family, and they'd made jokes about race all evening. Murphy had nudged Lolia when they drove by a police car, making a crack about how the cop would arrest her. Lolia had leaned over in the middle of the movie and whispered, "I bet you love this," implying that Murphy was enjoying the racism depicted in the film.

That kind of humor felt okay because they trusted each other. Murphy was one of Sita's and Lolia's closest friends. Baby-faced and rosy-cheeked, with thick, sandy-brown hair that he had a habit of running his hands through while talking, he could be both intolerably obnoxious and disarmingly sweet. He was a button pusher, the kind of kid who thought it was funny to yell an anti–Hillary Clinton slogan out the window of the car when driving through liberal Berkeley or to set off M-80s behind the Albany pool. But he was also the friend who listened when you told him about your problems and checked in on you later to see how you were doing. When Sita messaged him on Thanksgiving asking if he had any pumpkin pie, Murphy came by in minutes with two giant slices slathered in whipped cream.

After the movie, the three of them went over to Sita's house and hung out in her room, talking about the sleepover they were planning to have at Charles's the next weekend. The way Murphy tells it, he and Sita had traded phones and were lying on the bed scrolling through each other's Instagram feeds when she stopped on one of the posts and asked him what it was. According to a document that was later filed in court, Sita and Lolia told a school official that Murphy showed them the account on his own, after telling them that Charles and his friends felt that the Black girls in their circle were inferior because their hair was too nappy and their skin was too dark.

However it happened, Lolia and Sita ended up with Murphy's phone in their hands, scrolling through a private Instagram account that Charles had made. Murphy says that his decision to show them was born out of the closeness he had felt with both girls all day, his feeling that there shouldn't be secrets among them. Looking back, he's not sure how he expected them to react. He just remembers thinking, *Maybe you should see what's happening behind your back.*

WHAT THEY SAW

A PHOTO OF ANDREA PAIRED WITH A PHOTO OF A GORILLA.

A photo of Lolia with her hair loose and curly next to a picture of someone napping—Murphy had to explain that the juxtaposition was supposed to mean she had nappy hair.

Photos of a good friend of theirs, an Asian girl, paired with pictures of Jabba the Hutt and cottage cheese as a way of saying she was fat.

And worst of all: a picture captioned *twinning is winning* that showed Lolia and her basketball coach with nooses drawn around their necks.

BETRAYAL

The roar in your ears.
The gallop in your chest.
No breath.

Heart squeezed.
Belly queasy.
Sinking to the bottom of the sea.

Swim, you tell yourself.
Find the air.
But it isn't there.

The sky is sand.
The waves are clouds.
How can you tell
which way is up?

WHAT A NOOSE SAYS

A NOOSE IS JUST A ROPE WITH A KNOT THAT CAN BE TIGHTENED. BUT IN America it's a rope that tells a story. The story is about lynching—the practice of mob murder, usually by hanging but also by burning, shooting, drowning, beating, or being dragged behind a car. Between 1887 and 1950, at least 4,384 Black people were lynched in the United States—the true number is probably higher—in public displays of brutality and terror.

The vast majority of lynchings took place in the South, where white people used the noose as a means of intimidation and control. While lynching victims were usually accused of committing a crime like rape or murder, there was no need for anyone to produce evidence or witnesses. The accusation was enough. Black people could be lynched for being too successful or too outspoken, for owning property that white people wanted, for attempting to collect their wages or other debts from white people who didn't want to pay, for asking for food, or simply for being in the wrong place at the wrong time.

While lynchings sometimes happened under cover of darkness, they were often public occasions in which the person who was lynched was tortured and dismembered before a mob of enthusiastic onlookers. Sometimes they were advertised in advance so that photographers would have time to set up their equipment. Later, photos of the corpses would be sold as souvenirs.

"On the average, a black man, woman or child was murdered nearly once a week, every week, between 1882 and 1930 by a hate-driven white mob," sociologists Stewart E. Tolnay and E. M. Beck write in *A Festival of Violence: An Analysis of Southern Lynchings, 1882–1930.* Black artists and activists like journalist Ida B. Wells, essayist W.E.B. Du Bois, and singer Billie Holiday worked to make the scourge of lynchings visible to the world, just like Black Lives Matter activists have worked to call attention to the unarmed Black people who are killed by police. (The U.S. Congress didn't pass a federal anti-lynching law until 2022, despite more than two hundred attempts over more than a hundred years.) But even after lynchings stopped being a weekly occurrence, hate groups like the Ku Klux Klan continued to use the noose to menace and intimidate. So did individuals who wanted to tell Black neighbors or co-workers that they weren't welcome. They didn't need words to do it. All they needed was a length of rope.

A noose is just a rope with a knot that can be tightened, but in America, it's a rope that delivers a message. A noose says: *Be afraid*. It says: *I could kill you*. It says: *You are powerless and your life doesn't matter.*

PROCESSING

(March 18, 2017)

MURPHY HADN'T REALLY GIVEN MUCH THOUGHT TO THE ACCOUNT UNTIL Sita and Lolia began asking him questions: How long had it been around? What was the point of it?

"I didn't really register that, like, there's a bunch of photos that are targeting your friends," he explains now. "It was just Charles being Charles."

And to his eyes, the girls didn't seem that upset. They kept their anguish hidden, their faces smiling, and since he'd never spent much time thinking about the ways their experience of the world differed from his own, he assumed they saw the humor in it, the way his guy friends did. Before he left, they promised they wouldn't tell anyone what they had seen, because the account was supposed to be a secret.

WHISPERS

(March 18, 2017)

THAT NIGHT, ANDREA SAW SOME POSTS ON SNAPCHAT OR INSTAGRAM by Lolia and Sita. Something about people assuming someone was stupid because of their color. Something vague about not trusting people, about thinking you know people and discovering you're wrong. She DM'd Sita and asked what it was about.

Sita didn't reply.

You don't want to tell me, Andrea thought. *I don't care. It's fine.* It was probably just some relationship drama anyway.

PART 2

THE ACCOUNT

DO YOU REALLY THO?

IT HAD STARTED A COUPLE MONTHS EARLIER, AT A RESTAURANT CALLED The Melt that was known for its grilled cheese sandwiches. Charles was sitting in one of the restaurant's blond-wood booths with Greg, Steven, and Patrick. Steven and Patrick were both Asian, the children of first-generation immigrants from China. They had all been friends since middle school. Greg was the most recent addition to their group, the white boy among the other three Asian boys, and carried the cachet of also being friends with the popular kids. It was a winter weekend day sometime late in 2016 or maybe early in 2017, and the four boys were doing what they always did when they were together: trying to make each other laugh. As they waited for their food, Charles scrolled through pictures on his phone—memes he'd made, photos he'd collected that might be used for future memes. His model was the stuff he saw online, in YouTube videos and subreddits, some of which was funny precisely because it was offensive. Charles didn't think too deeply about the morality of that kind of thing. What mattered was that these memes made his friends laugh and their laughter was a shot of pleasure and power and affirmation and love, a fighter pilot takeoff crossed with a slow-motion squad walk, reckless and cool at once.

He showed them a photo of Ana in a little black dress and

a white coat. She'd posted it on Instagram with the caption: *i wanna go back to the old way.*

"Does she really, though?" he said. Maybe he spelled out the joke a little more: If they really went back to the old way, Ana would be a slave.

Whatever he said, the others laughed. So he turned the joke into a meme, right there at The Melt, stitching Ana's post to an old-fashioned engraving of a naked Black man hanging from a tree while being beaten by a white man. He captioned it: *Do you really tho?*

"You should post these somewhere," Greg said. Charles already had a spam account in addition to his main one, but Greg suggested he make a second one expressly for this kind of "edgier" content.

"If I made one, would you follow it?" Charles asked.

They all said they would.

So Charles made a new account and called it @yungcavage, a play on "young savage." Unlike his other accounts, he made this one private.

THE RULES OF INSTAGRAM

(Circa 2017)

1. Your main account is perfectly curated: photos of you, your family, your pets. This is the account your relatives and people from other schools will follow. You'll add flattering pictures from photo shoots and a few travel shots plus the occasional birthday posts for your closest friends.
2. Your spam account or "finsta" (fake Insta) is where you post weird candids, memes, selfies, rants, and anything else not suitable for your "rinsta" or regular account. This is the account people who really know you follow, the place where you spill tea and air out whatever is taking up space in your head. Party photos and attention-getting statements like "lost a friend today" go here. So does that picture of a dog humping your friend's leg and the photo of the slippers you wore on a middle-of-the-night trip to CVS.
3. Roast posts go on your spam account. That's where you make fun of someone's appearance, usually one of your close friends, by comparing them to something else: an object, an animal, a cartoon character, a celebrity.
4. Follows are easy to get but there's an element of exchange

to it. If you follow someone and they don't follow back, they're low-key making a statement. Following doesn't mean that much anyway. Not everyone who follows you will see what you post: Most people follow hundreds or even thousands of accounts and rarely see more than a fraction of them. The algorithm has its own way of deciding which posts show up in your feed. But still, it feels good when your follower count gets above five hundred and even better when it goes above a thousand. Followers = popularity.

5. Likes are worth more than follows. When one of your posts gets a lot of likes, it means people actually saw what you posted and took the time to let you know. Except when it doesn't. Some people sprinkle likes with careless abandon, double tapping on every post they scroll past, giving likes in the hopes of getting some of their own. Others are stingy with the like button, only bestowing their approval on a worthy few. Likes are open to interpretation, and you will absolutely try to interpret them, particularly when you're not getting any.
6. Comments are worth more than likes, but the language of comments is complicated. By commenting, you're communicating to the world that you have some connection to the poster. If the two of you are good friends, you might drop an in-joke in the comments, something not everyone will understand. Other commenting options: cleverness, snark, compliments (mostly for girls), emojis. Commenting is a bid for attention, a way of saying, "Hey, I'm here." That makes it a gamble. A funny comment attracts likes, but if the

joke falls flat, you'll look like you're trying too hard. Sometimes it's safer just to silently scroll by.

7. The more you interact with an account, the more you're likely to see it in the future. It's possible to follow an account but never see it, but it's also possible to follow hundreds of accounts and have certain ones appear in your feed every time something new is posted. Those are the algorithm's choices, not yours.
8. Everything we do online is noticed—every click, every tap, every search—our interests tracked by algorithms designed to keep us scrolling and clicking, turning our attention into dollars.
9. In April 2017, Instagram was reporting 700 million active users. By June 2018, that figure had reached 1 billion. That same month, the app's estimated worth was over $100 billion. What makes it so valuable? You. Your data. Your attention. Your time. By 2018, Instagram had earmarked most of its $390 million marketing budget for attracting and retaining teenage users. An internal presentation described the migration of young people to other platforms as "an existential threat."
10. Until this moment, it's quite possible you've never thought about the value of your attention—what it earns and what it costs. Maybe you'll start thinking about it now. When you follow, like, comment, what exactly are you saying? What are you saying when you don't say anything at all?

FOLLOWERS

AFTER CHARLES MADE THE ACCOUNT, HE BEGAN ADDING POSTS. HE'D make them during the week and then post them in batches. Afterward, he couldn't really explain the logic he used to determine which posts went on which account because he certainly made racial jokes on his regular spam account, particularly Asian jokes. He roasted his friends on both accounts too, showing embarrassing pictures of the guys in his inner circle. But the @yungcavage account was definitely for the posts that crossed a line, although to be honest, Charles wasn't really thinking about how far over the line he'd gone.

"I don't think I really cared about the line or anything," he says now. "Just because I thought no one was going to see it anyway."

By March @yungcavage had fourteen followers, including Charles himself. The first few people who followed the account were Charles's close friends, all juniors, like him: Greg, Murphy, Patrick, Steven, Otis, and Wyatt. They started following it just after it was created, before there was much on it. (Jon followed later and never interacted with the account.)

The remaining six followers weren't in Charles's inner circle. Three were juniors he was friends with but didn't spend a lot of time with outside of school, one of whom was white, one of whom was Middle Eastern, and one of whom was white and Latinx. The other three were sophomores he had met because one of them was in his Mandarin class, a white boy, an Asian girl, and a boy who was of mixed Asian, Latinx, and European heritage. In at least one case, a follower received an invitation to join the account without knowing who had sent it.

"Pls tell me who's the owner to this amazing account?" a white junior named Riley commented when he responded to an invitation and landed on a post entitled "20 Things The World Wouldn't Have If Black People Didn't Exist." (The original headline was taken from a *BuzzFeed* article about the contributions of Black inventors, but the @yungcavage post suggested the following answers: the Ku Klux Klan, an average U.S. IQ of 98, and men in prison uniforms.) Asked to guess whose account it was, Riley immediately suggested Patrick, who was known at school for making racist jokes. Once, Patrick had made a presentation in a U.S. History class on the topic of "Controversies About the College Admissions Process," which took a sharp turn midway through when he began to compare the IQs of different racial groups. (Patrick declined multiple requests for interviews.)

Afterward, people who witnessed it couldn't remember how overtly racist the presentation had been, but it was discomfiting enough that the teacher went straight to the administration seeking advice about how to handle it.

"He was basically promoting that Asian Americans are superior and they are getting cheated out of what they work hard for by other groups that get the easy street," the teacher of the class recalls. She knocked his grade down a point for using bad data, but that was all she felt she could do. You weren't supposed to give bad grades just because a student expressed an opinion you didn't like.

The stereotype that Patrick was invoking is a familiar one. Often referred to as the "model minority myth," it portrays Asian Americans as uniformly hardworking and successful, and blames the struggles of Black Americans on laziness or lack of aptitude rather than on the discriminatory policies that have often kept their efforts from yielding the same results. But even after that presentation, most students at Albany High School didn't take Patrick's remarks seriously. Sure he was known for making offensive remarks, but he was also a class clown who did all kinds of out-of-pocket stuff to get a laugh.

"People knew he *said* stuff like that and it was really edgy, but no one would connect the dots and think like, 'Oh, this guy's a racist,'" explains one of the other account followers. "People would think like, 'Oh he just has a high tolerance for humor. That's jokes to him."

One of the things that made the situation confusing was that people made Asian jokes all the time. The school had almost as many Asian students as white ones, so cracks about being bad at driving or good at math were pretty commonplace. Those stereotypes were too cartoonish to be hurtful, Charles says, and it was easy to assume that other people felt the same when he joked about *their* ethnicities.

"We were so comfortable in the fact that we knew no one actually believed these things," Charles says, "that we could say it freely and knowing it was a joke."

Or at least, that's how he justified it in his head.

TURNING ON THE TAPS

Tap, click, send.
A packet of poison.
A dagger of damage. It feels
like power it feels like tapping
a vein when I tap those keys,
sending a quip, a snicker,
a gif, a meme. I'm
not alone if you laugh
when I turn on the tap
each post a drop
until the drops make a flood
we're dot-dot-dashing the code
that makes us one and you
zero. It feels like singing like tap
dancing every staccato
click is stiletto sharp it feels
good to tap these keys
because from way over here I can
hold you down
and never have to see you
gasp for air.

PART 3

REVEALED

TALKING

(March 19, 2017)

ON SUNDAY, MARCH 19, TWO STUDENTS NAMED EREN AND ROSIE WERE at Eren's house, doing homework. Rosie, who is white, was a junior, with long russet hair and blue-green eyes. Eren was a sophomore and young for his grade. He had an openhearted smile, hazel eyes, and olive skin that reflected his mixed Asian, Latinx, and European heritage.

Back then, Eren says, he sometimes felt like he was in a stereotypical high school movie. Picture him walking through the halls during the opening credits, high-fiving and waving at people from every social clique while the movie's theme song pulses in the background. It wasn't exactly like that, of course. His core group of friends were mostly nerdier types. But he was also a self-declared social butterfly, with a blend of sweetness and coolness that made him appealing to both teachers and students. He was a talented hip-hop dancer and a stylish dresser and was a member of the school's Youth and Government delegation, which is where he'd met Rosie.

That Sunday night, Eren and Rosie sat on the couch, talking. They had been good friends, and then they'd dated for a few weeks, and then Rosie had decided that she just wanted to be friends again. For a while it had been awkward between them. But that night, things felt the way they had at the beginning—relaxed and intimate. They talked about Rosie's struggles with anxiety, the way the year had gone for each of them, how they were feeling about their lives. Eren was a good listener, supportive and warm. On her way home that night, Rosie reflected on how happy she felt to be close with him again.

"I was like, oh my god, we might still have a good, solid friendship," she recalls. "It's ironic, looking back on it. Because that was the night before."

FIRST PERIOD

(March 20, 2017)

CHARLES SAT DOWN TO WORK ON THE "DO NOW" ASSIGNMENT ON THE white board when he came into history class on Monday, March 20, so it wasn't until there was a break midway through class that he noticed that Sita was acting distant. He'd gone over to say hi and she'd walked away without replying.

"What's going on?" he asked her after class. "What did I do?"

No answer.

WE HAVE TO TELL YOU

(March 20, 2017)

ANDREA WAS IN THE ART BUILDING, JUST OUTSIDE THE CULINARY ARTS classroom, when she was approached by a group of girls: Lolia, Ana, Sita, and another friend of theirs, a Black girl named McKenna.

"Okay, we've got to tell you something. Like we *have* to tell you."

Andrea waited impatiently, thinking it was going to be some kind of boy drama.

But it wasn't. Not the kind of boy drama she was expecting, anyway.

There's a racist Instagram account, they told her. *A ton of people are following it. And there are pictures of you on it.*

The hallway walls were covered with murals of giant faces, all of which seemed to be staring at her. She tried to take in what her friends were saying, but everyone was talking at once.

News of the account had spread like wildfire among the Black girls and their close friends, and now several more people came to join them. One of them was Rina, the junior class president. A dancer and flute player who seemed to be friends with everyone in their grade, she had heard about the account from a friend and hadn't been able to concentrate all morning. Kerry remembers seeing her tear up in English class.

"They don't like me," she'd said. "They don't like me because I'm Black." She was one of the darkest-skinned girls in school and she had always been secretly convinced that everyone thought she was ugly.

As school officials would later describe in court documents, it wasn't long before there were close to a dozen girls talking and crying, their voices growing louder and louder as they shared their hurt and indignation. The next period had started, but it was clear that nobody was going to class. The culinary arts teacher slammed her classroom door shut, annoyed they were making so much noise.

Andrea was sobbing but she was also furious. Of all of them, she was the only one who wasn't surprised. She'd already known what those boys were capable of. She slammed her fist into one of the murals' smiling faces. Why the hell should she have to go through this? Why wouldn't those boys leave her alone?

I should have listened to my mom, she thought. *I should have done something to prevent this.*

HAIR STORY (2)

(October 2016)

IT HAD STARTED BACK IN THE FALL, IN ALGEBRA 2. SHE WAS DEEP IN her own thoughts when she felt a hand in her hair. It was Greg, a kid she was sort of friendly with because he was friends with other friends of hers. She swatted his hand away. Being pawed like this wasn't new—whenever she changed her hairstyle someone's hands would be in it. She wasn't about to make a big deal about it because it was the middle of class, and anyway if she got into it with every person who tried to touch her hair, she'd be exhausted.

That was the extent of the interaction. Until a little while later, when she was walking with Wyatt to his house to do homework.

"Did you see what Charles posted on his spam account?" he asked.

Andrea didn't follow Charles, so she shook her head. "Show me."

And there it was. A video of Greg touching her hair. Charles had taken it from the hallway. He'd captioned it, *Touching the nap.*

Andrea kept walking. She didn't want Wyatt to see her upset.

"Do you want him to take it down?" Wyatt asked.

"I don't really care," she insisted.

But she stewed on it all afternoon, especially as more people began asking if she'd seen it. Ana and Rina both commented on the post, telling Charles to delete it. Finally Andrea snapchatted him directly, asking him to take it down.

Andrea:

You know what that isn't a lot to ask I wouldn't just come up and touch you without asking it's a violation of my personal space

Charles:

Lmao I wasn't the one touching you

I never told him to do that

You think I instigated this

Greg chose to do this so don't get all up in my business about it

You tell greg not to touch you

Not me

Andrea:

You posted the video you are instigating it

Charles:

This was after it was done

And no one following my spams gonna watch that video and be like, oh that's funny

Finally, after some more back and forth, Charles deleted the video.

The next day, Andrea spoke with Greg after class. "You know that's not okay, right? Like you know that you shouldn't do that."

"Obviously I know that," she remembers him saying. "I'm not going to do it again."

He'd already gotten an earful from Rina, who had taken him aside to talk to him about it. Rina and Greg were good friends and she'd always seen him as an ally, so she figured if she explained why his actions were disrespectful, he'd understand.

"It makes us feel like objects," she told him. "It's really annoying. We don't know where your hands have been."

That should have been the end of it.

But it wasn't. Andrea was self-conscious about her hair now and began wearing it in a bun instead of leaving it out. And a few days after the video incident, Andrea heard that Charles had posted another photo of her on his spam account. This one was a screenshot of a Snapchat post that just showed the back of her head: her bun, her ear, the hood of her sweatshirt. It had been taken in class, by someone sitting in the desk behind her. From the angle, she could tell it was Murphy. The caption on the post: *Tiana or andrea?*

Charles had a class right next-door to Andrea's algebra class, so this time she confronted him in person. "Delete it," she said. "Show me right now."

He did.

"Don't post anything else," she told him. "We are not cool. Don't talk about me."

But the feeling of being watched lingered. The feeling that every inch of her was being assessed, analyzed, judged, and then dismissed as unworthy. It made it hard to go to school. Sometimes she just stayed home.

Her mother, Natalie, begged her to report what had happened. She could see the change in Andrea, the way her light seemed to have dimmed. "It's obviously affecting you," she said.

Andrea didn't want to be talking to her mother about some stupid thing that had happened at school. She didn't *want* it to be affecting her. But after Natalie told one of the school's vice principals about the incident, the vice principal called Andrea into the office to talk. As the administrator would later explain in legal filings, Andrea told her what had happened, but said she didn't want the school to take any action.

"I just kind of took that as an opportunity for me to vent," Andrea says. "At least have it down on paper that they were doing inappropriate stuff." Anything more than that, she thought, would only makes things worse. "I didn't want more repercussions," she says.

Anyway, she thought she'd taken care of it on her own. *At least I handled this as maturely as I could have*, she told herself. *At least they got the message that I'm not to be fucked with.*

But on March 20, as she stood in the hallway with the other girls, she understood that the opposite was true. They hadn't gotten the message at all.

WRITE DOWN EVERYTHING

(March 20, 2017)

BY NOW, THE COMMOTION HAD ATTRACTED THE ATTENTION OF THE school's security guard, Josette Wheaton, who ushered the entire group of girls from the Art Building to the main office. There were too many of them for a single office, so they wound up in a conference room with two vice principals, Tami Benau and Melisa Pfohl. Pfohl was biracial, white and Asian, and Benau was white.

Everyone was talking at once; many were crying. The two administrators had no idea what was going on, and the chaos made it hard to piece together the narrative. Eventually, Ms. Pfohl distributed Incident Witness forms for the girls to write down what had happened. Some were too upset to write. Others unleashed a torrent of words—all the racist remarks they'd let go by over the past weeks and months. The way Murphy tried to incorporate fried chicken into food conversations, for instance. That time Charles had texted Tiana the N-word and then said that Patrick had taken his phone and sent the text just to get a reaction out of Charles. Suddenly everything looked completely different. They'd assumed those things were slipups, errors of judgment. Just boys being dumb.

But now it was clear those boys had never been their friends at all.

The problem was, they didn't have any evidence of what was on the account. Just Lolia and Sita's memories of what they'd seen on Murphy's phone. Already it was starting to feel hopeless, impossible. The girls' words against the boys'. But still, they wrote down what they could on Incident Witness forms. These forms would later turn up in court:

Private Instagram account of disgusting racist images about multiple black girls in my grade making my very close friends ball their eyes out and have fits of rage

Boys saying inconsiderate/demeaning things in passing about colored people AND women

They call them all racist names and make remarks about the "KKK" and lynching

They body shame

I've heard multiple racist comments made to my friends

This also affects me b/c I am a Black Girl, already am self-conscious of my self.

NOTHING'S GOING TO HAPPEN

IT WASN'T THE FIRST TIME THIS KIND OF THING HAD HAPPENED AT Albany High School. It seemed like there was a social media scandal every couple of years. In 2012, a group of junior and senior boys set up a competition to see who could have sex with the most ninth- and tenth-grade girls, keeping score on Twitter. In 2015, a group of twelfth-graders created an account on Instagram they called Broke Boys where they posted degrading pictures of female classmates. In each case, the administration's response seemed lackadaisical at best.

"A lot of powerful, popular boys were involved or implicated, and I remember the prevailing wisdom was, nothing's going to happen to them," says Ned Purdom, who taught AP Literature, English, and Journalism at the high school when the Broke Boys account was discovered. That year, the school newspaper published a blistering editorial written by a senior named Ya Davis, taking the administration to task for letting these events go by, year after year.

"By not addressing cyberbullying, we are perpetuating the problem and unconsciously cultivating it by not taking proper action," Davis wrote. "We are giving males a false sense of security and a confidence to move on with and even escalate their actions, but more importantly, we're desensitizing women to these issues by making it seem 'normal' for these things to happen."

She wasn't wrong, as Ted Barone, who was then the school principal, admitted.

"I will acknowledge that our response to the earlier cases of gender-based cyberbullying was not as swift or strong as it should have been," he wrote in response to the editorial. "It's a complicated task to investigate allegations of cyberbullying. Snapchats disappear, DM groups are closed to outsiders, and people are often afraid of providing evidence to administration because of concerns about retribution."

He urged students to do their part by "acting quickly to capture incriminating posts" and provide administrators with copies to use as evidence.

EVIDENCE

(March 20, 2017)

KERRY HADN'T GONE TO CULINARY ARTS CLASS WITH THE OTHERS AND she wasn't in the conference room now. Instead, she was thinking about evidence. How could she get copies of the pictures Lolia and Sita had seen? She remembered hearing about something similar happening at another school—a bunch of boys on a group chat saying horrible things about some of their female classmates. A friend of hers had swiped one of their phones at a party and taken screenshots. What if she did something like that?

As she walked to her fifth-period class, she pulled out her phone and found the account on Instagram. It was private, but the app listed the names of people she followed who also followed it. One name stood out: a boy named Eren. She hardly knew him—they'd only spoken once or twice—but they were mutuals on Instagram and her friend Rosie had dated him, just for a few weeks. Both of them were in her next class: psychology.

When she walked into class, she pulled Rosie aside.

"Could you ask Eren to borrow his phone to make a call or something and meet me in the restroom?"

Rosie looked puzzled, so Kerry explained. "There's this racist Instagram account. I think Eren's following it."

Class was starting, so Rosie slid into her seat in the back row, next to Eren. She didn't really understand what Kerry was saying, but about fifteen minutes into class, she whispered the request.

Eren and Rosie have different memories of what she said. Rosie says she asked him straight up: "Kerry says there's this weird racist Instagram account you're following. Can I look at your phone?" Eren remembers her offering a made-up excuse: "Hey, my phone just died and I need to call my parents."

Either way, Eren unlocked his phone and handed it to her. Then Kerry and Rosie both excused themselves and went to the bathroom across the hall.

THREE MINUTES

(March 20, 2017)

THE FLOOR OF THE BATHROOM WAS POURED CONCRETE. THE DOORS OF the stalls were black. Kerry and Rosie stood in the middle of the room, their images reflected in the mirror over the porcelain sink: one Asian girl, one white one, their heads bent over Eren's phone. Kerry took pictures of the screen with her own phone as Rosie looked over her shoulder and scrolled through the posts on the account. Some of the posts were the kinds of things you would see on any other spam account—memes, guys roasting each other, the regular kind of dumb. But at least half of the posts were horrifyingly racist: Black men being lynched and whipped, jokes about the Ku Klux Klan and the N-word, a screenshot of the Snapchat conversation between Charles and Andrea about the hair-touching video that was captioned *Holy shit I'm on the edge of bringing my rope to school on Monday*.

"It was so much worse than I anticipated," Kerry says. "I didn't think I would react that badly, but I was physically shaking." Her heart was pounding. Her armpits prickled with sweat. "I was just, like, not prepared to see that."

They didn't have much time. If they were gone for long, their teacher would notice. Rosie scrolled, Kerry photographed.

She took pictures of the twenty-four most offensive posts. She took pictures of the comments and the list of followers.

In three minutes, they were done. Then they went back to class. Rosie handed the phone back to Eren.

"Is everything okay?" he asked.

She nodded. "Yeah. I think so."

DEACTIVATED

(March 20, 2017)

MURPHY HAD BEEN CALLED DOWN TO THE OFFICE BY VICE PRINCIPAL Benau and asked about the account during fifth period. (Benau did not respond to interview requests, but court documents confirm this account.) He'd tried to walk a middle line between telling and not telling, showing the vice principal some posts on his phone but not revealing who had made them or providing the screenshots Benau had requested. Meanwhile, his friends were growing increasingly anxious. They knew the word was out, but they didn't know how it had happened. Murphy was not about to tell them. Everyone was texting each other, unsure whether they should even be seen together.

Eventually, Charles, Jon, Patrick, Wyatt, and Murphy decided to go off campus to get boba at the 99 Ranch Market in Richmond. But once they were there, they were all too nervous to order. What should they do? Should they unfollow the account? Murphy worried that if he did, it would be awkward to ask Charles to let him back in, so he decided not to do anything.

After lunch, Greg approached Charles and encouraged him to deactivate the account.

"Dude, they figured out what it is," he said. "They know what it is."

Charles still didn't think it was going to be that big a deal, but he removed all the followers so the account wouldn't be visible.

A PHOTO IN THE SNOW

(March 20, 2017)

WHEN KERRY TRIES TO REMEMBER HOW SHE GOT FROM THE HALLWAY outside her class to the conference room where the girls were writing their witness statements, the whole thing is a blur. Her heart was still pounding from her secret mission and the conference room was chaos, with all the girls talking at once.

"I have all the pictures," she announced. "I have everything."

She air-dropped the images to Ms. Pfohl and some of the other girls, and they began going through them. Lolia wrote the screen names of the account followers on the conference room white board so that they could match them to the names of boys at school.

As she scrolled through the images, Andrea was having trouble processing what she saw. A photo of a white hood, a Black doll, a torch, and a noose captioned *ku klux starter pack.* Pictures of the back of her head with captions like *fucking nappy ass piece of shit.* An unflattering closeup of Wyatt with the comment "extra chromosome ass."

But then she saw a familiar photo. It had been taken from her own Instagram account—her favorite picture from a photo shoot she'd done on a trip to Tahoe with Lydia. It had been paired with a photo of a gorilla.

"I just got this stomach feeling of like, 'Wow, basically anything I do is not going to be good enough for these people,'" Andrea says. "I can't even take a picture of myself in the snow, looking how I look, and post it on Instagram."

Somewhere at her core, she knew she looked beautiful in that photo, no matter what anyone said. "There was part of me where I was like, *I don't even fucking look like a gorilla*," she says. "Like, *You guys are tripping*."

At least now, nobody could accuse her of being oversensitive. *This is bad enough for other people to be upset about it*, she thought. *They probably will do at least* something *about it, because these are* blatantly *racist.*

That's when she thought about her father. Her one Black parent.

"If my dad were alive, it would be so bad," she said aloud. "He would probably be in jail if he found out. He'd burn this school to the ground."

CHOKING

ANDREA AND HER FATHER HAD BEEN LIKE MIRROR IMAGES: BOTH STUB-born to their core. "I wear his face so we're always going to be very similar," she says. "And for a while I really resented that, resented that we had so many common qualities."

Her father, Harrison, had grown up in Richmond, just to the north of Albany, and had joined the marines right out of high school. He loved the Marvel universe, cooking, and martial arts, particularly karate, in which he had competed when he was in the military. Like Andrea, he had a probing and investigating intelligence that loved to get to the bottom of things, to discover the meaning behind people's words. He was good-humored and outgoing, especially when he suspected that people might be judging him because of the color of his skin. In those situations, he would go out of his way to be friendly, defusing any tension by making a joke or by finding a point of similarity.

When Andrea was little, her father had worked as a laborer for the railroad, but then he was sidelined by an aortic aneurysm that prevented him from doing any heavy lifting. The aneurysm could have killed him, but doctors had saved his life, opening his chest and replacing part of his aorta with a Teflon graft.

He'll be lucky to live ten years, the doctors said, but he did live, and life continued to go on, in both good ways and bad. Andrea's younger sister, Rachel, was born, and then Andrea's mother, Natalie, got thyroid cancer. After that it was Harrison who took care of the household as best he could while his wife went through years of treatments: four surgeries plus radioactive iodine therapy that required her to be quarantined from her family so she wouldn't expose them to radiation.

Looking back, Andrea thinks her father was probably depressed, in addition to having anger issues. When he wasn't cooking or hanging out with friends and family, the genial, funny facade would fall away and the man who remained seemed dimmed, exhausted. Maybe if he'd gotten some therapy, she says, things might have gone differently for both of them. Maybe if he hadn't had to work so hard to get respect from the outside world, he wouldn't have demanded it so forcefully from his three daughters, born eight years apart, who were taught to always answer him with a "yes, sir" or "no, sir."

But as it was, Harrison was a strict disciplinarian. He didn't tolerate raised voices or emotional outbursts. TV shows like *Hannah Montana*, *iCarly*, and *Wizards of Waverly Place* weren't allowed in his house because the girls on those programs were far too sassy for his taste. Andrea remembers her older sister waking up at the crack of the dawn so she could sneak off to school wearing makeup, and their father waiting for her at the door to make her turn around and wash it off.

"If she talked back, or if it got to the point where he felt like he had to discipline her, it was either with his belt or with a hard hand that wasn't just going to hit you once," Andrea says.

Andrea was spared the belt, but as she grew older, she and

her father clashed with increasing frequency. Minor disagreements had a way of escalating. Her father said she was rude, which she doesn't doubt.

"I'm sure I was," she says. "But at the same time, respect shouldn't be commanded, it should be earned."

The breaking point came when Andrea was in sixth grade. Harrison had told her twice not to Rollerblade through the kitchen while he was cooking, but she did it anyway. Later he would say that he was worried she would fall on a knife, but Andrea doesn't remember seeing any knives. What she remembers is her father's hands around her throat, choking her until she almost fainted.

It took a couple of months for her parents to separate after that. Natalie was in love with her husband; she wanted to believe him when he said that Andrea was overreacting, that he'd just grabbed her to protect her. But Andrea was afraid, and she was angry, and eventually Natalie concluded that Harrison had crossed a line that could not be ignored.

Still, the separation was meant to be temporary. Harrison moved in with his mother in Richmond, but he still took care of Rachel every day. Harrison, Natalie, Andrea, and Rachel continued to have meals together and to go on outings as a family. Harrison was going to culinary school now, with plans to open a barbecue business so he could contribute financially, something he hadn't been able to do since leaving the railroad. But the fights between him and Andrea continued, leaving her in a roil of conflicting emotions. She worried about him, especially as she saw him not taking care of himself, but she was also furious at him for choking her, furious that he still didn't seem to respect her autonomy.

Once, he came over to the home she shared with her mother and Rachel for a birthday celebration, and the two of them got into another argument. Andrea remembers that Natalie stepped between them so that Andrea could get to her room safely. But even then, with her mom standing in front of her, she didn't want to walk away. Instead she shouted at her father over Natalie's shoulder, "You can't talk to me like this anymore!" because she wanted him to see her, see her independence and her strength, see that he couldn't push her around.

And then, the summer before high school, Harrison had a second aneurysm and died. Nine years and seven months had passed since the first one, so maybe it was just that his time was up. But it was hard not to think about the Nation's and Burger King receipts Natalie had found in his car, receipts for hamburgers he had eaten the night before his death. He had to have known that he wouldn't be able to tolerate the sodium.

What was Andrea supposed to do with her feelings now? Where was she supposed to take the anger, the disappointment, the brokenness? How was she supposed to react when people talked about him like he had been an angel, when she knew he hadn't been? How could she love him and miss him and yet also want to rage at him for not being who she needed him to be, for vanishing before anything was resolved? Part of her was relieved that the person who had frightened her so badly was gone, and so for months she didn't cry, didn't tell anyone what had happened, just moved through the world in a state of numb shock.

It wasn't until months into their friendship that she had

finally told her best friend, Lydia, her tone so deadpan that Lydia didn't believe her at first.

"You're lying," Lydia said.

It was only then that Andrea began to cry.

"Oh my god," Lydia said as the tears streamed down her friend's face. "You're *not* lying."

Now, as Andrea stood in the Albany High School conference room, scrolling through the images from the account, it was her father's anger she kept thinking about. What it would feel like to have his rage turned on her enemies. Someone to protect her, like the other Black fathers who were already showing up at the school to protect *their* daughters. Someone whose anger was big enough to burn away her own, big enough to catch her and hold her and let her rest.

But none of that was going to happen.

Instead, she was going to have to walk through the world alone, wearing his face, like a mirror without a reflection.

PRETTY SERIOUS

(March 20, 2017)

ONCE KERRY AIR-DROPPED HER THE PHOTOGRAPHS SHE'D TAKEN OF the account, Tami Benau, the vice principal, decided to call the police. As she would later explain in a declaration filed in court, both the phrase "on the edge of bringing my rope to school" and the drawing of nooses around the necks of Lolia and her coach could be construed as threats of violence. By seventh period, when Murphy was called back down to the office for another interview, there were two police officers waiting for him.

Suddenly, it didn't seem like a good idea to withhold information.

"I was kind of figuring, *Okay, at this point if the cops are involved, I don't want to lie to the cops*," he says. "*Because it seems pretty serious.*"

POLICE

(March 20, 2017)

THE COPS INTERVIEWED THE GIRLS AS WELL, ASKING IF THEY'D EVER been physically harmed or threatened. Had they ever felt like their lives were in danger?

No, of course they hadn't. For many of them, it was just the opposite. These boys had been their friends, or the friends of their friends. They'd slept over at one another's houses, chatted with one another's parents, hung out together at school. And all the while those boys had been thinking of them as monkeys and imagining them being lynched.

As the police shook their heads and shrugged, the girls felt a sense of defeat. No one was talking about making arrests, or charging people with hate crimes. What Charles had posted on the account was horrifying, but it wasn't against the law.

"It's not like they could have taken them away in handcuffs and been like, 'Okay you're going to jail for three years for being an asshole,'" Andrea says. Still, she wished the police had given her some advice or encouragement, told her what to do next, where to go to find justice.

Because if the police weren't the answer, what was?

RAIN

(March 20, 2017)

IT WAS A GLOOMY DAY, THE CLOUDS LOW AND GRAY. AS ANA WALKED home through the drizzle with her father, Lewis, she felt calm for the first time since that morning. She talked about how hard it was to wrap her mind around what she'd seen on the account and how it seemed like Andrea had gotten the worst of it. There had been more posts about Andrea than anyone, pictures of her taken in class with terrible captions. What had Andrea ever done to deserve that?

With her father next to her and the rain whispering onto the pavement, even these horrifying things felt manageable. Something would happen. All this would be taken care of. A stillness settled over her like a long exhale.

But as soon as she was home, she was in it again. Her phone was blowing up with texts. And whenever she shut her eyes, she kept seeing the picture of Lolia with a noose around her neck.

WHAT HER PARENTS SAID

(March 20, 2017)

RINA'S MOM WAS MORE VISIBLY UPSET ABOUT THE ACCOUNT THAN HER dad. A surgical nurse, she would later say that the pain of learning what Rina and her friends were going through felt like having her chest cracked open.

Rina's dad was more stoic. Rina thought that this was because he'd grown up in a racist town, unlike her mother, who had spent her life in liberal places like Albany. Her dad knew better than to be surprised.

"Calm down," Rina remembers him telling her. "Don't let them see you hurt. They *want* to see you like this. This is not the only time this is going to happen."

RACISM AT ITS FINEST

(March 20, 2017)

THAT NIGHT, MANY OF THE GIRLS POSTED THE SAME IMAGE ON Snapchat: a knife dripping blood and the words "Racism at its finest."

Rina posted on Snapchat:

> Today was a very hard day and I know there are speculations as to why but I want to be clear, BLACK IS BEAUTIFUL, EVERYONE IS EQUAL, and lastly BE MINDFUL OF WHAT YOU PUT OUT INTO THE WORLD

Meanwhile, followers of the account were scrambling to distance themselves. Some pointed the finger at Charles. Others posted blanket apologies or denials on Snapchat or Instagram. A few sent personal messages to the girls who had been targeted that were half apologies and half excuses.

I know I'm probably the last person you want to hear from. I followed the account, I knew it was wrong, and I didn't say anything because I wanted to protect some of my closest friends. I never commented or liked anything on the account. You and others targeted have always been some of the nicest and best people to me. Especially you, I've always considered you a homie. I know that I don't deserve to be forgiven and that we won't be cool anymore, but I just have to apologize. Im sorry.

SKULL ISLAND

(March 20, 2017)

THAT EVENING, EREN WENT TO SEE *KONG: SKULL ISLAND* WITH HIS friends Gabriel, who was white, and Lucy, who was Chinese American. In the middle of the movie, Lucy's phone began to buzz.

"Guys," she whispered. "Come on. You have to see this."

Out in the lobby of the theater, she showed them. Her phone was blowing up with questions, comments, and accusations. *Racist*, they said. *Is this your account?*

Eren and Gabriel looked at their phones. The same thing was happening to them. It had something to do with an Instagram account they'd followed, Charles's spam account. People seemed to think it was theirs, or that they were intimately involved, which none of them could figure out. They barely knew Charles, who was a grade above them. Lucy had him in her Mandarin class and he'd suggested she follow his spam Instagram account. Eren and Gabriel had followed too, because the three of them did almost everything together.

What was on the account? None of them could remember much about it and when they went to look, it had already been deleted. Eren was following more than a thousand accounts, and he says it was only later, when he saw Kerry's photos of the posts, that he realized he'd interacted with the @yungcavage account at all. (In fact, he'd liked many of the posts and commented on two of them.) But now, standing in the lobby of the theater, he couldn't remember much besides the fact that it had seemed "edgy." Eren liked edgy humor—he followed YouTubers like iDubbbz and Filthy Frank who were known for their provocative antics. From what he could remember, the @yungcavage account had felt like it was in the same vein.

"It was never anything that I'd ever actively look up and peruse through, or honestly thought about deeply," Eren says now. He was a default double-tapper, who scrolled and liked, scrolled and liked. Later, he would ask himself why that was. "I've wondered why, back then, I didn't recognize that [account] as problematic? Why did I entertain that? Why did I not say anything?"

But on March 20, 2017, Eren wasn't ready to interrogate his own failings. All he was thinking about was how to control the damage. He still didn't know the role his phone had played in revealing the account. He just knew that he was getting a blizzard of condemning texts and he was far more interested in figuring out how to survive the storm than he was in understanding what had caused it.

"I was trying to save my perceived popularity and public image," he says. "This was directly attacking that—and me as a person. So I felt the need to defend that."

That night when he got home, he posted on his main Instagram account, which had around 1,200 followers. "I did not create this account. I do not condone what was posted on this account." And so on. He had labored over the caption for hours, boiling it down to a paragraph-length defense against the accusation that he was racist.

If anything, his post made things worse, judging by the comments.

"By knowing about it and not saying anything about it, you *are* condoning this," someone wrote.

That stopped Eren cold. He couldn't argue with the logic. He *had* condoned it. He'd double-tapped, making the little heart icon turn bright red. It was, he says now, an *aha* moment.

"I recognized then: Yes, I did have a role in it. Being a follower of the account, liking, commenting, everything like that, that holds weight," he says. "And that kind of prompted immediate introspection, like what does that mean for me as a person and my morals?"

That night, he paced back and forth in his room, unable to sleep. It was still a child's room—the walls covered with book fair posters from elementary school, the shelves laden with Bionicles and stuffed animals: a shark he'd won as a carnival prize at the Beach Boardwalk in Santa Cruz, a teddy bear his godfather had given him, some Plants vs. Zombies plushies from China. His bed was a mattress in the middle of the room, at floor level so that his blind and elderly cat, one year older than he was, could easily climb aboard. Now he circled around the bed, his steps powered by a surge of self-loathing and anxiety.

What have I done? He didn't want to tell his parents, didn't want to risk them seeing him as he suddenly saw himself.

"I was scared that they were going to think I was racist," he says. "In my self-reflection, that was a big question. *Am I racist? What makes someone racist?*"

WHAT MAKES SOMEONE RACIST?

RACISM SEEMS LIKE AN EASY WORD TO DEFINE, BUT PEOPLE USE IT IN so many different ways that its meanings shatter and refract and multiply and sometimes contradict each other.

There's no excuse for still being racist in the 21st century.
and
You can't live in 21st century America without being racist.

Racism begins at home.
and
Racism is in the culture.

Children aren't born racist; they have to be taught.
and
All of us are racist; it has to be unlearned.

Racism is using slurs and burning crosses.
and
Racism is microaggressions like describing a Black person as "articulate."

Racism is interpersonal
and
Racism is institutional.

Racism is about education.
and
Racism is about morality.

Racism is human nature.
and
Racism is in the past.

At its most basic level, racism starts with the notion that human beings can be divided into categories based on physical attributes like skin pigment, hair texture, and the shape of eyes, noses, and lips. There's no biological or scientific basis for these categories. They were developed over time, starting in the mid-1200s in European religious texts, and then were used to make racially discriminatory laws starting in the mid-1600s. *Racism* is thus the idea that human abilities and behaviors are determined by this made-up thing called race and that races can be ranked as superior and inferior.

The majority of Americans now say that they don't believe in superior or inferior races. Most people know that this isn't a good way to think, which isn't at all the same as not thinking it. But the word *racism* also describes the ways one's behavior can reinforce or reflect the idea that some races are better than others, *regardless* of a person's intentions or awareness. So here's a better definition: *Racism* is a system of advantages based on race. A person can contribute to that system of advantages by actively stereotyping or discriminating, but they can also do so by feeling a lack of interest in or empathy for the experiences of people of other races. They can even do so by not wanting to expend the energy necessary to make a situation fairer and more inclusive because it's working out fine for *them*.

When you think of *racism* as a system, rather than as a state of mind, it can help sort out all those contradictory definitions. The word can describe the most vile and horrific kind of human behaviors: slavery, lynching, discrimination. It can describe appalling attitudes like hatred, cruelty, and contempt. But it can also describe behaviors and attitudes that are more like being selfish, or rude, or clueless—harmful, but also commonplace and potentially inadvertent. It's not that all of those things are the same. It's that all of them contribute to that system of advantages.

WATCHING

SOME OF THE ACCOUNT FOLLOWERS TOLD THEIR PARENTS. SOME OF them didn't, thinking they could ride it out on their own. Most of them watched their phones all evening. Watched their names show up on posts about who was involved. Watched their follower counts dwindle on Instagram as people unfollowed them by the dozens. Watched their friends—now former friends—fleeing group chats. Watched the posts on social media, the statements in favor of Black Lives, and thought, *Oh my god, this is targeted at me. Everyone at my school thinks I'm racist.*

RED B EMOJI

(March 20, 2017)

ROSIE HAD BEEN MAKING EXCUSES TO HERSELF ABOUT EREN. MAYBE he'd just scrolled by it. Maybe he'd never really seen it. But that night, one of her friends texted her a picture of a comment Eren had made on the account.

The post was a screenshot of an iPhone text replacement page, showing that the phone would replace the two g's in the N-word with the red B emojis that were a wildly popular 2017 meme on the subreddit /r/dankmemes and elsewhere online. The post was captioned *Making my texts more black friendly*.

Eren had commented, "stupid ni🅱🅱er." He says now that the comment was solely a signal that he also knew the meme, a reference to a controversy involving the YouTuber Keemstar, who, in a 2010 feud with the moderator AlexXx8, had famously encouraged his followers to type "Alex is a stupid n*****" into the chat bar during a livestream. Rosie didn't know the reference, and it probably wouldn't have made any difference if she had.

"That comment," she says. "There's no justification for this whatsoever."

WORST-CASE SCENARIO

(March 20, 2017)

JEFF ANDERSON, THE HIGH SCHOOL PRINCIPAL, WAS TEXTING WITH VAL Williams, the district superintendent. It was just after 9 P.M., and the two administrators, one white, one Asian, were discussing what to do about the Instagram account.

"If evidence is strong," Anderson said, they should take "steps beyond suspension"—in other words, expulsion.

They hadn't yet interviewed most of the followers on the account or pinpointed who had created it. But they wanted to move quickly.

"Worst case we can revoke a suspension if we learn that one or two had tangential involvement," Williams replied. (Williams did not respond to interview requests.)

But determining what *tangential involvement* meant wasn't easy. None of the administrators had much familiarity with social media and the ways teenagers used it. And even if they had, they might still have been hard-pressed to assign specific levels of culpability to each of the account's thirteen followers. Was someone who followed the account but never liked or commented on a single post the same as someone who commented frequently? What about people who hit the like button but never commented? What about the people who commented but didn't say anything racist?

Which of these people would be considered tangential?

All of them?

None of them?

DENIALS

(March 20, 2017)

CHARLES STOOD IN THE BATHROOM STARING AT HIS PHONE AS THE texts came in, one after another. Everything seemed to be unfolding at warp speed. When he left school, he hadn't been called into the office like most of his other friends, and so he'd been thinking maybe he was safe. But now his friends were texting him. Kerry. Ana. Sita. Lolia.

"Like six people who I was super close with, just expressing this immense disappointment. And it was pretty insane how terrible that was," he says. "The main theme of their texts was just disbelief. They couldn't wrap their head around why or how, or what the reason behind everything was."

Kerry was one of the first people to contact him. *Charles, did you do it?*

By now he'd deleted the account completely. It was gone. There was no proof that it was his.

He texted back, denying everything. *I don't know why everyone thinks I did it.*

If you did it, you have to come forward, Kerry texted him. *You have to be honest.*

At last, Charles came clean. *Yeah, it was me.*

After that, all he could do was apologize. "Trying to find

ways to not lose this person in my life because of how important they were to me," he recalls. "But obviously I wasn't going to get that."

Charles's mother poked her head around the bathroom door. The vice principal had called. She and Charles were expected in the principal's office first thing the next morning.

That was bad. But what was happening on his phone was worse.

REALLY BAD

(March 20, 2017)

THAT NIGHT, CHARLES CALLED HIS SISTER, ELIZA, AT COLLEGE, SOBbing. She wasn't that alarmed at first, because he'd called her crying plenty of times, usually after getting into a fight with their mother. She was always the one who talked him down, who watched out for him when things in the family seemed to be going off the rails. His protector.

"Just tell me what happened," she said.

"It's really bad," Charles told her. "This time it's really bad."

"What's really bad?" Eliza asked. "Tell me what happened."

"It's really bad," he kept repeating. "I did something really bad."

"What did you do?"

But he couldn't tell her. All she could hear was the sound of him crying.

"I'm going to hurt myself," he told her.

"No, you're not," she said. "You're fine. You're going to be fine. Everything is going to be fine."

He believed her. She had gotten him through so much already. "We're going to figure this out," she told him when he finally told her about the account. She suggested he start by taking responsibility. He wrote his apology with her on the phone, the two of them editing it together.

That night, he posted it on Instagram.

> I completely betrayed people who considered me a friend and I cannot even begin to explain how disgusting I feel. All the things that were portrayed on the account do not actually portray my true feelings about people of color. I want to be someone with integrity, someone who cares about all people and someone who people can trust. I have not lived up to that at all. There's no way for me to rationalize why I did what I did. It was all just my stupid judgment of what would entertain my friends. I cannot express enough that no one but me deserves any hostility or consequences. I don't expect forgiveness because my actions are unforgivable.

Then, exhausted from crying, he fell asleep.

PART 4

UNDISCUSSED

AGAIN

(March 20, 2017)

AGAIN, ELIZA THOUGHT AFTER TALKING TO CHARLES THAT NIGHT. *Something* again.

She had thought the worst was over for their family.

She had thought she'd succeeded in protecting Charles.

Now he was going to be in the spotlight, just like she had been.

And nobody but her would care what happened to him.

THINGS THEY DIDN'T TALK ABOUT (1)

(February 2012)

CHARLES WAS IN SIXTH GRADE AND ELIZA WAS A HIGH SCHOOL JUNIOR when the police arrived with a warrant. It was a February afternoon and their mother was still at the hospital where she worked. Charles and Eliza didn't know it at the time, but the police had been to their house once that day already, to arrest their father. Now they stood in the living room as the police started searching the house.

"Do me and my brother have to be here?" Eliza asked. "Can I take him somewhere?"

She took him to Solano Avenue, their usual escape. They sat at a coffee shop and drank mochas until their mother came home from work and the police had gone. It was Eliza who had to bail their dad out of jail. Their mother refused to do it, but a friend of her father's wired Eliza the $20,000 bond. After that, her father disappeared. Eliza didn't care where he was, so she didn't go searching.

And then the newspaper article came out, revealing that their father had been arrested for possessing child pornography. It even said what street they lived on. Soon Eliza began getting anonymous messages saying horrible things about her father, as if she were the one to blame. There were messages from people she knew, as well: "Is it true?"

Eliza didn't respond to any of them. She did what she'd always done: tried to keep Charles from noticing that something was wrong. She and her mother debated whether to allow him to go to school that day. Were kids his age old enough to know what was going on? Would somebody say something to him? They decided that not sending him would attract more attention than sending him, and then Eliza anxiously waited for him to come home.

"So what happened at school today? How are things with your friends?"

He said everything was fine. So they didn't talk about it. Never mentioned it again. Anytime Charles asked where his father was, his mother would say something like, "Dad made a mistake."

Eventually their father resurfaced—he was depressed and suicidal but he had a place to stay with a friend in Chicago. In time, his mental health stabilized and he moved to Los Angeles after serving a short stint in jail. Meanwhile, Eliza had moved in with her best friend, whose parents had urged her to put some distance between herself and her family so that she could focus on finishing high school and applying to college. Eliza was that kind of kid—she was in student leadership, played sports, was outgoing, popular. People rallied around her to make sure she'd be okay.

As for Charles, he did what his mother and sister hoped he would do. He stayed ignorant, never learning the reason for his father's arrest and disappearance. "Basically, for that whole section of my life, I didn't understand at all what was going on," he says. He didn't really *want* to understand, he explains. "It was more of just trying to keep everything together."

His father was gone. His house was gone. His sister was gone. So he focused on his friends.

THINGS THEY DIDN'T TALK ABOUT (2)

(October 2012)

JAMES IZUMIZAKI TAUGHT SIXTH-GRADE MATH, LANGUAGE ARTS, AND science at Albany Middle School. He was a young teacher, just twenty-eight, and he seemed to be involved in everything, serving as athletic director and coaching sports teams at both the middle school and the high school. He coached both Eliza's and Charles's basketball teams, but he was more like an uncle to them than a coach, an Asian American father figure who brought some lighthearted cheer to a household that was still reeling from the events of the previous months. On the nights when Charles's mother was working late, Izumizaki was the one who drove Charles to and from basketball practice, sometimes stopping to get burgers on the way.

He had an easy charm to him, goofing around in ways both Eliza and Charles thought were hilarious. Once Charles left a sandwich to rot in the backseat of his car and Izumizaki roasted Charles about the smell for weeks.

And then, on the afternoon of October 1, 2012, the Albany Unified School District sent out a robocall to every family in the district.

"This is an important message from Albany Unified School District with very sensitive information. It is with great sadness that we inform you that according to Albany Police Department, Albany Middle School 6th grade teacher James Izumizaki passed away. The Alameda County Sheriff's Department is investigating the death as a possible suicide. We have no other information at this time."

Izumizaki had been arrested the previous week for molesting two of his former students, but many in the community, including Eliza, hadn't believed that it was true. When he was released from jail, the district's teachers and coaches gathered at one of the teachers' homes to figure out how to raise money for his legal defense. Eliza was there along with her best friend.

"We never asked him, 'What happened?'" she says. "We just said, 'You didn't do this. You would never do that. This didn't happen. They're all lying. How could they say this about you?' Which, I realize now, is a really huge mistake because two days later, he was dead in his car."

Eliza got the news from the robocall. "I was just losing my freaking mind," she says. "I was just crying, crying, crying, crying, like really confused crying." But even in that moment, her first thought was of Charles. She wanted to be there when he got home, to make sure he didn't listen to the robocall. She was relieved to see that Charles was behaving as if nothing had happened. For a while she wasn't even sure he knew.

He did know, though. One of his friends had gotten a text about it after school. They thought it was a joke at first and after that—it was just hard to take in.

"It didn't really hit me until later that day," Charles says. "The fact that it was someone that was so close to me was just unbelievable."

Today, Charles describes the experience as "super hard," but he didn't grieve openly like his sister did. Whatever he felt, he kept it locked away.

"He never cried in front of us, never showed any type of grief or anything, which became very worrisome for me and my mom," Eliza says. "And I remember my mom tried to send him to therapy a few times but my interpretation of what happened was, he was just in so much shock still and he was so young that he wasn't ready to talk about anything."

Once, Charles had a sleepover at a friend's and the friend's mother called Eliza and her mother to say she'd heard Charles crying. She was pretty sure he and his friend had been talking about Izumizaki. Eliza was relieved to hear that he'd been able to express his grief. But that was the only time.

It had been less than a year since their father's arrest, a topic that no one in the family had ever discussed. If it was possible to make sense of Izumizaki's arrest and suicide, they were both going to have to do it on their own.

"Everyone makes mistakes," Charles decided. "I don't agree with what happened. I'm not saying it's okay. But I'm not going to think differently about him. I don't think he's less of a good person."

You could say that shows a lack of empathy for the young people Izumizaki had victimized, and you wouldn't be wrong. There was something in Charles that flinched away from the harm that people close to him had caused. Maybe this was because the only people whose feelings really mattered to him were the men and boys he was close to. Or maybe he had concluded that if he cut people out of his heart when they disappointed him, he would wind up having no one at all.

THINGS THEY DIDN'T TALK ABOUT (3)

(2016)

IT WASN'T UNTIL CHARLES WAS SIXTEEN THAT HE GREW CURIOUS enough to try and find some answers about his father's arrest. It didn't take much sleuthing. A Google search turned up the information right away.

He never said anything to his mother and sister, just let them assume he still didn't know why his father was arrested.

"I never wanted to talk about it with anyone in my family," he says. "I don't think I ever will."

He didn't talk about it with his friends either. He kept it to himself. It had happened a long time ago. And truthfully, he really didn't want to think about it.

PART 5

INVESTIGATION

BLACKOUT

(March 21, 2017)

THE GIRLS WORE BLACK TO SCHOOL ON TUESDAY. THEY DIDN'T WEAR makeup, didn't worry about their hair. None of them could concentrate. In every class, their teachers were asking questions, wanting to know who exactly was involved and what they had done. The administration hadn't told them anything, so they were just as hungry for information as the students—more so, because they weren't on social media.

Ana was afraid to go to her second-period class because one of the account followers was in the class. Nobody looked the same to her now. Suddenly she was questioning everything.

WE'RE GOING TO FIGURE THIS OUT

(March 21, 2017)

CHARLES AND HIS MOTHER ARRIVED AFTER SCHOOL HAD STARTED, when most people were in class. He was so anxious, it felt like his entire body was made of electricity. Just the walk from the car to the school was terrifying. What did people know? What did they think of him?

"Every person that I saw at school, I felt kind of threatened by," he recalls.

Sitting at the table were the principal, Jeff Anderson, and vice principal Melisa Pfohl. Two police officers stood just beside Charles. He didn't really understand why they were there, but he figured it out quickly enough by their questions. Did he intend to harm people? Did he own weapons? When Charles said no, they grew silent and let Ms. Pfohl take the lead. She'd been Charles's teacher in third and fifth grades, and he felt close to her. Now she spoke to him and his mother like a family friend, sympathetically, gently.

Charles took full responsibility. It was his account, he told them. He'd made the posts. Afterward, Principal Anderson took Charles into a room by himself and had him write down everything he'd done on a piece of a paper and sign it. (Anderson declined to be interviewed.)

"At that point, I was so overwhelmed and just wanted to accept my punishment and be done with it," Charles says.

As he was walking down the steps of the school, Pfohl caught up with him. "'You know we're going to figure this out,'" he remembers her saying. Then she gave him a hug.

He was told that he would be suspended for five days. After that, he assumed, he could pick up the pieces and start rebuilding.

INTERVIEWS

(March 21, 2017)

GREG AND PATRICK WERE INTERVIEWED THE SAME MORNING AS Charles. Based on what they had heard the day before, school administrators considered those three to be the most serious offenders—Greg because he had touched Andrea's hair, and Patrick because he had made the most offensive comments on the posts. Greg came to school with both his parents, who stated at the outset that Greg was not going to make any statement. What they could say was this: Greg had not created the account or posted on it.

Patrick came in with his father. He admitted to making "a few irresponsible comments, intended to be edgy jokes towards my friends," as he wrote in a statement a few days later that was eventually filed in court. As for that presentation he'd made in social studies, he noted that he'd gotten a B on it, "a very acceptable grade," and said that the teacher had made no effort to speak with him afterward. (The teacher says she did speak to him, but didn't feel like she made an impact.)

One by one, the other followers were called into the office. None of the rest of them had their parents with them. One remembers the police handing him a brochure about hate crimes and thinking he was about to be arrested and charged with one.

Most of the followers told what they knew: that they followed the account, whether they personally had liked or commented on any posts, who else was involved. By the end of the week, every follower on the account had received either a two- or three-day suspension, depending on their level of involvement.

HAVE YOU SEEN THE PICTURE?

(March 22, 2017)

BRUTSRI WAS IN ALGEBRA CLASS WHEN ANDREA ASKED HIM IF HE'D seen the picture.

He had no idea what she was talking about. Nobody from the school had contacted him to tell him about the account.

"There's a picture of you," she said, and showed him the post on her phone. "Sorry."

The picture was taken from Brutsri's Instagram feed—it showed him and his girlfriend at a softball game, holding up a sign he had made rooting for her. The letters of the sign had been written in gold spray paint, but in the photo they looked brown, which explained the caption: *Did he color in that sign with his skin color.*

Brutsri didn't get it at first. But eventually it dawned on him: He was being mocked for being dark-skinned. It wasn't the first time. He was Sri Lankan American, but even just walking around Albany he'd had people roll down their car windows to yell the N-word at him.

Andrea was watching him. He was tall, broad-shouldered, and deep-voiced, with square-jawed good looks and an affable, even-keeled temperament. What would his anger look like? Would he storm out of the room? Punch a wall?

But Brutsri didn't do any of that. Instead, he shrugged.

"I really pushed it off," he says now. "I'm like, 'Shitty people saying shitty things. I don't care.'"

It annoyed Andrea, to be honest. She felt like Brutsri was holding himself apart, refusing to recognize racism when it was staring him in the face. She could tell he was hurt because he kept talking about it, but still.

"I feel like a lot of immigrant parents have conditioned their kids to be so tough that they don't view discrepancies as real," she says.

But Brutsri didn't want to go there.

"I was like, you know what? This isn't going to affect me," he says. "I'm not going to let this tear me down."

THE BATHROOM STALL

(March 21, 2017)

BILLIE WAS LATE TO THE LUNCHTIME MEETING OF THE FEMINIST CLUB because she'd been practicing her dance for a diversity assembly that was happening the following week. She was in ninth grade, a funny, brainy, vulnerable girl whose expressive eyes were framed by large round glasses. She felt awkward coming in late, but then, she felt awkward most of the time. She'd only moved to Albany the year before, and coming into a town where everyone seemed to have known each other since birth hadn't been easy. Plus, Albany was her first majority white school. She was biracial, Black and Jewish, and in the San Francisco schools, she had been surrounded by people who looked like her—Black kids, Latinx kids, biracial kids. Now she was one of only a handful of Black girls in her grade.

"What are we talking about?" she asked as she slid into her seat. She could tell that emotions in the room were running high.

So they filled her in. A racist Instagram account had been discovered. There were screenshots of the posts and they were terrible. Then a girl looked over at her.

"Oh my god, I think I saw a picture of you on it."

Forty pairs of eyes focused on Billie, who froze, unable to

speak. The first chance she got, she bolted to her next class, which was PE. She beelined for a stall in the locker room bathroom and started to change into her PE clothes, questions tumbling around in her mind like clothes in a dryer.

Why me?

Of course me.

But like, how?

What is this picture of me?

What even is this account?

She'd been bullied her whole life, at every school she'd ever attended, but in the past it had been about being gay and skinny and having mental health issues. Being targeted for her race was something new.

The bathroom stall felt safe. Enclosed. She was in her PE clothes now, but that didn't seem like any reason to open the door. Billie's older sister thought otherwise. She had PE at the same time, and she was in the midst of trying to coax Billie to come out and talk to her when Josette Wheaton, the school security guard, showed up.

"I need to walk you somewhere," Wheaton said.

When Billie refused, Wheaton just opened the door. "Don't worry. I got you," she said.

Despite the short amount of time Billie had been in high school, she and Wheaton were well acquainted. Not only was Wheaton one of the few Black adults on campus, she was also an expert at calming students who were overwhelmed by their emotions, a situation Billie frequently found herself in. Sometimes Wheaton referred to Billie as "a rogue child" because of her habit of leaving class to go wander the hallway or visit a friend in another classroom. When that happened,

Wheaton usually walked Billie over to the counseling office because her mental health was fairly precarious.

But this time Wheaton escorted her to Ms. Pfohl, the vice principal, who gave her the official notification that she was pictured on the account. (Because of concerns about her emotional well-being, Billie was never shown the post, which mocked her hair.)

"Do you want us to call your mom?" Ms. Pfohl asked.

Billie nodded, because she had no words to make the call herself. Words had flown away.

Instead, she just sat in her PE uniform, staring into space and watching her mind hopscotch from thought to thought, question to question.

She thought about the account and why she would be on it.

She thought about what she might eat for dinner that night.

She thought about the freshman debates, which were coming up the following week. Every ninth-grader participated, debating a preassigned topic. Billie's topic was whether Confederate flags and statues should be removed from college campuses.

It seemed ironic, to say the least.

STAFF MEETING

(March 21, 2017)

TEACHERS AT THE HIGH SCHOOL HAD ALMOST NO IDEA WHAT WAS GOING on. A few saw a sample of the posts on the phones of their students. Many saw signs of distress in their classrooms or in the corridors. But it wasn't until the end of the day that they were given an official briefing, in a short after-school faculty meeting. There, Principal Anderson explained that a racist Instagram account had been discovered that targeted certain students.

Even after the meeting, teachers still felt in the dark. Anderson wouldn't say which students were following the account or who had been targeted, but they were seeing interactions all over campus in which kids were confronting each other and accusing one another of being racist. They could feel the mood on campus—outraged and angry, hurt and frightened.

"There was just this confusion brewing, and sense of unease," recalls Ginny Tremblay Geoghegan, who was an art teacher at the high school at the time. "A school is an ecosystem. Everyone is affected by this. It's very triggering for everybody."

HOW TO SEEM OKAY (1)

WHEN YOU WAKE IN THE MORNING, YOU MIGHT HAVE A MOMENT OR TWO before the memory of what happened presses you to the bed and flattens your lungs. The weight of it will be so heavy, you'll be sure you can't possibly sit up, but you're going to have to. You're going to have to walk into that same school today, tomorrow, the next day, and the day after that, five days a week, six hours a day. You're going to have to move down those same hallways and take a seat at those same desks and greet the same people and try to be the person you were before.

First step: Get dressed, do something with your hair. You know how to do that, don't you? You used to do it every morning. But now, when you look in the mirror, you're going to see your reflection through the eyes of the boys who were on the account: too dark, too curvy, too curly, too Black. Strain to hear the voices of your friends, your parents, your siblings, all the people trying to remind you how beautiful you are and have always been. If you squint, maybe you can see yourself in the mirror the way they do. But it takes so much effort to keep that picture in focus. Relax your gaze and it fades away, and the images from the account will be there instead.

Pull your hair into a bun. Put on sweat pants and an oversize T. Why bother trying to look cute when nothing you do is ever going to be good enough? You used to spend so much energy trying to make yourself appealing. You're done with that now. Just getting to school takes everything you have.

Take a seat at your desk even as your skin prickles and your heart pounds and your awareness roams around the room, trying to assess the danger. Which one of these people might have known? Which one of them might be taking your picture right now? By now your heart will be stampeding in your chest and you'll have the urge to run out of the room. When you look up, your teacher will be eyeing you with concern.

Take the pass she offers. Go to the bathroom. Go to the mental health office. Gather in the empty corridors with your friends, the only other people who understand what it's like because they were on the account too.

When the bell rings for your next class, you'll have to do it all again.

Everybody will be sorry about what happened. Everybody will be shocked and angry. Everybody will tell you they feel sick inside. The support will feel good, and it will also feel terrible. Every time someone's eyes fill with tears, they'll yank a brick out of the wall you've constructed, the wall between you and the emotions you can't be feeling if you want to get through the day. You can't let those boys see how vulnerable you are, how weak you feel. You have to seem okay.

COACH

(March 22, 2017)

COACH RAY NEWSOME HAD BEEN COACHING GIRLS' BASKETBALL AT THE high school for fourteen years, one of the few Black employees in the school district. That year he'd taken the team to the league championships. He'd been thinking about retiring, but his players had made him promise that if they won the league title, he'd stay another year.

They'd won. So he'd agreed to stay.

It wasn't long after the team celebration that he got a call from an acquaintance telling him that his picture was on a racist Instagram account alongside one of his players.

"Instead of me trying to describe it to you, let me text it to you," she said.

Seconds later the picture was there on his phone. He and Lolia, with nooses drawn around their necks. His heart sank, not just on his own behalf, but on behalf of Lolia, his player, a bubbly extrovert whom he described as "sunshine." More pictures kept coming, arriving with a musical *ding* each time: Black men being beaten, the KKK, gorillas. A parade of horrors.

Later, he'd find out who was behind them, which made the whole thing even harder to fathom. The thing was, he knew Charles. He'd coached his sister, Eliza.

What could possibly have motivated him to do something like that?

LISTENING

(March 22, 2017)

UNDERNEATH THE POST COMPARING ANDREA TO A GORILLA, PATRICK had commented, "Its too good."

Below that was a series of comments from Wyatt:

"Hey not funny."

"Fuck you."

"Delete this."

To which Patrick had responded, "No fuck YOU you dirty zookeeping son of a bitch."

Reading the exchange, Andrea felt briefly pleased to see that Wyatt was sticking up for her. But him having spoken up once in her defense seemed so meager in the context of all the other posts he'd let go by. It was as if she was the only Black person he cared about.

"I felt like, *You're just defending me because you see some type of reflection of yourself in me in that we're friends. But like, you should be defending all these other people*," she says.

A day or two after the account was revealed, she texted him. *I want to talk to you.*

They met in the gym lobby, a wide expanse of red-and-white-checked linoleum with a big glassed-in trophy case in one corner that stretched from the floor almost to the ceiling.

"How could you have done something like that?" she demanded. "I feel like you know me enough to know better. You're a better person than that."

Her body was too small for all the feelings packed inside it: anger, disappointment, grief, and hurt. Why hadn't Wyatt been the person to report it? Why hadn't he held himself apart? At the very least, he could have unfollowed the account. She stood up for *him* on the daily, whenever she saw those people abusing him. How could he not have done the same for her? Who even *was* he?

As much as she tried to hold them in, the tears were spilling down her face. One of her teachers, Kevin James, was getting something from the vending machines across from them. He looked up and saw that she was crying.

"Are you okay?" he mouthed.

Andrea nodded and tried to make herself look as if she was, in fact, okay, because she hated people watching her have any kind of emotion at all. Something about the reflection of her sorrow in another person's face only made her sadder.

"I'm sorry," she remembers Wyatt saying. Mostly he listened as she told him how she felt. (From his vantage point by the vending machine, Mr. James remembers thinking, *Good for you that you're listening. If you've got a brain in your head, kid, do not talk, just listen.*)

But when Andrea started to cry, Wyatt reached out a hand.

She swatted it away.

"Don't touch me," she said, and left, because nothing he could do now would make up for what he hadn't done then.

WHAT A GORILLA SAYS

A GORILLA IS AN ANIMAL, A PRIMATE, A COUSIN FROM OUR DISTANT past, but in America, it's an animal that tells a story. The story is one that Europeans told about Africans as far back as the 1600s, a story in which Africans were more savage and primitive than Europeans, more closely related to the great apes that lived on the same continent. In this story, a gorilla is a savage brute, a monster, something less than human but also something more, brimming with menacing power and strength.

The story itself was as strong as an ape and as agile as a monkey. It could be put to all kinds of uses. Its particular talent, though, was that it justified enslaving and brutalizing Black people on the grounds that they were fit for nothing better. As the formerly enslaved abolitionist Frederick Douglass wrote in 1854, "The whole argument in defense of slavery, becomes utterly worthless the moment the African is proved to be equally a man with the Anglo-Saxon. The temptation therefore, to read the Negro out of the human family is exceedingly strong."

The story about white women was that they were delicate and vulnerable, innocent and pure, but according to the gorilla story, Black women were tireless, strong, and impervious to pain—more "masculine" than women of other races but also more sexual and less intelligent, more like animals.

Studies have found that these stereotypes persist to this day. Black feminist scholar Moya Bailey coined the term *misogynoir*—a combination of the word *misogyny* and the French word *noir* ("black")—to describe the particular ways that Black women are stereotyped and dehumanized. You can see misogynoir in dating apps, where Black women are often seen as less "feminine" and thus less desirable, or else as hypersexual and ready for anything. You can see it in doctors' offices, where Black women are less likely to be treated for pain than other women. You can see it in schools, where adults often perceive Black girls as young as five as being older, less innocent, and less in need of comfort and protection than white girls, a phenomenon called *adultification*.

A gorilla is an animal, a primate, a cousin from our distant past, but in America it's an animal that tells a story. The story begins: *You aren't human*. It ends: *And so you can't be hurt*.

APOLOGIES

The apologies came too soon, or maybe too late.
They sounded too hasty, or else too polished.
Just a bunch of smart words grouped together.
Cut and pasted. They came by text
when they should have come in person.
They came in letters that were never sent.
Not everybody gave one, so nobody gave one.
They were scattershot. They were stilted.
They were composed of words,
but there were no words.
Not everybody received one, so nobody received one.
Sure, there were a few—if you asked,
a few people remembered. That one, that very
good one, heartfelt, handwritten, personal.
Face-to-face, no excuses, asking for nothing.
But it lasted no longer than your breath
on a window, a snowflake on your cheek.
And then it was gone. Too soon. Too late.

WELFARE CHECK

(March 21-22, 2017)

CHARLES WAS TALKING ABOUT KILLING HIMSELF. HE'D TEXTED AS MUCH to his friend Otis, who kept trying to talk to the school administrators about it while they were interviewing him about the account.

"I was just freaking out and I was trying to tell them, like, 'Is Charles okay? Do you know anything about him?' And they kept trying to ask me, 'Who's running the account? Who's involved?'"

Kerry was worried too. She ran into Otis in the school atrium and they watched Charles walking out of the main office with his mom. He looked shattered.

"I just don't want him to hurt himself," Kerry said. She remembers how gloomy it was outside, even though it was spring. How gray everything felt.

"I know. I'm really worried about him," Otis said.

Charles's mother was worried too. Before leaving the office, she'd told Anderson that she was concerned her son was having suicidal thoughts. The next day, three police officers came to his house to do a welfare check. Charles assured them that he was okay, and they left.

The day after that, the school recommended that he be expelled.

PART 6

LAUGHING

IT SOUNDS LIKE I'M MAKING EXCUSES

CHARLES KNOWS THAT IF HE SAW THE ACCOUNT AS AN OUTSIDER, HE'D conclude that the person who made it was a bona fide, card-carrying, unapologetic white nationalist.

"Oh, yeah," he'd say. "This is coming from a place of hate."

Not just because of the content of the pictures, which were bad enough, but also the fact that he targeted specific people, including his close friends.

"The fact that it was people that I had interactions with on a daily basis definitely made it look like I hated these people," he says. "Which I don't."

He knows this is hard to believe. He knows that it sounds like he's making excuses.

"It's super messed up," he says. "All the pictures are super messed up. It's definitely racist. I'm not in denial about that, but the way I explain it, I feel like it still makes it seem like I am."

Because his explanation sounds something like this: "I'm not racist, but I posted these really racist pictures, but I didn't mean it."

"That just sounds so bad," he says. "Because that's what everyone says, you know?"

IT BEGAN WITH A PENCIL

CHARLES CAN REMEMBER THE PRECISE MOMENT THAT RACIST JOKES entered his circle. It was sophomore year. He, Jon, and Patrick were walking into Taco Bell after school. There, in the brick-red interior, Jon began talking about Lolia, who he said had taken his pencil in class. He called her the N-word and talked about Black people having a low IQ. (Jon remembers this conversation happening somewhere else.)

"It caught me off-guard, because they were pretty offensive," Charles says of Jon's remarks. "I was like, *What's going on?*"

But Charles didn't say anything. Jon was just joking around, he told himself, and Patrick wasn't bothered, so why should he be? He didn't think about how Lolia would feel if she heard what Jon had said. He didn't think how Ana would feel, or Tiana, or any of the other girls in his circle. He was focused on Patrick and Jon, whose opinions were the only ones that really mattered to him. "It was hard for me to speak my mind and I think that's how it works in our friend group," he says now. "There's a majority. The minority doesn't really have a place."

So Charles made a quick calculation: *If this is what our group's humor is going to be, then I guess I'm okay with that.* Soon he was making the same jokes, which meant that other friends were faced with the same choice he'd been faced with: Speak up or laugh along? And like Charles, most decided to go with the majority. Plus Charles had Black friends, so people tended to conclude that if *he* thought it was okay to make those jokes, it probably was.

"Those types of racial jokes became more and more prominent in our friend group," Charles says. "And everyone caught on to that—or mostly everyone."

Wyatt didn't think it was okay, and he said so fairly often. But nobody took Wyatt seriously.

"There were definitely friends who had more power than other friends," Charles says. "It was pretty clear who had a say in what, and in that situation we didn't view Wyatt as having much of a say."

If Patrick had said something, or Greg, or Murphy, that would have been different, Charles explains. "Because they were the type of people to really go along with the humor. And so if I heard them say like, 'Oh I think this is a little too far,' then yeah, okay, *you're* saying it, so it's probably a little too far."

But Wyatt? They were used to ignoring Wyatt.

"He was the only one that was uncomfortable with it the entire time," Charles says. "But again, because he was the only one, no one really cared or listened to him."

FUNNY

"FOR BOYS, BEING FUNNY IS LIKE A COMMODITY," SAYS ROSALIND Wiseman, author of *Masterminds and Wingmen*, an exploration of teen boy culture. "You are never going to be thrown out, never going to be socially isolated as a boy if you are funny. And if you can be *competitively* funny, that's even better. And this is why boys get into so much trouble."

Because to be funny is to be admired. And to be funnier than someone else is to win. The stakes keep going up. Be funny. Be funnier. And by all means, don't be the person who complains about the joke. Because boy culture says that *everything* is funny.

"Girls have a little bit more space to say, 'That's not funny,'" says Wiseman. "In boy world, everything has to be funny or else your heterosexuality and your masculinity is questioned. Everything has to be funny or you're being a little bitch."

HOW DOES A JOKE BECOME FUNNY?

LOOKING BACK, CHARLES THINKS IT STARTED WITH VIDEO GAMES, because if you played a single game of League of Legends online, you were almost guaranteed to hear a barrage of N-words and homophobic slurs.

In the online kingdom where the edgelords reigned, you gained citizenship by laughing at these kinds of things. It was a boy's land, a *white* boy's land mostly, a sly playground of jokes and roasts where taking anything too seriously was a sign that you didn't belong. To be offended was to be excluded, to be cast off among the grown-ups and the girls, the social justice warriors and snowflakes. Men were not supposed to mind anything except attacks on their own manhood.

Once he knew the kingdom existed, Charles could recognize its citizens. On Reddit's front page were memes that had been "voted up" by a lot of people, and in 2017 a lot of those memes found humor in things that objectively weren't funny, which was kind of the point.

Racist jokes. Jokes about suicide, pedophilia, rape, incest, mass shootings, the Holocaust, people with disabilities. It was easy to laugh at those things when they weren't about you—and you could prove you belonged in the kingdom by laughing even if they were.

"Like with all these jokes, in the back of my mind, I know

it's wrong," he explains. "It's offensive. That's part of what the humor comes from."

Something about the surprise of it. Something about it being transgressive, shocking, not meant to be said or even thought. Which meant that the worse it was, the funnier it would be.

"I don't really know how it starts," he says. Maybe one person found those things funny and shared the joke and other people found it funny too. "Or everyone just thinks it's funny because they think other people think it's funny."

Either way, he says, "I guess the humor just got darker and darker as I explored more of the Internet."

That brand of humor was pretty mainstream in their high school, at least among white and Asian boys. Nobody took it as far as Charles did on the @yungcavage account, but they took it far enough. Shortly after the account was discovered, a senior named Jillian Guffy talked about the popularity of "edgy" memes in an article in the Albany High School newspaper entitled "What Does It All Meme?"

"The constant exchange of offensive memes breeds a vicious competition where the jokes get increasingly more shocking until the initial jokes are no longer very outrageous," she wrote. "This is classic desensitization, especially when considering how young people rely on their smart phones. If every time we open our social media accounts we are met with offensive memes, it's only natural for us to get used to that type of media. Because most adults are completely clueless of this world, our online activity goes unregulated and we remain unaccountable."

POE'S LAW

IRONIC RACISM FEELS LIKE SOMETHING THAT JUST HAPPENED, A strange bird that hatched in the peculiar incubator of cultural references, digital gags, and detached exaggeration that is Gen Z culture. But the truth is that however this kind of humor first originated, organized hate groups have capitalized on its popularity.

"It's a fairly explicit strategy from some groups to draw in young people who are interested in pushing boundaries or being edgy," explains Lindsay Schubiner, program director at the Western States Center, which has created a tool kit for combating hate at schools. Hate groups of all kinds have discovered that messages that are disguised as humor, irony, or trolling are far more persuasive and attractive to young people than straightforward racism. Take, for example, the neo-Nazi website The Daily Stormer, which its editor, Andrew Anglin, once described as "non-ironic Nazism masquerading as ironic Nazism."

In 2018, a reporter named Ashley Feinberg obtained a copy of the website's style guide, a handbook for its writers on everything from punctuation to the proper formatting of hyperlinks. The style guide also included some notes on strategy, including a section called "Lulz."

> *The tone of the site should be light. Most people are not comfortable with material that comes across as vitriolic, raging, non-ironic hatred. The unindoctrinated should not be able to tell if we are joking or not.*

In other words, if you want to make the unthinkable thinkable, make it sound like a joke.

The most successful trolls live in a shadowland where everything is ambiguous. Are you being racist to be racist, or racist to make fun of political correctness, or even racist to make fun of racism? Who knows? And as long as it's funny, who cares? (The idea that it's impossible to know what anyone really means online is sometimes called "Poe's Law.")

Using irony as camouflage, far-right meme farms are now pumping out memes with the speed and volume of an Amazon warehouse. In 2018, a team of researchers that included Gianluca Stringhini, a Boston University professor who studies memes, found that a majority of the most widely circulated memes originated on a tiny number of right-wing forums on Reddit and 4chan that were dominated by hate content. These memes were then carried into other, more mainstream forums and platforms, where they continued to spread to a wider and wider audience. And since their origins were unknown, so were their intentions.

Not every racist meme is generated in a far-right meme factory, though. As Brian Friedberg, the senior researcher for the Technology and Social Change Research Project at the Harvard Kennedy School's Shorenstein Center observes,

"There's an ambient anti-Blackness in Internet culture that often goes uncritiqued, or largely unnoticed."

Friedberg and his boss, Joan Donovan, are working on a book about the past decade of meme wars, tracking the way memes are used to spread disinformation and manipulate public opinion. One thing they've noticed is how prevalent anti-Black racism is online, particularly on Reddit. He points to the "casualness and ubiquity" of the N-word as one example, but there are many.

"Any chance to make a Black person look dangerous or ridiculous, there's always going to be memes," he says.

There is now much more content moderation on Reddit than there was in 2017, and some anti-racist subreddits have formed that actively seek out hateful content and get it taken down. Much of the stuff that Charles and his friends used to see on Reddit has migrated to platforms like 9GAG and iFunny and Discord or transformed into videos on platforms like TikTok and Instagram. The app iFunny, for example, contains thousands of memes that glorify Nazis, mass shooters, race war, and armed insurrection, while the Institute for Strategic Dialogue, a think tank that tracks online extremism, has found white supremacist, antisemitic, transphobic, and pro-terrorism videos garnering millions of views on TikTok.

By 2016, three quarters of American youths ages fifteen to twenty-one had run into extremist content online, an increase of about 20 percent from 2013. (The percentages have likely gone up further since then.) Those online exposures inevitably bleed into the real world. In 2021, the U.S. Government Accountability Office released a report on bullying and hate speech in schools that found that during the 2018–19 school year, one in four students ages twelve to eighteen "saw hate words or symbols written in their schools, such as homophobic slurs and references to lynching."

The more online hate you see, the more you are likely to see in the future. The algorithmic filter bubbles that shape all of our online experiences are designed to serve up more and more of any content that a user engages with, funneling users into increasingly extreme echo chambers. The more you interact with it, the more normal it begins to feel, and the more likely it will be that your own views and opinions will begin to align with those of the online communities you're part of. Which can lead to some odd contradictions. During the period that Charles was posting racist images on his @yungcavage account, he also wrote a thoughtful essay about racism that connected the hypocrisy of U.S. founding fathers with the failures of Reconstruction and the present-day prison system. Perhaps the essay was a lie he told just to get a good grade. Or perhaps the two parts of his brain had found a way to coexist inside his skull, like neighbors who take the same elevator to side-by-side apartments in the same building but never engage in conversation.

STREAKS

CHARLES WANTED TO MAKE HIS FRIENDS LAUGH. AND RACIST JOKES got laughs. His beef with Andrea got laughs too, so he upped the intensity of it. In his memory, it had started with Wyatt telling him that Andrea had been saying negative things about him, that she had called him and his friends "immature." (Wyatt doesn't remember this.) He insists that he didn't actually hate Andrea but was just dramatizing their feud for comic effect. Half the time it was just the randomness of it that he thought was funny, like posting a picture of her eating a carrot captioned *she's eating a fucking carrot.*

He and his friends often sent one another meaningless pictures just to maintain their Snapchat streaks, which measured how many consecutive days they'd been in touch. A lot of the posts on the account came from streak photos, including the picture of Lolia and her coach. Charles screenshot it, and then later he drew in the nooses by hand. Because at that point, he had spent enough time looking at racist memes to know which images had power—monkeys, torches, nooses, white hoods.

And so it went, through post after post. His method was to take a random picture from Instagram or Snapchat and then add the most incendiary image or language he could.

"My main motive was to please my friends," he says. "And that's what got the job done."

PART 7

JUSTICE

FOUR KINDS OF JUSTICE

Punitive Justice

Live by the sword,
die by the sword.
Do the crime,
then do the time.
You reap what you sow.
An eye for an eye,
a tooth for a tooth.

Permissive Justice

Boys will be boys.
Let bygones be bygones.
It was a first offense
and he's a good kid
with a bright future
so let's not make
a big deal about it.

Restorative Justice

Who was harmed?
What do they need?

Whose obligation is it
to make it right?
Don't *feel* guilty;
you *are* guilty.
So do something about it.

Transformative Justice

The harm took place
in a house,
but what was going on
in the neighborhood?
Who built the house?
Who laid down the streets?
Who was looking the other way?

THE EVENING NEWS

(March 22, 2017)

ON WEDNESDAY NIGHT, A STORY ABOUT THE INSTAGRAM ACCOUNT RAN on the evening news. It featured Billie's mother.

"The mother of a student at Albany High School is speaking out tonight about racially offensive pictures that targeted her daughter and others at the school," said KTVU anchorman Frank Somerville. "In fact, we can't even show you some of the photos because they're so graphic."

The segment was about three minutes long. It showed partially blurred-out pictures of some of the posts, mentioned the involvement of the police, and included a clip of the district superintendent, Val Williams, in front of the school saying that she found the photos "disgusting."

"We're not going to tolerate racism," Williams said. "We're not going to tolerate bullying. We're not going to tolerate cyberbullying."

But what does *not tolerating* something actually look like?

"The mother wants these students expelled," crime reporter Henry Lee told Somerville at the end of the segment. "Whether that happens is another question. This investigation is ongoing."

THE MATRIX IS A GUIDE

(March 23–24, 2017)

AS NEWS OF THE ACCOUNT SPREAD, PARENTS AND COMMUNITY MEMbers began to contact the school board to demand that the district's response be swift and strong.

"Anyone who was a member of the site should be suspended for not less than two weeks, but any of the young people who created or posted racist memes MUST be expelled," a parent of a biracial girl wrote in a letter to the school board on March 24.

Many commenters seemed unaware that California state regulations ban suspensions of longer than five consecutive days and that suspensions are increasingly understood to be counterproductive. A 2021 study by the American Institutes for Research, for example, found that suspensions not only failed to reduce undesirable behavior, they actually increased the likelihood of negative behaviors down the line.

Meanwhile, school administrators and school board members were exchanging emails asking whether they were required to follow their own discipline matrix. Under the matrix, a first-time incident of cyberbullying would result in a two-day suspension.

"My sense from our conversation yesterday is that you

felt constrained and bound by the discipline matrix," Val Williams wrote Melisa Pfohl on Thursday, March 23. "Our attorney helped clarify that the matrix is a guide."

School administrators, as a group, like rules. And in the days, weeks, and months after the @yungcavage account was discovered, there would be a lot of discussion about what the rules—either the district's own policies or the California education code—required them to do. Albany was a tiny district, and few of its professional administrators or elected school board members had ever navigated a crisis of this magnitude. Most of them knew almost nothing about social media and the role it played in the lives of their students. The rules were the only guidebook they had.

But in this case, the rules weren't much help. The rules didn't tell an all-white school board and a mostly white administrative staff how to sort out their own feelings of anguish and alarm, their worries about how they would be perceived, their fears of getting it wrong. The rules didn't explain how to heal the wounds of the people who had been affected or how to put a fractured school community back together again. Nor did they explain how to respond to thirteen followers with different levels of participation and varying responses to the account's discovery, or how to protect student privacy while also responding to a community that wanted answers and accountability.

All the rules could tell them was how to punish.

"We can be confused that the number of days of suspension—whether it's three or five or ten or a hundred—is what will make it right and how justice will be served," Pfohl says, recalling the pressure administrators were under to act decisively. "But it doesn't. It's so much more complicated than that."

CHARLES'S MOTHER AND STEPFATHER OFFERED TO WITHDRAW CHARLES from school right away and have him finish junior and senior year online.

"He's done something just egregious here," his stepfather, Alexander, remembers saying. "We'd like to pull him out of school and we'd like to start the withdrawal process."

But according to Alexander, school officials were not interested in this solution. They insisted on expulsion. "They wanted some kind of retribution," he says.

This seemed unnecessarily punitive to him. He argued that having to leave school was a sufficiently severe punishment without it being on Charles's permanent record. "He'll have no junior prom memories. He'll have no high school sweetheart. When they have a high school reunion, he won't be invited," he said. "I think that's enough."

Meanwhile, members of the school board were receiving correspondence making the exact opposite argument.

"These guys deserve to be expelled (and without that expulsion being 'stayed')," a former school board member wrote in an email to a current board member, "and if they aren't expelled, the message of white privilege and rich white people getting away with stuff, and the message that Albany is a racist city and a racist school, will reverberate around the country. Our district and our city will be tarnished for the foreseeable future."

VIDEO

IT WAS ANDREA'S IDEA TO MAKE A VIDEO, BUT ANA WAS THE ONE WHO had the skills to make it happen. Over the course of five or six days, she interviewed Andrea, Brutsri, Lolia, and a few other students of color, putting them in front of a plain, mustard-yellow wall that threw their anger and hurt into stark relief. In the video, each of the students speaks about their reaction to discovering the account, their feelings about the likers and followers who did nothing, and their ideas about what should happen now.

"Really there's no form of punishment that will teach them how to accept people," says one student, a Black boy who wasn't pictured on the account. "Expelling them may seem appropriate, but that's not going to teach them how to accept people. That's just going to teach them that they don't belong somewhere, that their views don't belong somewhere. They have to go through programs and meetings and circles and they have to talk things out." He paused. "If they truly want to change. I can't help it if they don't want to change."

The last quote is from Andrea:

"It's like one of my deepest fears that I'm never going to be enough for someone. So when somebody pulls out your insecurity from the bottom of your heart and just puts it everywhere and, like, fully validates that that's actually true? Oh my god. It's awful."

THE DAGGER

THERE ARE LOTS OF WAYS TO HURT ANOTHER HUMAN BEING. YOU CAN do it directly, with violence or words. You can do it indirectly, through rumors or exclusion or assumptions. You can do it without doing anything, by failing to act. You can use the authorities to do it, wielding the power of the police, school officials, bosses, government agencies. Money will do it, by making it harder for someone to find housing or health care or get a job or a loan. You can even use the environment: Pollute the air or the water where they live, allow their streets to flood, fail to pick up the trash.

Racism, of course, has done all of that and more, which is one reason that it elicits such strong emotions. A slur, a stereotype, a joke, an assumption is never just itself. It's also everything that came before it, centuries of wounds, cuts on top of cuts on top of cuts.

So what do you do with all that history? The person who made the joke or used the slur didn't commit all of racism's many crimes, but they still used the same weapon, its blade honed by repeated use.

IT LIVES IN THE BODY

THE INSTAGRAM ACCOUNT WASN'T A HATE CRIME, AS MUCH AS PEOPLE sometimes said it was. Being racist and sexist isn't illegal, and even language like "on the verge of bringing my noose to school" didn't meet the standard for being a criminal threat, which California law says must be "so unequivocal, unconditional, immediate, and specific" that it communicates serious intention and the "immediate prospect" that the threat will be carried out.

But even if it wasn't a crime, the impact that the account had on the people who were targeted by it is similar to what has been found among people who have been targets of hate crimes either by being assaulted or by having their home, school, or workplace vandalized.

"Compared to other crimes, hate crimes have a more destructive impact on victims and communities because they target core aspects of our identity as human beings," Jessica Henderson Daniel, the president of the American Psychological Association, said in 2018. "Hate crimes also send the message to members of the victim's group that they are unwelcome in the community, decreasing feelings of safety and security."

A comparison of hate crime victims with the victims of other crimes in England and Wales found that hate crime victims were more than twice as likely to suffer a loss of confidence, an increased sense of vulnerability, anxiety, panic attacks, depression, and sleeplessness than other crime victims. Another study, this one of people in Sacramento, California, who were targeted because of their sexual orientation, found that these victims not only experienced more fear than other crime victims but also reported "significantly less belief in the benevolence of people." Being targeted had rearranged their entire view of the world, in other words, which now seemed more dangerous and less kind.

You don't have to be the victim of a hate *crime* to experience these kinds of impacts—hate alone will do the trick. People who have experienced race-based discrimination have higher blood pressures and shorter life spans, with their bodies showing premature aging at the cellular level. They tend to remain in a state of hypervigilance that can suppress the immune system and increase the risk of heart disease, which may explain why Black women in all income groups are more likely than white women to give birth prematurely. Other studies have found that feeling excluded or rejected can lead to chronic inflammation, which is implicated in a wide variety of diseases, from diabetes to cancer. Older Black women who contend with racism on a regular basis report nearly three times more trouble with cognitive function—the capacity for learning, concentrating, reasoning, remembering, and making decisions—than those who don't.

Some researchers have linked the health effects of racism to the impact of shame, which can put people at greater risk for depression, addiction, suicide, and anxiety. Other researchers have focused on feelings of powerlessness, which can afflict anyone who is categorized as low status, whether it's because of race, class, or bullying. Robert M. Sapolsky, a Stanford University neurology professor, has investigated the way feeling powerless affects baboons who in all other ways are living a pretty low-stress life on the Serengeti. Those who have lower status in their troop face a constant threat of petty violence from higher-status baboons to the point where even minor teasing produces an intense stress response in the bodies of the baboons who are used to getting picked on. That stress, which can be measured by the presence of the hormone cortisol, can lead to the same kinds of diseases you see in chronically stressed-out humans: hypertension, diabetes, inflammation, suppressed immunity.

All of these are different lenses for looking at the same phenomenon: When you are targeted for who you are, it doesn't just hurt your feelings. It hurts every cell in your body.

SQUISHY

ANDREA AND RINA WERE TALKING ABOUT BILLIE, THE ONLY FRESHMAN on the account. Billie's combination of toughness and vulnerability reminded Andrea of herself, and she wondered how Billie was doing. Did she know that it was okay to be angry? Did she know that she wasn't alone?

"We should probably go talk to her," Rina said.

They found her sitting at a table in a corner on the third floor, doing her math homework. They each pulled up a chair.

"We were also on the account," they said. "We wanted to tell you that we're here for you. We're going to help you out."

Just as Andrea had feared, Billie wasn't doing great.

"Everyone was treating me like I was all squishy and cracked," she recalls. She was new at the school, hadn't had time to create a persona for herself. Now this was it: Victim of Racist Cyberbullying.

"It's cool to be known at school, but not for this," she says. "Everyone knew I was on it. And so from that day everyone looked at me differently."

She appreciated that Andrea and Rina had reached out. But she didn't really know what to say to them. They were Albany people—they'd grown up in town. She was never going to be like them. She still felt so terribly alone.

ONE OF THE GOOD GUYS

(March 22–29, 2017)

MURPHY DIDN'T TELL HIS PARENTS THAT HE'D TALKED TO THE COPS ON Monday. But by Tuesday, the school had called to tell them he was involved with the account. When his dad sat him down for a talk, Murphy did what he could to pin the blame on Charles. But his father wasn't buying it.

"You didn't think this was bad?" he remembers his dad saying. "Someone tying a noose around a girl's neck? You don't think that's bad?"

"Yeah," Murphy admitted. "That doesn't sound too funny after you say it like that."

"Because it's not *supposed* to be funny," he remembers his dad saying. "That's racist. People would actually do those kinds of things. You think that's funny, for someone to die like that?"

His father's reaction made the situation feel more serious. But it was hard to sit with those feelings for long. He knew he'd screwed up big-time, but he was still hoping he could get out of it.

"I'm like, *Man, I'm about to lose all my friends*," Murphy recalls. "*I need to make sure I'm the one looking like the good guy.*"

He figured he could do it. He was the one who had blown

the whistle, after all. The girls had told him they'd have his back. And Murphy's understanding was that his cooperation meant he wouldn't be suspended. "I kind of had that mentality running through me the whole time," he says now. "Where it's like, *Okay, I'll be safe no matter what.*"

But his sense of invincibility didn't last long. School administrators said that since Murphy was a follower on the account, he was just like anyone else. He'd liked the picture comparing Andrea to a gorilla, and he'd taken the photograph of the back of Andrea's head that Charles had used in the "Tiana or Andrea" post. He'd taken it just to keep a Snapchat streak going with Charles, a quick snap of whatever happened to be in front of him in class. But still. He had to have known how it could be used.

Murphy received a two-day suspension on Wednesday—one day fewer than other followers. He spent Thursday and Friday doing yard work for his parents, who forbade him to see his friends or play video games. While he was out of school, Lolia asked him on Snapchat for help building a case. Could he send her anything else?

All of the account followers had been told not to have any contact with the people who had been targeted. The targets had been told the same. But Murphy was the good guy. He and Lolia and Sita were still friends.

He sent Lolia screenshots of two Snapchats in which followers of the account called each other the N-word as well as other insults, along with a screenshot from a group text conversation several months earlier that included a racist joke involving swimming emojis with dark skin tones.

According to one of the lawsuits that was subsequently

filed, when Murphy returned to school the following Monday, he went to the principal's office with his parents for a mandatory end-of-suspension meeting before he could return to class. In that meeting, the lawsuit contends, Principal Anderson told Murphy that the flames of the Instagram account controversy would have burned themselves out if Murphy hadn't "tossed gasoline on the fire" by responding to Lolia's request. (The district did not dispute this account.)

Anderson immediately suspended Murphy for an additional three days.

SUSPENDED ANIMATION

BEING SUSPENDED SUCKED, BUT NOT IN THE WAY IT WAS MEANT TO suck.

A few days off from school—that wasn't so terrible.

What sucked was knowing that people were talking about you while you were gone, that people were angry at you, that you couldn't explain.

It sucked not being at school, but it also sucked knowing you had to go back.

NO BIG DEAL

MURPHY'S DAD HAD A LOT TO SAY ABOUT MURPHY'S INVOLVEMENT IN the account. During his suspension, the lectures came daily, particularly as Murphy began to receive blowback from other students in the form of threats or angry messages.

"Well, now you see that you did something racist," his dad would say. "People don't find it funny. Clearly it's not a joke."

Murphy remembers his older brother interrupting one of these lectures to pose an objection. He had been part of the Broke Boys Instagram account two years earlier, and they'd posted the same kind of stuff, he said. Back then, nothing much had happened. Why was everyone making such a big deal about it this time?

Murphy didn't know what to think, so he just agreed with whoever he was talking to. If someone was mad about the account, he'd apologize. If they thought the account was no big deal, he'd shrug and roll his eyes. His main focus was getting back to school and putting the whole thing behind him. Whatever it took, that's what he would do.

THE HARMERS

(March 26, 2017)

BY NOW, THE SCHOOL'S TOP ADMINISTRATORS SEEMED TO HAVE LOST interest in sorting through the levels of culpability. On Sunday evening, after followers of the account had completed their three-day suspensions and were getting ready to return to school the next morning, Principal Jeff Anderson sent out a terse email informing them that their suspensions had been extended. Every student who followed the account was now receiving the maximum suspension allowed under California state regulations: five days.

For the parents of the less-involved students, this zero-tolerance approach was hard to swallow. Wyatt's father, Dennis, calls it "an utter failure" on the part of the administration.

"By grouping everybody together, they didn't even think or ask questions," he says. "And that just shows their level of understanding about everything from social media, to how these kids behave, to who is who in this whole organization. They just made decisions without getting to the bottom of everything."

Those decisions would end up having lasting repercussions. The key one was this: Because everybody got the same punishment, students and teachers concluded that everyone had the same level of involvement. From then on, all thirteen students who followed the account were in the same category, regardless of how central or tangential they had been. According to subsequent lawsuits, school officials began to refer to them collectively as the Harmers.

From then on, their fates were linked.

MESSAGE FROM THE SUPERINTENDENT

(March 28, 2017)

EIGHT DAYS AFTER THE INSTAGRAM ACCOUNT WAS DISCOVERED, the Albany Unified School District superintendent, Val Williams, sent out an email.

> AUSD Parents, Staff, Students & Community Members,
>
> The purpose of this letter is to inform you of an anti-semitic incident that occurred on the Albany High School campus. The situation, which I describe below, was handled the day that Principal Anderson and his co-administrators were alerted to this incident. Given our recent experiences and our reaffirmed commitment to safe and welcoming campuses, we are providing the details of this situation to you.
>
> On March 8th, AHS administrators were notified that a group of seven 9th graders has been engaging in Nazi salutes when passing

> in the halls. While administrators were alerted to this behavior on March 8th, upon further investigation, it was determined that these students were making these salutes to each other for several months. The vice principal immediately brought these students into the office, determined what occurred, contacted their parents, and took appropriate action.

The letter hit the community with the force of a bomb. First a racist Instagram account, and now Nazi salutes? How could this be happening?

BYSTANDER

A BLACK FRESHMAN NAMED DAMARI HAD SEEN THE NAZI SALUTES IN the hallways. The kids who were doing them were in his grade, and while he wasn't exactly friends with them, they'd grown up together.

"It definitely struck me as weird, seeing a bunch of kids marching and heiling through our school to try and be funny," he says.

But it didn't shock him. That mix of humor and racism was a normal part of life.

"In modern-day social media, there's a lot of dark humor," explains Damari. "A lot of those things are constantly joked about, especially in a group of all-white kids. It's very common."

So, he'd taken it in stride. Not like the Instagram account, which put him in "fighting mode." He saw the Nazi salutes as a lesser offense.

"I saw it and I didn't think 'Oh I absolutely hate them now' because I'm not Jewish. It didn't really affect me personally, but I could see how it affected other people."

Don't get him wrong; he knew it was messed up. Joking about genocide? Not cool.

Still, he didn't report it. Not because he's not Jewish but because he's not a snitch.

"I don't tell to higher authorities, ever," he says. "Police, principals, that's a straight line for me."

So did it make sense to him that nobody reported the @yungcavage Instagram account?

Not really.

"Following an account and seeing something with your naked eye are very different," he argues. "If you followed an Instagram account, you are personally going to that account and requesting that you want to join or be a part of that."

Whereas the Hitler salutes were just going on around him. He didn't ask to see them. So he continued going about his business.

He hesitates, seeming to replay the conversation in his mind.

"I guess it's definitely looked at similar," he says after a moment. "Being a bystander."

THE BYSTANDER EFFECT

IN FEBRUARY 2021, A THIRTY-SEVEN-YEAR-OLD MAN DIED ON A GRASSY traffic island in a busy part of San Francisco. For almost a full day, people walked and drove past his unmoving body without anyone stopping to check on his well-being. At last, a woman who had seen him from her window earlier in the day concluded that he wasn't just taking a nap and called 911. It took her roughly seven hours to make the call. She was the only one who did.

As shocking as this story is, it's actually an example of a well-known phenomenon known as the bystander effect. In study after study, social psychologists have found that people are less likely to intervene or offer help if there are other bystanders present. One reason for this is called "diffusion of responsibility." When lots of people *could* intervene, no individual feels that intervening is their responsibility. Another reason is that we tend to take our cues about how to react to a situation from other people. If no one else seems alarmed enough to act, we're less likely to be alarmed ourselves. Finally, we tend to worry about what other people think of us. If it feels like people might judge us harshly for acting, we won't act. In general, people are more likely to intervene if a situation is clearly dangerous, if the perpetrator is there in front of them, and if the cost of *not* acting seems higher than the cost of acting. All of which means that online bullying and bigotry are particularly prone to the bystander effect.

In 2014, Sarah E. Jones, a graduate student in the College of Communication and Information at the University of Kentucky, investigated college students' attitudes toward cyberbullying. She identified five principles that students used to decide whether they should intervene in something they saw online:

1. *Honor proximity*: Respond only if you are close to the victim or know the story behind the online interaction.
2. *Respond according to severity*: If it doesn't seem really harmful, keep scrolling.
3. *Embrace the cultural environment*: Base your actions on what is considered normal or acceptable in your peer group.
4. *Gauge from others' responses*: If somebody else says something, you can keep silent.
5. *Avoid personal consequences*: Make sure that you don't end up being the next victim.

These unwritten rules help explain why young people are slow to intervene when they see racism or harassment, either in person or on social media.

"When you're an adult, you don't tend to remember and appreciate the power dynamics that make it so difficult to feel that you have power in that situation," says Rosalind Wiseman, an expert on teen boy culture. "And as a young man in that situation, it's very easy to rationalize not doing anything, because you can say, 'I have no power' or 'Nothing's going to make a difference. They're not going to take it seriously, so why even try?'"

OPPORTUNITIES

NIGHT AFTER NIGHT, EREN TRIED TO LOOK INTO HIS OWN SOUL, TO inventory what he saw there. Did he feel prejudice or hate toward Black people? He didn't *think* so, but if he didn't, why hadn't he reacted to the images on the account? Why hadn't he said something?

His brain offered him a variety of logical explanations: The other account followers weren't his friends. He had thought of himself as peripheral, a sophomore eavesdropping on the conversations of a group of juniors. If someone was going to say something, shouldn't it be someone inside the group?

But what if those circumstances made him *more* responsible instead of less so? What if the fact that he didn't really know the account creator made him uniquely qualified to blow the whistle on the whole thing—or at least to separate himself from the situation? Why was he only thinking it over now?

"I felt like I had a lot of opportunities to unfollow this account that I didn't take," he explains. "And so with these opportunities passing me by, I was like, what does that mean for me? What does that mean *about* me?" Why had it taken getting called out directly for him to look closely at the account's "edgy humor"? Where was his own personal line between what was acceptable and what wasn't?

It was like a switch had flipped and he'd suddenly gone from relatively little self-awareness to deep self-scrutiny.

And so he paced. Back and forth. Around the bed.

Who was he?

How could he share a body with the person that he had been?

A CHANCE TO EXPLAIN

AS THE SECOND ROUND OF SUSPENSIONS BEGAN WINDING DOWN, ADMINistrators found another problem staring them in the face. Somehow the kids who followed the account and the kids who were impacted by it were going to have to go to school together.

Charles, Patrick, and Greg, the three students considered to be the most responsible, were not coming back to school—at least not anytime soon. Charles and Patrick were facing expulsion, and the school had suggested to Greg's family that he should go on independent study once he'd finished his five-day suspension.

But the other eleven followers of the account were going to have to return to school, and administrators were understandably nervous about how that would go. Eventually they hit upon a plan. A local nonprofit called SEEDS (Services that Encourage Effective Dialogue and Solutions) volunteered to hold a mediation session between the two groups of students on Thursday, March 30, the day the eleven followers, likers, and commenters were supposed to return to school.

The mediation was optional, but all eleven agreed to attend. Their motivations and expectations varied. Some wanted a chance to apologize to the girls in person, or to deliver the apology letters they had written. Others just wanted to get back to school. Most wanted to explain their particular role—how much or how little they had liked or commented.

"I was kind of looking forward to this, in a weird sense," Eren says. "As much as one can look forward to a mediation about this kind of thing. Because I thought this was going to be an opportunity to explain myself."

Looking back now, he can see that he was hoping to receive some kind of absolution, a way to get back to the life he'd had before. "I still definitely did not consider the full ramifications of everything," he says. "But I had this remorse that I wanted to try to right it, for my own self, in a selfish sense, to maybe stop this inner turmoil."

The students involved in the mediation had the option of going to class afterward or going home. One of the parents remembers talking it over with her son, who was eager to get back to school. She remembers telling him, "It's going to suck for a while. There's no way to sugarcoat it. It's absolutely going to suck for a while, but then hopefully less sucking, and then eventually no sucking, we hope."

That was the plan, such as it was. Go in, face the music, and get on with whatever period of sucking lay ahead.

HARSH CONSEQUENCES

(March 28, 2017)

NORMALLY A TUESDAY NIGHT SCHOOL BOARD MEETING DIDN'T DRAW A big crowd, but March 28 was the first meeting since the Instagram account had been made public. Every one of the black plastic chairs in the room was full. Some people had spilled into the hallway. Others were sitting on the floor.

Seated at a curved dais beneath the city seal, the members of the board moved through the mundane items on their agenda until it was time for public comment. Over the next three hours and twenty minutes, some forty-five speakers shared their grief and rage not just about what had happened at Albany High School in the past week but also about what had happened over previous years and even decades. Many Black and Latinx speakers said that they had grown up in Albany or raised children and grandchildren there and had experienced racism or sexism or bullying that went unaddressed.

"This stuff is part of Albany's history and for you to say this is an isolated incident says more about *you* than it does about the history of this city," one speaker charged.

A Black Albany parent who had a daughter in second grade talked about growing up in Oakland, where he said he went to at least as many funerals as birthday parties. That's why he and his wife chose to raise their family in Albany, where his daughter would be safe.

"What's the point?" he asked. His voice thrummed with sorrow and fury. "What is the *point* of working hard in school and doing the things you have to do and then growing up and getting a good job and making enough money to send your kids to school in a place that's great if they're going to get treated like this?"

Over and over, speakers advocated for the harshest possible punishment. The account was so horrifying, the images so egregious, the harm to the people targeted so obvious, that the students responsible could never be allowed back at the school.

"When you do something this wrong? There are harsh consequences," the second-grade father said. "This is calculated. This is something that you know it's wrong and you do it anyway! That's something you can't fix with a suspension. You can't fix that with 'Let's sit down and talk a little bit.' That part is done."

Then Coach Ray stood up. He talked about going to a rally at the high school over the weekend, when more than three hundred people had joined hands to encircle the school in a gesture of solidarity. There he had encountered parents of some of the account followers. They'd come up to him to offer their apologies, and he had felt compassion for them because he could see the pain on their faces.

"But you know what?" he said. "Those parents are fighting for their kids. They are fighting for the reputation of their children. They want to make sure they get a chance to go to college. They don't want this situation to ruin that. But what about the parents of the kids that were targeted? Who's sticking up for them?"

He described the horror of having his image circulated with a noose drawn around his neck.

"Fourteen years and that's the image I'm leaving here?" he asked. "That will *never* go away. So the boys can come back to school after four to five days, after watching cartoons or whatever, planning their next dastardly deed, and forget about it. Well, I can't. These young ladies can't. We have to live with that for the rest of our lives."

SAY IT REAL SLOW

(March 28, 2017)

ABOUT TWO HOURS INTO THE MEETING, ANA'S FATHER, LEWIS, STEPPED up to the podium. A plant manager for an oil and gas company who had first moved to Albany while getting his mechanical engineering degree at UC Berkeley, he had an air of authority that had quickly established him as the spokesperson for the families of the affected girls.

Discipline must be meted out, he told the board, and it was clear to him that the appropriate discipline in this case was expulsion.

"So, the opportunities of the past—they may have been missed," he said, and gave a heavy sigh. "But in this time, space, and social climate, the course of action should leave *no doubt* about where this city stands," he said. "It should be Albany for all."

He raised a warning finger.

"And one last thing. I'm gonna say this one time and I'm gonna say it real slow: If we don't get the right decision here, may God have mercy on this city."

I WILL NOT STAND

(March 29, 2017)

THE NEXT DAY, THE HIGH SCHOOL HELD ITS ANNUAL DIVERSITY ASSEMBLY in the gym. Andrea stood up and read a piece she'd written called "I Will Not Stand," her voice trembling. She talked about a young boy of color who had come into the ice-cream parlor where she worked and whose mother had asked if Albany High School was a good place for him to go to school, how sad it made her not to be able to recommend her own school as a place where he could feel safe and accepted.

> So I will not stand for it.
> I will not stand for racism or sexism or
> homophobia,
> I will not stand for bullying or excuses,
> I will not stand for classism,
> I will not stand for feeling unsafe in your own
> school,
> I will not stand for being shamed for something
> so strong and beautiful,
> I will not stand for being belittled and beat down,
> I will not stand for people trying to shove me into
> their perfect little stereotype,

I will not stand for not being heard,
I will not stand for not being accepted for who I
am,
I will not stand for being dehumanized.

With the final "I will not stand," she sat down, cross-legged, on the gym floor. But then she got to her feet again to talk about the things she *would* stand for.

But for that little boy and his mom, I will stand.
I will stand and rise for people of color,
I will stand for immigrants,
I will stand for the LGBTQ+ community,
I will stand for anyone who is willing to fight for
what they believe in,
Because there are beautiful people inside and out
that are worth fighting for.

When she finished reading, it was Ana and Lolia she went to, her eyes filling up with tears.

THESE HARMERS SHOULD NOT BE LET BACK INTO OUR SCHOOL

(March 29, 2017)

THE DAY BEFORE THE MEDIATION SESSION, SOMEONE ASSOCIATED WITH the Albany High School Feminist Club sent out a text about a protest planned by two other student clubs: the Black Student Union and Amnesty International.

Tomorrow is the first day the "harmers" (so the racist students who played the part of bystanders) can be back at school. Some students from BSU and amnesty have told me to spread the word about taking part in a sit in tomorrow to protest letting these people come back to ahs. It'll start at the beginning of break with as many students as possible sitting in the main lobby basically making a point and making it hard for people to continue with their normal day. Ill be staying there past break and I can't make all of you skip your next class, but I can highly encourage you to. This statement will make a much bigger impact if it actually affects how our school runs for the day. Again, please share this with basically anyone you know who also believes these "harmers" should not be let back into our school. Choosing to stay silent puts them on the side of the oppressors—in this case that means fucking racists

The text was forwarded from phone to phone, spreading throughout the school. Eventually it was forwarded to one of the account followers, who sent it to the others via Snapchat.

"My reaction was like, 'Oh shit,'" Eren recalls. "This is getting more and more escalated. I'm still ready to go to this meeting, but I'm also now trying to prepare for this student protest specifically against us. So I was more than a little freaked out to go back."

School administrators got wind of the protest too. But they decided to go forward with the mediation, which would take place in the main building of the high school, just yards away from the main lobby, where the protest was going to take place.

PUNISHMENT AND ACCOUNTABILITY

EVERYONE WANTED TO SEE JUSTICE DONE, BUT WHAT DID THAT MEAN, exactly? Historically, justice has been meted out differently to different types of people. "The first thing that, as a society, we use for Black folks is punitiveness," observes Ashlee George, co-director of the Restorative Justice Project at Impact Justice, a research center focused on justice reform. "And it's harsh and it's extreme, and it's to the fullest amount. And historically, for white folks, it's been permissive. Wealthy white man, Christian, heterosexual, then there's so much permission to do harm."

But are those the only two choices—punish or don't punish?

"We have been conditioned that accountability means pain and punishment," observes Aishatu Yusuf, Impact Justice's vice president of Innovation Programs. She defines accountability differently—as "an understanding that a harm took place and that you are responsible for a piece of that harm."

"The conflation of accountability and punishment is what leads to continued, archaic activities that solve nothing," she says, asking, "Is our goal to prevent this crime or action from happening again, or just to punish an individual?"

But given the way that justice has been unequally applied over time, it can be hard to pass up the opportunity to apply punitive justice to a group of people who have historically been sheltered from it, which is one reason so many people wanted to see the Instagram kids receive the harshest possible punishment.

As a Black woman, Yusuf empathizes with this feeling. "It's the idea that there is no evidence to support the belief that the world is changing for *me*," she says. "And if the world isn't changing for me, and my people are going to keep being persecuted, oppressed, and killed, why do *I* have to act differently? Why do *we* need to forgive? Let's treat the oppressors how they treat us."

But, she says, the choice to respond to pain with pain has implications for everyone. Taking the punitive approach means allowing the cycle to continue, rather than building a society "where accountability is actually a conversation about what happened, why it happened, and how do we prevent it from happening again."

That can feel like a terrible response, she admits. "But," she says, "that's literally the only answer. And I think we conflate working toward a better world with being silent. We conflate working toward a better world with being accepting of bad behavior. We conflate working toward a better world with being docile. They are not the same."

PART 8

SEEDS OF DESTRUCTION

QUESTIONS OF HARM

WERE YOU HARMED IF YOUR PICTURE WASN'T ON THE ACCOUNT BUT your name was?

Were you harmed if your picture wasn't on the account but your race was?

Were you harmed if your picture *was* on the account but you were Asian or white?

Were you harmed if you were male?

Were you harmed if people said you were on the account but you never saw the post?

Were you harmed if your best friends couldn't stop crying?

Were you harmed if you'd once shrugged off the jokes?

Were you harmed if everything looks different now?

Were you harmed if you decided to forgive?

Would you have been harmed if the account had never been hidden?

Would you have been harmed if it had never been found?

A COMPLETELY DIFFERENT VIBE

(March 30, 2017)

THE ELEVEN ACCOUNT FOLLOWERS ARRIVED ONE BY ONE. SOME CAR-pooled, some were dropped off by their parents, some walked. Some came with apology letters, others with ideas about what they wanted to say. Gabriel's father later recounted watching his son square his shoulders as he walked to the door of the school and feeling a swell of pride that he was doing this hard thing. Murphy remembers greeting random people as he arrived at school, getting hellos and handshakes as if nothing had happened.

"I was thinking to myself, *Oh, this is going to be a walk in the park,*" Murphy says. "*I'm going to go into this meeting, have the meeting, go out, and then go to my classes and pretend like nothing ever happened almost.*"

The account followers went into one room to be prepped. The students who had been impacted went into another. Both were given similar instructions. The account followers—ten boys plus Lucy, the sophomore girl—were told to be respectful and serious. The account targets—Lolia, Ana, Andrea, Tiana, Billie, and Brutsri—and their friends were told that they'd have a chance to ask the account followers some questions, but that they needed to do it one at a time.

"You guys can't be yelling at them and stuff," one supporter remembers the mediators saying.

Billie hadn't been told about the SEEDS mediation. She had been focused on preparing for the freshman debates, which were being held that day. But at the last minute she was flagged down by a girl she knew from basketball and pulled into the room with the others.

The room was more crowded than anyone expected. Most of the people pictured on the account had brought along a friend or two for support. The result was that the mediation event was not the small, focused conversation between harmers and harmed that the boys had been expecting.

"It was two to one," Murphy said. "Two girls to one guy, which made it a completely different vibe when you walked into the room."

Murphy wasn't the only one who was shocked by the numbers when the two groups came together. Brutsri had had no idea how many account followers there were until he saw them all.

Oh damn, that's a lot bigger than I thought, he remembers thinking. "You see faces that you know, and they're looking back at you, and you're like, 'I thought you were my friend.'"

He'd helped one kid put together his campaign for Youth and Government. He'd been on a soccer team with another. His parents were good friends with the parents of a third. These were the people he chatted with in class, greeted in the halls. Nobody was a stranger to him. "Oh man," he thought. "I talked with you guys all the time. That was *you guys*."

ROOM 104

(March 30, 2017)

ROOM 104, WHERE THE MEDIATION TOOK PLACE, WAS A GOOD-SIZED classroom—big enough to have a couple of saggy couches and an oversized armchair pushed up against the windows on the back wall. It had the school's signature red-and-white-checked linoleum floor and a series of chair-desks with red plastic seats. Posters on the walls featured books, movies, and athletes, and there was a bulletin board with pictures of students from prom and graduation.

The eleven Instagram followers sat in chair-desks on the side of the room closer to the door. The targets and their supporters sat across from them. The moderators sat at either end. The girls had been in high spirits before the session began, snapping photos, buoyed by both jitters and hopefulness. But now the tension in the room was palpable.

"I could feel the angry, anxious, nervous energy everyone was feeling," Ana remembers. "It was hella strong."

According to a time line created by SEEDS and later filed in court, the moderators started with what was supposed to be a neutral, low-impact question—"What are some of the things you really like about Albany High School?" They passed a rock around the room to give each person a chance to reply. That part went well enough, although a number of the girls on the targeted side of the room opted to pass the rock along without speaking.

Then the moderators asked the people who had been affected by the account to talk about how they felt when the account was discovered and how they'd been impacted since.

Andrea remembers saying that her sister, Rachel, had asked her why she was so sad all the time.

"I shouldn't have to tell an eight-year-old that I'm being bullied and I can't feel good about myself," she said. "I shouldn't have to say that!"

According to the SEEDS time line, "The Instagram group listened quietly and nervously."

The girls cried. They yelled. They explained how deeply betrayed they felt. After everyone had spoken, the Instagram group was asked to respond.

That's when things began to go terribly, horribly wrong.

The SEEDS mediation was often described as restorative justice, but it wasn't really. Restorative justice is a carefully structured process that requires a lot of preparation. Typically, both the person who was harmed and the person who did the harm would spend weeks getting ready before they met, and both would have people there to support them. Nobody would be thrown into a room together and expected to figure it out on the fly, particularly not people who were already scared and angry and hurt.

But that's exactly what happened. Maybe it would have gone differently if more time had passed since the account's discovery, or if the Instagram followers had been more prepared for the intensity of the emotions they would face and the kind of apology they needed to make, or if each of the account followers had been able to meet with each of the targets one-on-one instead of in a group. Maybe if they had met off campus, in a more neutral environment, away from the growing crowd of protesters in the hallway outside, or if participation had been limited to people directly involved with the account, or if the mediators had been more skilled. But as it was, the whole thing was a train wreck. An unmitigated disaster.

"It made it a thousand, million times worse," Ana says. "I don't think anything good came out of that meeting."

The first problem was that the main culprits weren't in the room. Charles had made the posts. Patrick had egged him on. Greg had touched Andrea's hair. But because the mediation was for students who were returning to school, those three hadn't been invited. The eleven followers who came to the mediation kept wanting to explain the limits of their involvement, to point out that they weren't the ones in charge. One boy had only just started following the account. Another didn't even go on Instagram. A couple of others said they had liked the posts without really taking in the contents.

It wasn't me, they each wanted to say. *I'm not the one who did this. I'm not a racist.*

But the distinctions that felt so important to the account followers meant little to the people who'd been targeted. Who cared which one of them drew the noose around Lolia's neck or compared Andrea to a gorilla? The point was that the people in that room had seen those things done and had given it their overt or implied approval. What else was there to talk about?

"I really thought they would own up to what they did and you know, kind of apologize," Andrea told a news crew later that day. "And a lot of it was them defending themselves and constantly saying, 'Well, I didn't really add to it by liking and commenting, I didn't really think I was a part of it.' And none of them were like, 'I'm so sorry, I'm taking full responsibility, I hate what I did, I don't agree with it.' I didn't hear that."

MATTERS OF GUILT

DOES IT MATTER IF YOU DIDN'T MEAN TO HURT ANYONE?

Does it matter if you thought no one besides your friends would see it?

Does it matter if it was supposed to be a joke?

Does it matter if you laughed?

Does it matter if you never commented?

Does it matter if you never saw a post?

Does it matter if you knew it was wrong but you said nothing?

Does it matter if you said something but no one listened?

Does it matter if they bullied you?

Does it matter that they're still your friends?

Does it matter that you're a teenager?

Does it matter if you're sorry?

SHUTTING DOWN, STORMING OUT

(March 30, 2017)

"SOME PEOPLE OFFERED HEARTFELT APOLOGIES," BRUTSRI RECALLS. "One of them walked up to me and gave me an apology and I was like, 'You know what? I respect that and I forgive you.'"

But the others? "Other ones, not a huge fan of them," he says. "A lot of them just tried to pretend like they weren't responsible for what they did."

To Andrea, all of it just seemed fake.

"It was for appearances. None of them were actually sorry," she says. "It impacted their lives negatively and in that way they wished they hadn't done it, but they hadn't realized the impact of what they had done and how vile their behavior was."

The girls who had been targeted were angry and passionate. So were their friends, who were often more vocal than the targets had been. They wanted answers: *Why did you follow it? Why didn't you report it?* They asked the account followers questions like "Are you sorry about what you did or are you sorry you got caught?" and then didn't let them reply.

"While the questions were pointed and powerful," the SEEDS narrative reads, "I don't believe those harmed were ready to listen to the answers regardless of the responses' sincerity or honesty."

The account-impacted people interrupted because they had more to say. They interrupted because the responses the account followers gave seemed flimsy and absurd, like when one follower said something like, "I'm a really sick person. I just like things that are weird." A lot of account followers wouldn't look up or meet the eyes of their accusers. Some of them smirked or chuckled, maybe out of nervousness, maybe out of exasperation, maybe out of sheer douchiness.

"I was so unapologetic that one of the restorative justice guys took me aside and said, 'Listen, you've got to be a little more sympathetic. Try to understand what they're going through,'" admits Jon. Being insolent was a way of being edgy, he says now, but it was also a reflection of how little importance he assigned to the girls and their feelings.

"It didn't really occur to me to even try to put myself in their shoes," he says. "They were minor characters in my mind. It was about me, mainly, and my friends."

The more emotional the girls got, the more some of the boys settled into a stance of removed rationality, focusing entirely on their own level of culpability rather than on the pain and hurt in front of them.

"'Bro, chill,'" is how Andrea characterizes it. "'Why are you taking it so seriously?'"

"Some of the boys definitely were just like, 'We don't care,'" says Angela, one of the friends who was there. "And then the guys that were known as the sweethearts, as the kind ones that were in that room, they were like, 'Sorry.' I mean, it's terrifying having another human being, whether they be a woman or a man, yelling and crying. It's a lot. So what else are they going to do? Either they're going to try to feel this pain and go through the stress that this woman is going through or they're gonna shut down. And then you're shutting down everything, right? You don't have the mental capacity. You don't have the empathetic skills in order to process what's going on in front of you. So you're going to go blank."

The SEEDS time line describes the account followers as listening "stoically," which seems to indicate that they were indeed shutting down.

"It became clear to me at a certain point that nothing was going to happen like I had anticipated and like I'd hoped," Eren says. "And that caused me to hold my tongue. At that point, I just wanted to be out of there and I didn't want to say anything else that would further exacerbate the situation for me."

But the more removed the boys behaved, the more furious the girls felt. The more furious the girls got, the more awkward and distant the boys became.

It would have been different, Murphy said, if they'd been able to talk one-on-one. Then he wouldn't have been so worried about what his friends thought of him.

"I think it's because we're guys," Murphy says. "Where it's like we don't want to show weakness almost. I don't want to show sympathy or sadness or remorse."

At the same time, he says, "if you do feel those things, it would be very appreciated and actually have some value to the other person." And he insists that he tried, at least at the beginning, to deliver a good apology. "I didn't want it to be short and sweet and to the point. I wanted to be like, 'Oh, I'm sorry for all of this, this, and this. I didn't mean it. I'm sorry. It was a bad idea.' I tried to be sincere. It's not like I wasn't trying, but I don't think they took it as a very sincere and acceptable apology."

He's right. Nobody remembers him as being sincere that day. They remember him smirking, laughing, rolling his eyes.

"Murphy was, like, giggling whenever people freaked out—he just couldn't take it seriously," one of the other boys says. "Maybe it was his response to the pressure that came from it, and it was like he cracked and couldn't help himself. That's how he dealt with the stress of being in there."

Another person who seemed to have trouble knowing what to do with his face was Wyatt.

"He was just looking to the side, hella awkward. Like, *I don't want to be here and this is uncomfortable*," Ana says.

She felt enraged on Andrea's behalf. "Would you look at her? *Look at her*," she yelled. "She's crying right now because of you!"

Wyatt tried to reply, but at some point he started to say "you people," a phrase that can communicate white separateness and condescension. People on the other side of the room responded with fury and disbelief.

"I don't think he understood why 'you people' was bad, or that he used it in that way," Kerry says. "I don't think he was educated on that at all. But even if you don't mean something, sometimes it's taken in that way."

That's in retrospect. In the moment, she felt like she was part of a collective panic attack. The emotions that had been building inside her body since the day she stood in the bathroom photographing the posts with Rosie now burst out of her mouth in a kind of howl.

"I thought I *knew* you guys!" she remembers yelling. "I was going to go to *prom* with you!"

Where the adults were in all of this is a bit of a mystery. No one from the high school had thought to stick around, and by the end, the two outside mediators seem to have lost control of the session completely.

A ROPE IN A TREE

(March 29, 2017)

MEMORIAL PARK IS RIGHT NEXT DOOR TO ALBANY HIGH SCHOOL. IT HAS tall, leafy trees and wide lawns, a playground with a spiral slide, a baseball field, and a Spanish-style Veterans' Memorial Building where people hold weddings and quinceañeras. It was near the Veterans' Memorial Building that an anonymous caller to the Albany Police Department reported having seen a noose dangling from a tree. It was the evening of March 29, the day before the account followers were supposed to return to school and attend the mediation session.

Officer Carlos Ordaz was sent to investigate. A choir was performing in the building that night, and he threaded among a scattering of event-goers as he scanned the trees, searching for the rope. When he found it, it did, in fact, appear to be a noose. The rope was about seven feet long and high enough in the tree that Ordaz called the Fire Department so he could use their ladder to reach it and cut it down. Then he bagged it up as evidence.

Early the next morning, school district superintendent Val Williams received an email from someone who said he had found a second noose in the grass at the park the day before. The man had untied the knot that formed the noose and thrown it away in a compost bin near the playground. Another Albany police officer, John Geissberger, was sent to the park, where he retrieved this second rope and bagged it up as well. Then he walked around the park looking for more ropes or any other signs of wrongdoing. He didn't find any.

A REPORT OF A ROPE

(March 30, 2017)

AT 10:15 ON THE MORNING OF THE MEDIATION, OFFICER GEISSBERGER returned to the park to examine the scene where the suspected nooses had been found. He took note of fresh scuff marks in an arching pattern on the ground below the tree where the first rope had been found and noticed it was consistent with someone dragging their shoe on the ground. He took photos of the scene, but a theory was already developing in his mind. The scuff marks looked an awful lot like the marks you see underneath a rope swing.

At 10:49, right as the BSU/Amnesty International sit-in was about to begin, Superintendent Val Williams sent out an email to the entire school community—students, staff, and parents—telling them that the police were "investigating a report of a rope that looked like a noose tied to a tree in the park next to the school."

In an email to the school board sent later that day, Williams admitted that the police had advised her not to send out any communications until they'd had a chance to investigate more thoroughly. But, she wrote, "there was no way I could not send something out in the next few minutes."

YOU DID THIS

(March 30, 2017)

VAL WILLIAMS'S EMAIL LANDED LIKE AN EXPLOSION INSIDE ROOM 104. The eleven account followers had surrendered their phones to the mediators, but many of the account's targets and their friends had not. At some point, one of the girls received a text about the reports of a noose and shared the news with the others in the room. Everyone ran to the window to look.

The idea of a noose hanging in the park would have seemed farfetched a month before, but now it seemed utterly plausible. After all, the Instagram account had contained not one but *two* references to nooses.

The targets and their friends turned to look at the account followers.

"You did this!" someone said.

To the Instagram followers, the accusation seemed absurd. A noose? Of *course* they hadn't hung up a noose. *They* weren't the ones who had made those Instagram posts; that person wasn't even here. And how exactly did anyone think they'd managed to string up a noose in the park when they'd been in the mediation session all morning?

Murphy says that his attitude about the noose report was probably the thing that moved him from the category of "good guy" to the category of "bad guy" once and for all. He was sick of being yelled at and annoyed that no one would accept his apology. Seeing how heated people were getting about the noose, he exaggerated his own tranquility. Rolled his eyes. Snickered.

"There's no frickin' noose," he said.

"'Calm down,'" Rina remembers him saying. "'There's no reason to get so mad. You're doing the most.'"

Rina, the junior class president who never lost her temper with anyone, was incensed. She came at him full force, standing inches away from his face, clapping her hands at him.

"Are you kidding me, Murphy? Really? Are you really going to say this stuff right now?"

"Okay, Rina, back up," one of the other boys said. "Don't hit him."

"My cheek is right here," Murphy said, deliberately provocative. "What are you going to do?"

That's when Rina stormed out. Several of the other girls followed her.

OUTSIDE

(March 30, 2017)

SHORTLY AFTER WILLIAMS'S EMAIL WENT OUT, A GROUP OF FIVE HIGH school students sought out Principal Jeff Anderson. They'd heard about the noose report and wanted him to know that they were the ones who had put the rope in the tree at lunchtime the previous day. They'd found the rope in the grass and had been using it as a rope swing. Other kids had been using it as well, including some who'd gone to the choir recital the previous night.

But why was a rope swing tied like a noose? Officer Geissberger checked the logs for the veterans' building and discovered that a Scout troop met there every Tuesday night. A call to the assistant scout master confirmed that a group of eleven- to thirteen-year-olds had been practicing tying knots out on the grass, including a knot called the taut line hitch, which slips up and down like a noose. It was dark when they finished and apparently some of the lengths of rope they'd used for practice had been left behind when the kids were cleaning up.

A left-behind rope had then been strung up in a tree the next day to be used as a swing.

A knot in a rope. A swing on a tree.

A lesson. A toy. A threat.

The rope was what it was, but it was also what it was seen to be.

An hour after sending her initial email, Val Williams sent a follow-up, explaining that the noose wasn't actually a noose. "Per the Albany Police Department, upon further investigation, including several interviews with first-hand witnesses, the Albany Police Department is convinced that the rope found in the park was, in fact, only a swing that children were playing with yesterday," she wrote.

But the damage had already been done.

U.S. District Court judge James Donato would later sum up the situation like this: "Given the highly charged atmosphere at AHS, and the offensive racial content of the Instagram posts, spreading a rumor about a suspected noose near AHS was like throwing a match into a powder keg."

FIERCE

(March 30, 2017)

BY 11 A.M., STUDENT PROTESTERS WERE SEATED ON THE FLOOR OF THE main building, just a few yards from Room 104, where the mediation session was still underway. The building's entryway was called the atrium because of the floor-to-ceiling windows that made up one wall. Students sat cross-legged on the red-and-white-checked floor with their backpacks beside them or on their laps, taking up every inch of space. More protesters had taken over the bright red staircase that led to the upper floors. The majority were upperclassmen. A few held signs that said things like I WILL NOT STAND FOR RACISM or WE ARE THE HUMAN RACE, but most just crowded together in a disorderly jumble of shoulders and knees, confident that their presence was message enough.

"It was silent," one teacher recalls. "And the expression on their faces was just fierce. Like, 'You can't intimidate us.' It was powerful."

Billie remembers being shocked by the size of it when she stepped out of Room 104 to get a breath of air.

"The entire school is just sitting there staring at me," she recalls. "Even the teachers were participating in it."

Several girls had come bursting out of the room, frustrated

and overwhelmed by what was happening inside. It felt amazing to them to see all those supportive faces. To feel the love and know that people cared about what had happened to them and their friends. Some of the them began venting their frustration to the crowd, describing how unapologetic the boys were being.

The protesters listened, growing increasingly riled as one girl after another came out to share her fury.

Then the bell rang for the start of the next period.

Students looked around, as if to ask each other, “What now? Do we go to class?”

But no one got up.

SHOCK

(March 30, 2017)

INSIDE ROOM 104, THE ACCOUNT FOLLOWERS COULD HEAR THE GIRLS yelling to the crowd, and the crowd's answering murmurs.

"You guys need to see what you've caused at the school," one of the girls said when she returned to the room. "It's time to get out in the hallway and stand in front of that crowd so everyone can see your faces."

The Instagram followers looked to the two mediators for guidance. None was forthcoming. One of the mediators said they shouldn't go out, because not everyone in the room had agreed. At that, another girl went to each of the impacted girls in the room: "Do you agree? Do you agree? Do you agree?"

They did. She turned to the Instagram followers. "Everybody agrees. Get the fuck up and go outside."

Ten of the eleven followers did as they were told. Only Jon refused to go.

"I got the impression that we should just comply," Eren says. "Just go along with it."

He was the first one to step out of the room.

"Everyone's head turned to look at me," he remembers. What he saw on the protesters' faces was shock.

"Shock that it's me, shock, disgust, anger, just stupefied looks. And I'm just staring at everyone, I'm looking, because that's all I could do, really."

WE JUST HAD TO TAKE IT

(March 30, 2017)

THERE ARE TWO VERSIONS OF WHAT HAPPENED NEXT. IN DECLARATIONS filed in court, school administrators say that the roughly 250 students at the sit-in "remained quiet and respectful." Steven, one of the account followers, said the same. But others who were there—students, parents, and staff—say that the room didn't stay silent for long. Ned Purdom, the journalism teacher, remembers hearing a rumble move through the crowd as the perpetrators came out.

"For a few seconds it was very quiet. Just this silent standoff," he says. "Then the shouting started."

Look what people think of you! You're a fucking racist!

"Everyone was hurling insults at us," Murphy says. "Everyone was just bashing on us. They had us in a line in front of the whole school almost. We came face-to-face with everyone and just had to take it. And if you did anything up there, if you smirked or did anything kind of like *fuck off*, you'd get more hate for it."

Not that he was thinking that clearly at the time. In the moment, he was only trying to look brave, to look as if the vitriol didn't matter to him, like maybe he even enjoyed it. Steven, who had been eating a sandwich when they were sent out to face the crowd, continued to eat his sandwich. Steven had already struck many of the people impacted by the account as unremorseful after he and Jon had tried to play tennis on the courts directly adjacent to the high school on the first day of their suspension. His sandwich-eating would soon acquire a legendary status—every bite he took felt like a provocation.

Brittany, a Black girl who wasn't targeted but had attended the mediation as a supporter, remembers feeling a surge of satisfaction when she saw the account followers standing before the hostile crowd.

"I think they deserved all that," she says. "I think everyone in the school should have seen who this problem was about. You made this account, you thought it was funny. So since you think it's funny, why don't you stand in front of everybody, so they can see your faces?"

Like Brittany, Billie enjoyed the idea of the Instagram followers having to face the entire school. *Ha, fuckers! Explain yourselves!* is how she characterizes it. But when she was actually presented with the spectacle of the boys' humiliation, it didn't feel as good as she'd anticipated.

"It literally felt like we were in the medieval days and we're stoning someone," she says. "I don't think you can do that."

A FOLLOWER REMEMBERS: STANDING THERE

(March 30, 2017)

It felt like we were about to be
executed or something.
We were just
standing there.
None of us knew
what to do. It was so loud
and they were all just
screaming and taking
videos of us: “Fuck you,
disgusting racists.”
That’s the part that probably
has left the most damage on me.
It honestly felt
out-of-body. I was
standing there with
a blank expression
on my face and in my mind.
There were no thoughts
of me trying to remember
the faces of the people there.
There was no,

"Oh god, I'm so scared."
I was just
standing there,
and it felt like a long time.

IS THIS REALLY HAPPENING?

(March 30, 2017)

EVERYONE AGREES THAT THE TEN INSTAGRAM FOLLOWERS WEREN'T out there for very long. But if you're a teenager standing in front of a hostile crowd of a couple hundred of your peers, it doesn't matter whether it's for thirty seconds or three minutes. It's going to feel like an eternity.

Eren's body was buzzing with adrenaline. His heart pounded in his chest. But his mind was utterly blank. He kept asking himself, *Is this really happening right now?*

"I was just completely shut off, very disassociated, detached from the whole thing because it didn't feel real," he recalls. "That's easily the most surreal experience I've had in my life, because these are all people that I've known forever, some since kindergarten. People that I thought knew me, that I thought I knew. And now we're here and they were looking at me like this."

His teachers were there. Even his friends. (Later these friends would explain that they'd tried to go to class but had been told by their instructors to attend the protest instead.)

And then something happened that made the whole thing feel even more surreal.

His mother began shouting from the back of the room,

trying to get Principal Jeff Anderson, who was standing near the front, to get the Instagram group back into the room. She had come to the school with Eren's grandmother to pick him up at the end of the mediation and had witnessed the whole thing.

"Get them out of here!" she yelled. "This isn't safe!"

But nobody in a position of authority seemed inclined to do anything except watch the scene unfold.

Eren's mother pushed through the crowd until she stood between her son and the protesters with her arms thrown wide, as if she could shield him with her body.

"What are you doing?" she demanded of the protesters. "This is bullying!"

Eren's first thought was, *This is my mom in front of the whole school, embarrassing me.*

"Stop," he said to his mother, or maybe he just thought it. "Don't."

His mind was still posing the same question over and over, repeating it like a mantra: *Is this really happening right now?*

"You guys are monsters!" his mother was saying. "*You're* the bullies. You don't even know what they did."

And now one of the account-affected girls was on her feet, yelling at Eren's mother.

"Shut up, bitch! Shut the fuck up! You don't know what you're talking about! Racism is not the same as getting fucking yelled at, okay?"

Is this really happening right now?

"*You* hung that noose," somebody yelled. "Whose mom are you?"

When the targets of the account tell the story, Eren's mom

is a weird shrieky lady who tried to act like her kid was innocent. But for Eren, his mom was a hero: the one person in the entire room who actually stood up for him. Because the principal of the school was there. Eren's teachers were there. His friends were there. And nobody did anything to make it stop.

"Everyone was in a state of shock or a weird trance and my mom kind of shattered that," he says. "And then the administration was like, *Okay, get them to this room*. Ushered us out."

THE POINT WAS FELT

(March 30, 2017)

IT'S HARD TO FIGURE OUT THE EXACT SEQUENCE OF WHAT HAPPENED next, as people's memories and the sworn statements of various school and district officials contradict one another. But by noon, the mediation session had collapsed completely. Andrea, Ana, Billie, Lolia, Tiana, Sita, Rina, and many of their friends went to join the protest. The Instagram followers were taken into another conference room for safekeeping. It was a smaller room, without enough chairs for everyone. There was a white board on the wall that had their names on it under the heading *Harmers*. Nobody said anything at first. Then someone said what Eren had been thinking: "Is this really happening?"

And then the dam burst and they exploded into hysterical laughter. Not *this is funny* laughter, but *what the hell just happened* laughter. The kind of laughter that's almost like a scream.

At some point, Eren must have gotten his phone back because he remembers texting his mom.

I'm going to need to change schools.

INSIDE THE STOREROOM

(March 30, 2017)

EREN'S MOM TEXTED HIM BACK FROM A TINY BACK ROOM NEAR THE school's attendance office. She and Eren's grandma, along with Lucy's and Gabriel's moms, had all been hustled into this room by a school staffer who couldn't figure out how to get them to their children, or their children to them, or where to put them where they'd be safe.

The room was tiny and seemed to be used as a storage room, given the motley collection of items packed inside: amplifiers and speakers of varying sizes, some tripods, a dolly, a fabric screen, a couch, cardboard boxes. There was a small sink in there and an examination table, which indicated maybe it had been used by the school nurse, and one tiny window that didn't open, which a staffer eventually covered with paper because students kept banging on the glass and staring in at them as if the three mothers and one grandmother were in a tank at the aquarium. There weren't many places to sit, so the three moms gave Eren's grandma the sofa and traded off sitting on the exam table. Otherwise they stood.

It was hot in the room, and they were hungry and thirsty.

At some point, someone from the school came in and brought them some mini water bottles and two bananas, which they split four ways. Then they went back to waiting.

PIZZA

(March 30, 2017)

IT WAS QUICKLY BECOMING CLEAR THAT THIS WAS NOT GOING TO BE A normal school day. Both Principal Anderson and Superintendent Williams had asked students to go back to class, but nobody had moved. Meanwhile, the freshmen were still pacing outside the school's Little Theater, murmuring their speeches under their breath as they prepared for the debates.

By lunchtime, those debates would be canceled. Across campus, school was proceeding in a haphazard fashion, with some teachers canceling classes and others soldiering on, even as fewer and fewer students showed up. Nobody from the administration had sent out any information about what was happening or what was expected of them, and so each member of the faculty was left to figure it out for themselves.

"I felt like I was being gaslit by my administration," one teacher remembers. "There was nothing over the intercom. I didn't receive a call. No runner came to my classroom to say we are going to stop classes."

A couple of the Instagram followers had left the school—one with a plainclothes police officer as an escort—but most were still holed up in the conference room waiting for the moment when it would be safe to leave.

At some point, Superintendent Val Williams asked them if they were hungry. They were. In court documents, Williams says that she asked someone to get the students lunch from the school cafeteria, but soon a delivery guy made his way through the crowd of seated protesters with a stack of hot pizzas. It's unclear now whether the pizzas were ordered for the boys or had been intended for other students, but whatever their original destination, the pizzas ended up in the conference room with the account followers. This did not go over well.

"I just remember sitting there for hours," Rina says. "We were hungry. We were getting heated because we saw someone bring pizza in for the boys. Then everyone's like, 'They're getting pizza and we have nothing.' We don't even have chips. You all couldn't get us chips? We were pissed. Of course *they* got food—really good food."

Then one of the account followers had the bright idea to post a photo on Snapchat of an empty pizza box with a few crumbs and a squashed soda can alongside a caption like *just chillin eating pizza* or maybe *livin' life*. (Memories differ as to the phrasing.) This show of bravado enraged the protesters. Soon, students were banging on the window of the conference room as if they were going to bust through.

Teachers did their best to help maintain order, handing out bags of chips, granola bars, juice boxes, and bottles of water, often drawing on their own personal supplies.

And still, no one was going back to class.

"Nobody was ever in charge to disperse them," says another teacher, who also asked not to be identified. "They let angry, hurt, confused kids be in charge. And that's why it went so horribly wrong."

SHIT SHOW

(March 30, 2017)

BY EARLY AFTERNOON, HUNDREDS OF STUDENTS WERE OUT OF CLASS. (Estimates range from three hundred to seven hundred.) The bulk were participating in the sit-in, but a sizable number were milling around in groups, intoxicated by the intense emotions of the day and the sudden absence of restrictions. Administrators from other Albany schools showed up to try to help corral the students, but they were no match for the sheer numbers of kids who were out of class or the intensity of the students' feelings.

Ned Purdom, the journalism teacher, remembers seeing Principal Anderson physically blocking one of the doorways as one of Purdom's favorite students, a Black boy, was being restrained by some of his friends. This was a kid Purdom had never seen lose his cool, an honors student and peer helper who was known for his sweetness. He had no idea what the interaction was about, but the anguish on the boy's face was unforgettable.

"He was shredded," Purdom recalls. "I don't know if he was trying to be violent toward anybody, but his anger was manifesting physically and his friends were doing all they could to try and calm him down and get him out of there."

Coach Ray had gotten a text at work from Natalie, Andrea's mom, telling him that the mediation session had gone terribly and that things at the school were now getting out of hand. Alarmed, he left his office in Pleasanton, about forty-five minutes away, and drove over to the school to see if he could calm the waters.

The situation was worse than he'd anticipated. "Oh, it was crazy," he says. "It was chaos."

Students were now camped outside the doors of the school, waiting for the Instagram followers to come out. After an administrator told them that they had to clear a path so as not to create a fire hazard, the students had obediently done so—a long strip of pavement that extended from the school steps to the curb with protesters seated on either side. The goal was for the Instagram followers to walk this gauntlet. The protesters insisted no harm would come to them if they did. They just wanted the account followers to see how hurt they were, they told the administration.

The account followers and their parents were having trouble accepting these assurances. In the rooms where they were sequestered, they could hear students pounding on the windows. It didn't seem like they just wanted to say hi.

As the day unfolded, Ginny Tremblay Geoghegan, the art teacher, felt pulled in multiple directions. She supported the students' right to protest and agreed that there should be no business as usual after what had happened. At the same time, the whole thing felt dangerous and out of control. She saw one group of kids try to set a fire in a hallway.

"It was a shit show," she says.

Purdom, the journalism teacher, agrees. He described his feelings in the moment like this: "*These kids aren't safe, I don't feel safe*, everything kept getting worse."

Students running through the school. Students sobbing. Students slamming doors. Students pacing. Students who didn't seem to recognize their own teachers. Students coming into classrooms to rest and regroup, desperate for a sanctuary where they could take a calming breath. Students who were friends with the Instagram followers who had made the calculation that they'd better be out there protesting if they didn't want to be branded as racists. And hundreds of students sitting in the atrium and on the steps and on the school's front lawn, waiting for the boys to come out.

WALK OF SHAME

(March 30, 2017)

BY NOW, NEWS CREWS HAD GOTTEN WIND OF THE SITUATION. TV VANS lined up in front of the school. A news helicopter circled, its blades slicing the air. Superintendent Williams went out to the sidewalk to talk with the reporters. So did Andrea and her mom, who wept through the entire interview.

At the same time, the demonstration was getting larger. As the school day wound down, students from nearby high schools who had heard about the protest on social media began to show up, gathering on the nearby corners.

At around 2:22 P.M., the Albany Police Department was contacted by an unidentified caller who then handed the phone to Principal Anderson. Anderson reported "a disturbance" at the school and said they "needed some support." According to a police department narrative, "all available APD resources" were immediately deployed to the area around the high school, including some officers who had been scheduled to attend a training outside the city. A nearby intersection was blocked off.

School officials told the police that they were concerned about how to get the Instagram followers out of the school safely. The gauntlet that the students had created was still waiting for its star attraction, and the protesters were starting to get testy.

"Everyone was like, 'We just want them to come out so they can do a walk of shame. But no one is going to say anything. Everyone has agreed to just be quiet,'" Ana remembers. "As long as they just have a walk of shame in front of everybody."

But the longer they waited, the angrier people got. It was hot out and they'd been sitting in the sun for hours. Officials from both the high school and the school district came and went, sometimes asking politely for the students to disperse, sometimes seeming to indicate that if the protesters waited long enough they would get to see the Instagram followers walk down the pathway they had made for them. Kids kept appearing at the school doors to announce that they were talking to school officials and the police and that the Instagram followers were going to be coming out at any moment. By now the idea of staying silent had lost its potency.

"They were like, 'Oh we can't wait for them to come out so we can say blah, blah, blah.'" Ana says. Tempers, already high, were starting to boil over.

It felt to her like the school was just trying to protect the account followers. Which, Ana realizes now, was part of their job.

"They have to," she says. "They didn't have a choice. But I don't think we really were thinking about that [when we were] waiting for them to come out."

News of the walk-of-shame plan had made it into the conference room where the account followers were hiding out.

"People were texting us while we were in there," Eren says. "And they were saying that there was a gauntlet for us outside the front entrance of the school. Like a walk of shame, a gauntlet of shame. Just two lines of people from the front entrance all the way down to the sidewalk leading out. And the expectation was that we were going to walk that. And I was like, *Fuck no, I'm not going to do that.* Because I was freaked out. I was scared. Scared people were going to grab me and very possibly beat the shit out of me."

Eren's mom and the other parents had similar fears. They had been trapped in the storage room for close to three hours now, and they were demanding that the school do something—tell the students to go to class, or end the school day and tell them to leave school property, something. When administrators indicated that they didn't feel confident students would listen to their instructions, the parents asked for a police escort out of the building. Administrators didn't like this idea at all, and neither did the cops, who argued that a uniformed officer would only escalate the situation. In a declaration filed in court, Williams says the police chief informed her that "he could not just send two or three officers and that if he sent more officers it would have to be a full squad in riot gear." The police recommendation was for two plainclothes officers who were already on campus to escort the involved students outside via the back exit. Two marked patrol cars would be waiting for them.

It wasn't a great option. The back exit was by the gym, which meant that everyone was going to have to run across an open outdoor area called the Quad, through a set of double doors into the gym lobby, and then out another set of doors before running across an open plaza area to get to a car. But, as Anderson would write in an email to staff the next day,

"We decided to have the students exit through the gym lobby because there was no news crews."

Whatever was going to happen would at least happen off camera.

At around 2:50 P.M., Anderson made the call. It was time to go. A physical education teacher named Scott Shevelson arrived to escort the Instagram followers alongside the two plainclothes detectives.

The kids in the conference room shot across the hall to meet up with the parents who'd been in the storeroom and slip out through a back door onto the Quad. Then everyone just ran.

HOW'S IT FEEL TO BE A RACIST?

(March 30, 2017)

OUT FRONT, THE PROTESTING STUDENTS WERE STILL LINED UP, WAITing for the account followers to walk the gauntlet.

Then someone shouted from inside the building, "They're going out the back!"

A wave of students hurtled around the side of the school to the back entrance.

The Instagram followers made it across the Quad, but by the time they reached the gym lobby, a large crowd of students was waiting on the sidewalk, phones out, filming, yelling. An empty water bottle flew through the air and bonked one of the mothers on the head. The police escorts faded away.

"As soon as we got into the gym lobby, I saw the detectives kind of just bounce," Murphy says. "They were like, 'Oh, heck no.'"

It was too crowded to actually run, so the Instagram followers were shuffling in a line. The thing that made it so surreal was that everybody knew each other, had known each other most of their lives. As the followers and their parents moved through the crowd, they passed face after face that was both familiar and completely strange to them. It was like they were being carried away in flood, through a landscape that they'd walked through a thousand times but that was now unrecognizable.

A kid shoved his phone in Murphy's face. "How's it feel to be a racist?"

Murphy shot him his most insolent smile.

Record. Select. Post.

"That video just goes around to everyone," Murphy remembers. "Everyone had that video. It was posted everywhere. Everyone was like, 'Why are you smiling? Clearly you don't take the situation very seriously if you're going to smile about it.' And I'm just like, 'I'm not smiling about the situation, I was smiling about this kid who had his stupid phone in my face trying to get me riled up, trying to get me to start doing something.'"

Meanwhile, they were still shuffling toward the waiting cars with the crowd pressed in around them.

"You basically walk into a mob while you're already in the mob," Murphy says. "It was almost like a wall you have to cross, which is pretty hard because it's people who are not wanting you to leave for some reason—even though they don't want you to be there."

Wyatt was near the front, being escorted by his mom. He kept his head down, his shoulders hunched, looking broken and defeated. Half the protesters followed him and his mom as they went to their car. The other half followed Murphy, Jon, Steven, and Riley.

Suddenly Murphy felt a sharp tug on his back. Mr. Shevelson had his hand on Murphy's backpack to keep him from getting sucked into the crowd, and he'd been pulled backwards himself. The next thing Murphy knew, someone had flipped him around.

It was Dominick, a white senior he was kind of friends with. The two of them used to smoke weed together, go into San Francisco and go shopping, but now Dominick was punching Murphy in the face. Another student, a Black kid named Keshawn, was throwing punches too. A blow grazed Steven's head and he stumbled into a hedge. In the chaos, Jon saw an opening and sprinted home, certain that he was being followed.

Then Mr. Shevelson was pushing Murphy and Steven away from the mob, urging them to go faster.

"Oh shit, your face!" Riley exclaimed. The punch had broken Murphy's nose. Blood gushed onto his shirt and his white Vans, puddling on the ground.

Wow, okay. So everyone hates me now, Murphy remembers thinking. *What do I even do at this point? What* is *there to do?*

SOME KIND OF TERRIBLE MOVIE

(March 30, 2017)

THE THREE SOPHOMORES HAD MADE IT TO EREN'S DAD'S MINIVAN ALONG with their mothers and Eren's grandmother. But almost immediately, the car was surrounded by people. Eren's dad's window was down and people were throwing things into the car, pressing their signs and their phones against the other windows, kicking the tires, pelting it with trash.

"We are one! We are one! We are one!" they chanted.

Eren's dad leaned on the horn, trying to clear a path, but well over a hundred kids were now blocking the street, pounding on the windows, shouting. Eren's dad turned on the radio to drown out the noise and some random Mexican rap music came on, providing a surreal soundtrack as the crowd began to rock the car.

"We're trapped. We can't move. We can't drive. They start shaking the car, pushing the car, and we're all sort of bouncing around inside and I just don't understand what the hell is happening. This is like some kind of terrible movie," recalls one of the parents. "I don't know how to describe how terrifying it was."

Nobody in the car spoke. Eren's dad inched forward as a police officer and an administrator from the high school peeled kids off the sides of the minivan. Patrol cars moved in with lights and sirens.

"Go! Go! Go!" the moms shouted, desperate to escape. And eventually he did.

BRITTANY REMEMBERS: HONESTLY

(March 30, 2017)

We wouldn't let them leave. Like
we were banging on the windows, banging
the front of the car, calling them all sorts of names,
yelling at them. We did not let them leave.
At the time, it felt good. We were all angry,
but then it was just like: We want justice.
That's all we wanted.
Honestly, all I can remember was
all of us gathering around that van and just
banging on the windows, banging
on the car. Everyone was recording.
Throwing things at the car.
Kicking the tires on the car.
Throwing paper. It was a lot.
I was like, *Wow. This is crazy.*
It was honestly really funny, though.
It was honestly—they deserved that.

OVER

(March 30, 2017)

AND THEN, SUDDENLY, IT WAS OVER. ONCE THE ELEVEN INSTAGRAM followers were gone, the other students began to disperse. Soon, there was no one left but the teachers and a few news anchors doing stand-ups in front of the high school.

The teachers hugged each other. Asked each other, "Are you okay?"

"What just happened?" one of the teachers asked Ned Purdom, the journalism teacher.

"What's *going* to happen is that we're all going to be paying private tuition for those boys," he replied.

It was obvious to him that lawsuits were coming. And when they came, they were going to be expensive.

MESSAGE FROM ALBANY UNIFIED SCHOOL DISTRICT

(March 30, 2017)

THAT AFTERNOON, SUPERINTENDENT VAL WILLIAMS SENT OUT AN EMAIL.

> AUSD Parents, Staff, Students, & Community,
>
> Today students at Albany High School peacefully demonstrated their solidarity against intolerance, racism, and hatred. Also on campus today, the students involved in an incident that occurred last week participated in a restorative justice process. What was made clear from these separate but related actions is that the student body stands together in its message that our school stands for inclusion. To any questions concerning consequences for the students whose online conduct prompted these events, our district administration and legal counsel are closely examining all available options.

At the end of the message, she mentioned having "been informed" that "there were altercations when students were exiting campus" and promised to conduct an investigation.

A FOLLOWER REMEMBERS: AFTERWARD

(March 30, 2017)

My mom and dad, they took me to this spot in
Berkeley,
'cause they were like, "Let's go get lunch or something.
Are you okay?"
I don't know what was happening to me, but
something was definitely wrong.
And I think that probably anyone
who would have gone through something like that
would probably be pretty messed up after it too.
But they took me to some café in Berkeley,
and then we sat on this little grassy field,
and my mind was totally empty.
I had a bagel. And I was eating the bagel
and it just tasted like nothing. I don't know
what I was even thinking about, but I just remember
I was sitting there, and my mom and dad
didn't even know what to say,
they were just looking at me.
And they tried to start a conversation, but
I was not really responsive.
And I don't know, I guess I looked—

my face was really pale.
And then my mom cried.
I don't know why, if it was
because of how I looked,
or if it was that she knew
what had happened.

SLUMBER PARTY

(March 30, 2017)

THEY WERE AFRAID TO GO HOME. AFRAID PEOPLE KNEW WHERE THEY lived, and of course they did. Albany's a small town.

They went to Eren's grandmother's house in Oakland, checking the rear windshield to make sure they weren't being followed.

"Finally, I could breathe," Eren remembers. He kept his phone turned off because he didn't think he could handle seeing everything that was coming his way.

After dinner they went to Gabriel's house, where the three sophomores slept together on the floor in a back room. The parents stayed in the living room with a phone and a baseball bat in case someone burst in during the night. So many impossible things had already happened that they no longer felt able to judge what was likely.

The sophomores stayed together for days. They were too afraid to leave the house and too afraid to go home, so they camped out in one room, their belongings strewn across the floor. After three days, a couple of the parents took them to San Francisco to play mini golf, just so they could get some fresh air. Then they all went back inside, to the room where they now lived.

Meanwhile, the parents of the account followers were talking among themselves, making contact with families they'd never spoken to, whose names they hadn't even known. On the phone, the mothers whispered to each other, trying not to be overheard by their teenagers. They all had the same fear: What if their kids tried to hurt themselves? One mother said that every time her son spent any time in the bathroom, she couldn't stop herself from asking through the door if he was okay. Another kept waking in the night to check on her sleeping son.

Nobody had any idea what to do next. It was clear that the Instagram followers couldn't go back to school on Monday, or perhaps ever. The girls who had been impacted by the account didn't want to see them and the kids who had followed the account were afraid of what would happen if they showed up. After some back and forth, district administrators agreed to put them all on twenty days of independent study. That would get them through April anyway. Maybe that would be enough time to get things sorted out.

A BOY WITH A KNIFE

(April 1, 2017)

TWO DAYS AFTER THE MEDIATION SESSION, A BOY WENT INTO THE bathroom with a knife.

Nobody was home. He knew what he needed to do. Get in the bathtub. Open the vein.

He took his shirt off.

He had the knife. Nobody was home.

He knew what he needed to do: Get in the bathtub. Open the vein.

He looked at himself in the mirror.

He had the knife. Nobody was home.

He knew what he—

A knock on the door. "Are you in there?"

Someone was home.

In the moment, it felt like a miracle. A message. *Don't.* But looking back, he thinks the message would probably have come to him even without the knock. As much as he was planning on it, as much as he wanted to, the thought would have come to him: *I'm in my family's house. Someone's going to come up here and find me. That's selfish. It'll just ruin the lives of my family too.*

He thinks it would have. He'll never know for sure.

But after that, as much as he thought about the knife, he knew he was never going to use it.

SHAME

THE FACT THAT SHAMING FEELS GOOD TO THE PEOPLE DOING THE shaming and bad to the people who are being shamed isn't much of a surprise. The whole *point* of shaming someone is to make them feel bad, particularly someone who seems like they're not going to feel that way on their own, someone who seems impervious, impenetrable, unreachable. A celebrity, say, or someone wealthy or powerful, or maybe just a cocky teenage boy.

Dr. Brené Brown, a research professor at the University of Houston who has spent her career studying shame and other emotions, draws a distinction between *guilt* and *shame*. *Guilt*, she says, is both helpful and healthy: "It's holding something we've done or failed to do up against our values and feeling psychological discomfort," she writes. *Shame*, on the other hand, is "the intensely painful feeling or experience of believing that we are flawed and therefore unworthy of love and belonging—something we've experienced, done, or failed to do makes us unworthy of connection."

Guilt focuses on the behavior. Shame focuses on the person.

The impulse to use public shaming as a punishment goes back for centuries. The pillory, a device for holding people in a stooped position while they were publicly taunted and tormented, wasn't banned by Congress until 1839 and was still used from time to time until 1905. Since then, public humiliation has periodically come back into favor, often popularized by tough-on-crime judges who think that shaming might succeed where other sanctions have failed. Publish the names of the johns who seek out prostitutes. Make shoplifters and drunk drivers stand on street corners with signs admitting their crimes. The particulars vary, but the impulse remains the same: If we can make someone feel terrible enough about what they've done, we can make sure that they won't do it again.

Some legal scholars have argued that public shaming is inherently bad for society because it normalizes cruelty and degrades human dignity. Humans are social animals, and when we feel that our connection to other humans is threatened, our bodies experience that as an existential threat. Shame of all kinds—including bullying—has been shown to increase the risk of depression, addiction, suicide, and anxiety.

Shaming is also a punishment that is rarely specific or proportional or temporary—once you hand punishment over to the general public, you rarely have any control over how long it will last or how severe it will be, and it can easily spill over to affect the designated wrongdoer's friends and family. Public shaming, particularly online, has no expiration date. "There is no rhyme or limit to the terms the public may impose," argues Yale Law School professor James Q. Whitman in an essay opposing public shaming. This is not only bad for the shamed, he says, it's also bad for society as a whole because it "invites the public to rummage in some of the ugliest corners of the human heart."

Another scholar, University of Chicago law professor Eric Posner, has highlighted a different problem with public shaming. He argues that people who weren't directly victimized by a crime or misdeed will participate in public shaming rituals not because they care about what happens to the person being shamed, but because they want to enhance their own reputation. Throw a tomato at the criminal languishing in the stocks in the public square and you've made a public statement that you yourself are a virtuous and upstanding citizen. Call someone out on Twitter, and you have allied yourself against whatever opinion or behavior you think is wrong. This means that bystanders are motivated to shame wrongdoers not to deter bad behavior but to feel better about themselves.

But even if you set aside these ethical or philosophical concerns, there's a more basic practical one. Does shaming actually work? Does it change people? Make them come to their senses? Prevent them from repeating the behavior that got them in trouble in the first place?

One person who has looked into this question is an Australian criminologist named John Braithwaite who has examined misbehavior in a variety of settings, from juveniles who commit crimes to nursing homes that violate safety standards. His conclusion is that people are more likely to turn around their behavior if they are treated with respect and praised for their improvements rather than humiliated for their shortcomings. In Braithwaite's experience, public shaming and labeling actually get in the way of a person feeling guilt for what they've done. If you tell someone that their actions prove that they're a terrible person, they have three choices. They can accept your verdict, which can lead to long-term mental health problems, loss of self-esteem, substance abuse, and repeat offenses ("I'm a bad person, so I can't help doing bad things"); they can shift blame by creating a narrative in which someone else is at fault and they are misunderstood or wrongly accused; or they can find people who will give them validation and praise for the exact behavior that caused other people to reject and stigmatize them.

"When people shame us in a degrading way, this poses a threat to our identity. One way we can deal with [this] threat is to reject our rejecters," Braithwaite writes. "Once I have labeled them as dirt, does it matter that they regard me as dirt?"

Shaming people can thus have the effect of making them double down on the behavior they're being shamed for, which is one reason that Loretta J. Ross, a professor at Smith College, has advocated a "calling in" approach to confronting bigotry and intolerance. "Calling out happens when we point out a mistake, not to address or rectify the damage, but instead to publicly shame the offender," she wrote in a piece for *Teaching Tolerance* magazine. "In calling out, a person or group uses tactics like humiliation, shunning, scapegoating or gossip to dominate others."

Calling in, by contrast, is always done "with love," she writes. It presumes a willingness on both sides to learn and to repair harm. But, she cautions, calling in isn't appropriate for every situation, particularly not ones where people refuse to accept responsibility or intentionally degrade other people. And she has no problem "punching up"—using callouts to go after powerful people whose positions allow them to do harm to others while insulating them from the consequences: CEOs, celebrities, politicians, etc.

But for most of us, being told that we've violated a community norm is quite enough to make us feel bad, without the need for a public dragging. That squirmy feeling of moral discomfort is hard to tolerate, which is why we need some support if we're going to move through it and make amends.

"When we do something wrong, the people who are in the best position to communicate the shamefulness of what we have done are those we love," Braithwaite writes. "A judge waving his finger at us from on high is in a rather poor position to be able to do this. We do not care so much about his opinion of us because we have been given no reason to respect him as a human being and we will probably never meet him again."

PART 9

PARENTS

IT HAS TO BE THE FAMILIES

KIDS AREN'T BORN RACIST, EVERYONE SAID. THEY HAVE TO BE TAUGHT. So those kids, they had to have learned it from their parents. Because how else would they have thought it was okay?

People said it at community meetings. They posted it online, on Nextdoor and Facebook. Parents said it to their children. Neighbors said it to their friends. Teachers said it to each other in the halls.

It has to be coming from the parents.

Those families, they've got to be racist families.

WHAT THE BODY REMEMBERS

LET'S SAY YOU WERE BULLIED WHEN YOU WERE IN HIGH SCHOOL AND you'd thanked your lucky stars that your own kid wasn't. Let's say the experience lives in your body, that feeling of being in the spotlight and yet also being made to disappear. Let's say the anxiety has fluttered inside you ever since.

Let's say that it's your kid who is now considered a bully, or at least a bystander who didn't speak up when someone else was being bullied. How hard this is to fathom! At the beginning, your thoughts are all about those girls, because you know what it's like when the fear thins you out into a wavery ghost, when the tears and the shaking seize you. Once when you were young, you saw a boy who'd assaulted you walking around in a department store and you hid in the dressing room for hours, afraid to come out. Let's say you want somehow to tell those girls, *I know this, I understand*, because even if you can't claim to know what it's like to be the victim of racism, you do know what it's like to be bullied.

Let's say your kid is hated by everyone now and hides in his room like you hid in that dressing room. Let's say loneliness infuses your house like the smell of burnt toast. You know that loneliness so deeply and so well, and you feel you will shatter from the weight of it, because how can this most precious person be broken the way you were broken without you being able to do a thing to help?

Let's say that fear is roaring in your ears.

Let's say it's so loud you can't hear anything else.

How do you know which side you're on?

How is it possible that you're not all on the same side?

ST. ALBAN'S

(April 2, 2017)

ON THE SUNDAY AFTER THE FAILED MEDIATION SESSION, A GROUP OF parents gathered in the library of St. Alban's Episcopal Church, a narrow, rectangular room with a sofa on one side and a few folding chairs on the other. In addition to a white volunteer facilitator named Bonnie Wolf, there were about two dozen people in attendance, squished in so tightly that it felt, in the words of one parent, "incredibly awkward." It would have been awkward even if the room had been larger, because the gathering included parents of both students who had been targeted and students who were part of the account. The idea for the meeting had been hatched by a few parents who knew one another, and then word spread informally, through personal connections. It turned out that both sets of parents had been interested in meeting one another but had been kept apart by school officials who had canceled a planned mediation session after the SEEDS event went haywire.

"Probably the parents of the harmers were so aghast and embarrassed with what their children had done, and knowing that it ran counter to their own values and what they thought the values of their home were," says Ana's father, Lewis. "And certainly, we wanted to have a word with them also, right?

Like, 'What is going on in your house? Talk to us. What is going on?'"

Not all the parents attended. About ten of the fourteen account-associated families were represented, but just three of the impacted families. Some didn't hear about the meeting until later, and others simply weren't ready. The atmosphere in the room wasn't tense exactly, but it was, in Lewis's words, "charged." Yet as anxious as the parents of the account-following kids were, many of them felt hopeful. Finally, the families were in the same room. Maybe now some kind of healing could begin.

The meeting began with people going around the room and introducing themselves. Many of the white and Asian parents of the Instagram kids felt the need to prove, in the words of Charles's stepfather, Alexander, "that I wasn't racist, that I was a good actor, and that I can be trusted to do the right thing." In his introduction, Alexander mentioned the fact that he had recently attended services at Acts Full Gospel, a Black church in Oakland, and had written a positive Yelp review about the experience.

"People are giving their bona fides in some degree, right?" Lewis recalls. "Hey, this is not how we are. My mother was this, and my grandmother, and we've lived in this area and this, that, and the other. People with left-liberal values who had no idea and they wanted to express that and say they were sorry."

The parents of the Black girls who had been targeted wept as they talked about the impacts of the posts. The parents of the Instagram kids wept as they shared their sorrow, shock, and remorse. Afterward, Ana's mother, Sheila, described the exchange as "a breath of fresh air."

"Everyone in the room felt the import of that meeting," agrees Wyatt's dad, Dennis. "And I can't speak for the group, but I kind of feel like everyone felt that was a good meeting. A good meeting of people coming together and talking about it. It was the first time. And there was a sense of optimism, I think, where we could continue to work together."

The group decided to write a joint letter that could be shared at the next school board meeting and distributed to the community that would let people know that they were committed to working together. And while it was clear that there were parents of targeted students who thought it was a little soon to be discussing a resolution, the parents of the account followers were hopeful that if they just kept meeting, if they just stayed in contact, eventually they would be able to mend what had been broken.

A WARNING AT TRADER JOE'S

(April 2, 2017)

EMAIL SENT FROM ONE PARENT OF AN ACCOUNT FOLLOWER TO ANOTHER:

> Hey I wanted to drop you a quick note because some stuff came up tonight I want to make sure you know about. It came up at the meeting tonight after ours at St Albans (and also from emails passed along by friends, and someone I barely even know came up to me at Trader Joe's this evening to warn me) that kids at AHS have said they will attack any returning suspendees. (Other kids are saying they will walk out of any class a returning suspendee shows up at.) At the dinner tonight with a bunch of the affected families, one brought their lawyer, who has seen similar cases and said "You'd be crazy to send your kids back into that"—because all it takes is one kid who doesn't want to let it go, and there's usually more than one. "The kids don't forget, they don't get over it. Some of them are going to hold onto it and it only

takes one. If you send your kid there you're a fool. You're setting your kid up for harm. I don't think anyone should go back, that's wishful thinking."

I know you have a lot of optimism about this, frankly I did too (especially after our meeting this afternoon), but this all gives me serious pause. (It also really depresses me.)

THE OPTICS WILL BE PROFOUND

(April 3, 2017)

FOR A COUPLE DAYS AFTER THE ST. ALBAN'S MEETING, EMAILS FLEW back and forth between the parents. In addition to drafting a letter, they talked about what kinds of changes they might want to see at the school, including changes to the curriculum. The group decided to read a joint statement at that Tuesday's school board meeting, alternating paragraphs between parents from the two sides.

"The optics and sound will be profound," Lewis wrote to the group, "and send a message that a 'coalition of the willing' is committed [to] find solutions to Diversity and Inclusion."

THE THIRD RAIL

(April 4, 2017)

THE APRIL 4 MEETING OF THE ALBANY SCHOOL BOARD WAS HELD AT Cornell Elementary School, in a room filled with brightly colored posters and hand-drawn flags from different countries. The board members sat at a skirted table with an array of puppets behind them, while the audience sat on metal folding chairs and spoke at a small wooden lectern. Once again, the room was filled to overflowing.

The parents who had met at St. Alban's lined up to read the letter they had written, alternating paragraphs just as they had planned.

"We want the Albany community to know that we are unified in our goal of capitalizing on this teachable moment by first healing and educating our children and secondly committing to long-term solutions that will prevent such incidents in the future," the letter said. "So far, our parent group has committed to continuing to meet together, to talking with our children about atonement and forgiveness, and to communicating with the community about our process."

When it was over, the spectators in the room got to their feet for an extended round of applause. The parents hugged and shook hands, faces somber, eyes brimming.

Ana's mother, Sheila, took the mic next, speaking in her distinct blend of American and Irish accents as she thanked the parents of the Instagram followers who had come to the meeting at St. Alban's.

"I was so thrilled to be in that room," she said. "And to listen to how heartfelt you guys were about the situation."

And, she added, "We do want their kids to come back to school, contrary to what people might be saying. Because they have to come back to get their education also."

Then her husband, Lewis, stood and went to the podium. His voice was soft and he held one arm folded over his chest as if cradling himself.

"This is heavy," he said. "This. Is. Heavy. The weight of American history. The weight of Albany history. If you don't know it, you need to learn it."

On that very day, forty-nine years before, Martin Luther King Jr. had been assassinated, he pointed out. And now, in 2017, the nation's first Black president had been succeeded by a man who openly endorsed racism and misogyny.

"These kids need to understand that they're not playing with toys," he said. "It's the hardest lesson in the world to learn. I feel for Charlie and the lessons that he's going to have to learn from this."

He looked at the other parents in the audience, who were sitting very still.

"I have a hard time thinking he was solely a mastermind," he said. "They are accomplices to it and should share the same fate. We can't absolve kids of that."

He turned to the board and told them that they had the power to send a message. "If you approach this line, the third rail in the electric power grid—there's no *degrees* of touching the third rail. If you touch the third rail, you will cease to exist."

In the audience, Wyatt's father, Dennis, leaned forward with his elbows resting on his knees. His wife ran a hand over his back.

"Sorry for the people who have to be the example," Lewis was saying. He took a step forward, toward the audience in their folding chairs. "Lord knows, any time a person who looked like me misstepped, it's time to make an example. Justice is blind. If the example has to be made, just think how lasting it will be."

AN UP-FRONT AND FRONT-ROW SEAT

(April 4, 2017)

"THIS DELICATE THING THAT HAD BEEN CONSTRUCTED OUT OF SAND AND petals just exploded, just got blown away in the wind of his oratory," a parent of one of the Instagram followers said later. "The only part of which I really remember, because it just paralyzed me, was his analogy that these kids should know that anybody who touches the third rail should cease to exist. Which is a very alarming thing to say about children. Children should cease to exist. I don't really like the sound of that, for anybody's kid. I don't care what they did."

When asked about this, Lewis chuckled. He saw his school board speech a bit differently.

"Welcome to your first experience of being on the wrong side of something you've watched on television and you thought, 'Oh my gosh!'" he said. "You have an up-front and front-row seat to race relations gone bad, or some other title fitting. And so you will hear the perspective of a Black man whose daughter was targeted."

In his view, the nice white and Asian parents in that room had made the mistake of thinking that the story of racism in America was finished and they didn't have to educate their children about something that every Black family in America already knew: that Black people in America have been catching hell since the first African was brought to this continent in chains. And like the unattended children in a horror movie who go off to explore the haunted house while their babysitter is napping, these nice white and Asian children had idly opened a box of cursed American artifacts.

"They thought it was a plaything," he says. "Look what we found! This is a meme!"

Now, he thought, these same parents were too eager to stuff everything back in its box and shut the lid.

"That's why I said you touched the third rail," he explains. "You can say, 'I just grazed it.' No, you *touched* it and you're going to *feel* it. They may have wanted immediate, expedient reconciliation and absolution, but sorry."

Fair enough. But how was his third-rail analogy supposed to be interpreted in the context of the letter they had all just read, a letter that talked about coming together for healing?

"Well, justice, right? Fairness," Lewis said. "When you do something wrong, there's consequences. God knows there's hundreds of thousands of Black people who did much less and got some really harsh justice or consequence. So maybe they were getting a little taste of that.

"Let me say this," he continued. "I did not say, 'Listen, let bygones be bygones. They're just kids. It's okay. You didn't mean it.' No. There was no agreement. The point of it is, we're going to come to a solution. We're going to deal with what this has drug up."

AN EXCHANGE BETWEEN TWO PARENTS

(April 6, 2017)

TWO DAYS AFTER THE SCHOOL BOARD MEETING, LEWIS SENT AN EMAIL to Charles's stepfather, Alexander, in which he made it clear he would be advocating that Charles, Greg, and Patrick be expelled.

"According to their student peers and friends, the accomplices' behavior and reputations are checkered with offenses that they have evaded discipline for," he wrote. He then asked Alexander to support expulsion for those who were "primary perpetrators."

Alexander wrote back a few hours later.

"Rest assured, Charlie is never going back to AHS. He will pay a steep price for allowing peer pressure to overwhelm his morality."

He then invited Lewis and the targeted girls to come over to the house to confront Charles, observing that "the girls might enjoy watching him cry."

Lewis replied at 9:01 that night with several questions. Did Alexander feel that Charles had acted on his own? Was expulsion a fait accompli? Did he think there were accomplices who deserved the same fate?

"Given your forthright involvement on Sunday and Tuesday, I'm simply curious to know your position and if your intent is to stand with the coalition of affected parents who feel expulsion is the appropriate discipline," he wrote. "This is the most immediate issue that will pave the path of reconciliation."

Alexander responded to Lewis's questions the next morning, explaining that he felt no loyalty to the families of the other account followers.

"They are pleased that Charlie is taking all the blame and have assumed no responsibility for their child's role," he wrote. "That said, it would still give me no satisfaction to see others expelled however complicit they may be." Instead, he advocated requiring them to perform community service, with expulsion hanging over their heads if they didn't do a good job.

"The main thing the racist kid learns about racism from expulsion is to be more discreet about their racism," he wrote. "That is why I believe that expulsion should be the last resort, not the first response."

Lewis did not reply.

NEXT MEETING?

(April 10, 2017)

ON APRIL 10, DENNIS, WYATT'S DAD, SENT OUT AN EMAIL ASKING ABOUT setting up another meeting of the families who had gathered at St. Alban's. Lewis replied the next day to say that the families of the impacted students preferred to meet on their own for the time being. It seemed to many of them that the parents of the boys were too eager to fix things, too unwilling to sit with the discomfort of their children's wrongdoing or to accept that the injuries would take time to repair.

"'You're bleeding. I just want to keep putting on Band-Aids and Band-Aids and Band-Aids'" is how Natalie, Andrea's mother, characterized the families of the Instagram followers. "But it's like, 'No, this is going to gush for a while.'"

Lewis suggested that the account-associated families continue meeting on their own. "I would imagine that your group's restorative path forward toward healing and atonement requires some collective reflection and expression."

He was also concerned, he said, that people in the community and at the district might interpret the St. Alban's statement to mean that everything was now resolved. To counter that impression, he suggested issuing a new joint statement "stating our collective demand for the School Board to expel the primary three perpetrators from AUSD."

Only one parent responded to Lewis's email. She said that she wouldn't want to sign an additional letter without having a chance to discuss the underlying issues in person. Then the conversation went dead.

GROUP PROJECT

THE PROBLEM WITH THE SUGGESTION THAT ALL THE INSTAGRAM PARents work together was that not all of them saw the situation in the same way. Dennis says he and another parent tried to explain that to Lewis. "His point, as I understood it, was: your group, go do your work and get back to us after you've done it," Dennis says. "But there was some misunderstanding there. Because we weren't a group."

Some families were devastated by what their children were part of and were eager to make amends. Others were defensive or indifferent. Then some of the families started lawyering up. Attorneys began showing up at public meetings to talk about free-speech rights.

"They weren't speaking for us, but it became this perception that everyone was aligned on our side," Dennis says. "And we weren't."

They were like students assigned to work together on a group project, graded together even though they couldn't agree on what the assignment was.

STRUGGLE SESSIONS

ONE PARENT AT THE ST. ALBAN'S MEETING HAD SEEMED MORE RESERVED than the others, less ready to apologize. This was Steven's father, Peter. At the St. Alban's meeting he had asked for evidence that Steven was actually involved. (In an email, he explained that as a computer engineer he knew that anything digital could be forged or doctored and was concerned that Steven's sole comment on the account, the word "yep" after the first post, might have been taken out of context.)

People on both sides of the incident were taken aback by this stance, which seemed uncaring and legalistic. Did he really think the screenshots of the posts had been forged? But every person who was impacted by the account was filtering the events through the lens of their particular history and life experience, and Peter was no exception. He had grown up under China's authoritarian brand of communism during the Cultural Revolution, the period between 1966 and 1976 when anyone accused of foreign, capitalist, or counter-revolutionary sympathies could be tortured, killed, imprisoned, or publicly humiliated. A million and a half people were killed, and millions more were punished in various ways, often through public "struggle sessions," where they were beaten and verbally abused by the crowd, sometimes for days on end.

All of this had made him an ardent believer in both free

speech and due process. He had seen too many people's lives ruined just because they'd been in the wrong place or said the wrong thing or associated with the wrong person—his elementary school PE teacher, for example, who was punished for having a cousin who was an anticommunist leader; his high school physics teacher, who was anonymously accused of planning to emigrate to Hong Kong with his girlfriend; a friend who was sentenced to spend ten years in a labor camp just for having been in China's Muslim region when an uprising occurred there; a co-worker who was branded an anticommunist after casually remarking that the shelves at the grocery store were empty that day. By the time Peter left China in 1983, he'd seen hundreds of examples.

"Each of them was dragged to the stage and publicly denounced, some for many days or weeks," he explained in an email. "Some of them committed suicide such as my PE teacher (some of my classmates said that he was pushed off the balcony so it was really a homicide)."

He himself had been accused in high school of being too interested in learning English, which was taken as evidence that he might be planning to defect to the United States. He'd avoided severe punishment by writing a paper acknowledging his mistakes and promising to spend more time studying communist literature.

Peter didn't share these experiences at the St. Alban's meeting, or afterward. He didn't like dwelling on his own story and resisted what he calls making "a big deal about some supposed personal injury." Instead, he took his demands for proof to Vice Principal Pfohl. The conversation did not go well. Afterward, Peter told his son that Pfohl was "a communist."

"I appreciated this country primarily because one is allowed to question anything without consequences but now I am certainly forced to admit that this might no longer be a good assumption," his email explained. He agreed that the account was wrong and that apologies were in order. But he thought the school had overreacted when it lumped all the followers into the same category regardless of the role they played.

As he was about to make abundantly clear.

PART 10

WHY CAN'T YOU JUST GET OVER IT?

BODYGUARDS

(April 17, 2017)

SPRING BREAK STARTED ON APRIL 10, PROVIDING A MUCH-NEEDED respite for the entire school. When classes started up again a week later, two of the boys who followed the Instagram account had returned to school. (The other twelve, including Charles, were still at home.) A month had passed since the discovery of the account, but the wounds still felt raw. That posed a dilemma for school administrators. Everybody—the followers of the account *and* the people the account had targeted—was legally entitled to a safe and secure learning environment. But most of the Black girls in the junior class didn't feel safe around anyone who had followed the account.

After the events of March 30, the day of the mediation and sit-in, the returning students didn't feel safe either. The school had hired security guards to make sure no one jumped them, but if anything, that made things worse. The security guards were muscular men who dressed in Albany High School basketball T-shirts, as if that would help them blend in. Students posted pictures of them on social media with captions about how the racists now had bodyguards. Many assumed that the families had hired the security guards themselves, which contributed to the narrative that they were entitled and unapologetic.

Adding to the difficulty was the fact that most of the kids on both sides were juniors. This was the year that everyone said was crucial for getting into college, the year when you were supposed to take the most challenging classes, get the best grades, rack up the most impressive résumé of clubs and activities. No pressure or anything, but this was the whole reason your parents had moved to Albany.

But Albany was a relatively small school. Most classes had only one or two sections, and many of the students on both sides were in small programs where they spent the entire school day with one cohort. So how exactly was this supposed to work?

THE SPY WHO LOVED ME

(April–June 2017)

ANDREA DIDN'T WANT TO GO OUTSIDE. IN THE HOUSE SHE WAS SAFE. Invisible. She could make her room spotless, fix her hair the way she liked it, or just lie in bed, not moving. Alone, she could be pristine. The mirror-smooth surface of a lake. An unwrinkled sheet.

Nobody's eyes raking over her body. Nobody's perceptions pricking her skin like a rain of needles. "I can't really hide my Blackness, shove it away, hide it under the couch," she says now. "There was no way I could take it off." But at home, no one expected her to. At home her Blackness was loved and cherished.

Sometimes she imagined being trained as a spy, so she would know how to respond to any situation. As a spy, she could read people's true intentions, discern their hidden motives. Or maybe she could be a billionaire, so rich she would never have to worry about anything or anyone. Money commanded respect. If you had enough of it, she thought, you could wear it like a suit of armor, confident and unafraid.

LET'S JUST BE CHILL

(April–June 2017)

ANA HAD NEVER BEEN BIG ON ACADEMICS, SO SHE JUST CHECKED OUT a little further. Smoked more weed, stayed high during school. She hated being in the spotlight for any reason, and she really didn't want to be known for being the victim of a racist Instagram account. Still, the discomfort warped everything. Her U.S. History class had one of the account followers in it, and as the teacher began to cover topics related to race and racism, she felt the anxiety coursing through her body, because here it was, the long, horrifying story of Black people in America, a story that kept wrapping around her like a boa constrictor, squeezing the breath from her lungs. Eventually she dropped the class, opting to take it online instead.

That first week, she went to a party and one of the boys was there.

"Let's just be chill," Ana told him. "I don't have a problem with you right now."

But then everyone was telling her how cool she was for being chill, which was exactly what she'd been trying to avoid. She hadn't done it for *him*, she'd done it for herself.

"Why would I want it to be hella awkward while I'm trying to have a good time?" she said. "I'm not trying to be thinking about that shit."

GROUP CHAT

RIGHT AFTER THE ACCOUNT WAS DISCOVERED, ANA HAD FORMED A group chat for the account-affected people and their friends, but by April, Andrea was finding the flow of messages overwhelming.

"It was just little constant reminders," she says. "And I was like, 'Okay, I can't constantly have notifications on my phone that make me irritated just popping up.' It was like, Yes, you're all bitter about it. Should we confer together and be bitter about it? Probably not. It would probably magnify the bitterness and make it even less productive than it already is."

She and Ana were both coping by trying to shut the incident out of their minds. Lolia and Tiana coped by talking about it. Neither approach was better or worse, but they were definitely not compatible.

"Even hanging out with those people, a lot of what they wanted to talk about, like what we ended up talking about, was that," Andrea says. "So I was like, I don't want to talk about that literally ever, basically. Or I only want to talk about it if *I* bring it up."

Over time, the differences in coping strategies would grow, driving a wedge between people who had started out as allies.

CRYING

(April–June 2017)

ROSIE COULDN'T STOP CRYING. SHE CRIED DURING THE SIT-IN. SHE cried as she walked home with one of her friends and then she sank to the floor in the kitchen and cried some more. She went to dance practice and cried there. She cried until she burst the blood vessels in her face, and she kept crying with her tear-slicked cheeks bright red.

She wasn't alone in crying that day. It felt like their entire community had shattered like window glass. But then the tears wouldn't stop. Days later, Rosie was still crying. She felt ashamed of this. *She* hadn't been targeted by the account. She wasn't a victim. Her grief felt presumptuous. What gave her the right to feel anything at all? She knew she had done the right thing in taking Eren's phone. She was proud of that, proud that she'd been able to do something to stand up against racism. But now Eren was gone and she missed him.

"I felt like he died," she says. "One day he was my best friend and then he never talked to me ever again. That was so painful. It took me a long time to accept that. To accept that I would never reconcile with him."

She'd seen him once, right after the account was discovered, and he'd apologized in a way she'd found half-hearted. At the time, she'd been too angry to do anything but stare at him, stone-faced. Now she messaged him on Snapchat. *Can we talk?*

No, Eren said. He can't remember exactly what he said, but the gist was this: *I don't really want to talk to you about anything ever.*

So she blocked him. But that wasn't what she wanted either.

At last, she wrote him a letter. She tried to tell him everything: how angry she was, how hurt, how much she missed him, how she hoped he was okay.

When she put the letter in his mailbox, it felt like releasing a caged bird, watching it flap upwards into the blankness of the sky. First a beating heart, then a pair of wings, then a blur, a speck, an absence.

This is done, she thought. *This is over.*

THE LITTLE SCHOOLHOUSE

(April-June 2017)

THEY CALLED GABRIEL'S HOUSE THE LITTLE SCHOOLHOUSE. THE THREE sophomores went there every day to do their schoolwork, sitting side by side on the big couch with their laptops. Gabriel's mom got the bell schedule from the school and tried to reproduce the flow of the day.

A few students had gotten in touch with Eren to say they were sorry for how out of hand everything had gotten on March 30, that they'd gotten caught up in the mob mentality when his father's car was surrounded. People said he should come back to school, that they knew his level of involvement had been minimal. But none of that meant anything to him. He couldn't see himself walking back onto that campus, certainly not when students were there.

"I went from being a sociable person and kind of on top of everything," he says, "to just instantly feeling like a pariah and unsafe to walk in my hometown. Did not want to be seen in public. Felt scared if I was seen in public. Just afraid to be out and be seen."

The three of them didn't leave the house. They didn't go to the store or to a movie or to grab a sandwich. They tried it once or twice, but they always turned back, either because someone yelled something at them or because they just felt too afraid.

But still, they had to get through the semester. A couple of teachers seemed to want to keep punishing them, sending homework home without any instructions or not sending it at all. But most of their teachers did their best to help them finish the term. Their chemistry teacher let them come to the lab after school, when everyone was gone. Their dance teacher said they could write a couple essays and then make a short video of themselves dancing.

But Eren—who had been an exuberant and accomplished hip-hop dancer—couldn't dance. The joy that had always powered his dancing was gone. He felt like a ghost, a scarecrow, a piece of furniture. In the end, he just sent in an old dance video he had on his phone. Judging by the grade he got, he doesn't think his teacher was fooled.

Later, he would realize that the name for what he was experiencing was depression, but at the time he just knew that he felt dead inside.

"I was miserable," he says. "I was upset at myself for putting myself into the situation and upset at the school and everyone else. I was very, very angry at everything, including myself. Maybe myself the most."

TEACHERS

THE TEACHERS AT ALBANY HIGH SCHOOL WERE STILL MOSTLY IN THE dark about what role different students had played in the Instagram account and so they didn't really know what to make of the school's response. How were they supposed to think about the students who followed the account? How much remorse were any of these kids really feeling?

Ginny Tremblay Geoghegan had had two of the account followers as students. "They were the sweetest kids I had ever worked with," she says. "It seems so out of character. It's really a mind trip. Because I'm like, *Did I know them? Were they secretly these really awful, awful people this whole time and I was just totally wrong about them?* But everyone's attacking them and hating on them and their community has really turned their back on them, and what if it was just a mistake and they never really knew what they were doing? But then I feel like I'm making excuses for them. It's just a mess."

She kept looking at the situation from different angles, trying to see it clearly.

"If they were really following this account in earnest, then I think what they went through is justified and good and I hope they learned their lesson and will change their lives. But if not, and they never had an opportunity to explain what happened, it just seems like a waste. Like a missed opportunity to teach kids how to be in the world."

Meanwhile, teachers themselves were struggling. Not only were they upset about the account themselves, but there was a gaping hole in the fabric of the school community and none of them knew how to fix it. Students were crying in the halls. Parents were outraged and blaming teachers for not having prevented campus racism. News vans were parked in front of the school. Faculty meeting after faculty meeting was devoted to the question of how to respond.

"For the balance of the year, this was the topic," Ned Purdom says. "How do we get to the end of the year? What is the status of the situation and the punishments? What do you do if you have a kid that's clearly not coping well? What should you expect of them academically?"

Teachers weren't sure how much to discuss the whole issue in the classroom, and since they got little direction from the administration, some did and some didn't. But whichever choice they made, there were students who were upset. Some complained that the school didn't care about racism and was sweeping the whole incident under the rug. Others complained that the issue was being overblown and they were tired of talking about it.

If there was a right path to take, no one had any idea what it was.

A CHANGE AT THE TOP

(April 20, 2017)

ON THE MONDAY AFTER SPRING BREAK, PRINCIPAL JEFF ANDERSON went to a meeting at district headquarters and then went home early. On Wednesday, April 20, teachers learned that he would not be returning to Albany High.

"AUSD did not release Mr. Anderson from employment," a district email emphasized. "He has been reassigned to another position within the district. We are glad that he is able to continue with us and use his skills to serve AUSD students in another capacity."

HOW TO SEEM OKAY (2)

ANOTHER DAY. ANOTHER DAY. ANOTHER DAY. YOU WERE SUPPOSED TO be okay by now. You'll keep trying to find your way through, but every path is a dead end. Every choice is the wrong one. The wrongness will feel like an ailment, like a bitter flavor you can't wash out of your mouth. You'll feel like *you're* the problem. Your emotions are too big, too messy, too loud.

By now you'll be starting to hate the people who give you sympathy and puppy-dog eyes almost as much as you hate the people who avert their gaze. You'll hate the kids who are all about the drama and the kids who act as if everything is normal. You don't know who to trust, and before long, you'll find that you don't trust anyone.

You'll begin opting out more and more often. Taking those sympathetic looks and cashing them in. Your teachers will go easy on you, thank god, not saying a word when they see you lingering in the halls. So go ahead, ditch class. Ditch school. Ditch your finals, your AP tests. Because you can't, you literally can't do it, can't calm your racing brain enough to concentrate, can't muster up the energy to put pencil to paper. This the only power you have left: the power to say, *Fuck it, none of this matters.*

Maybe you'll stop eating. Maybe you'll start throwing up after meals, the anxiety raising the bile in your throat, pushing the food out of your stomach. Maybe you'll stop sleeping. Maybe you'll sleep all the time, drink more liquor, smoke more weed. There are lots of ways to disappear, and disappearing's the only thing that will hold any appeal.

The adults will ask you: *What kind of help do you need? What do you want to happen next? How can we make our school more supportive?* When you look in their eyes, you'll see how desperately they want you to be okay. As the days stretch into weeks, the weeks into months, you'll feel like you're disappointing them. Shouldn't you be over it by now? How long is too long to feel like this? Because the truth is, you don't know how to be okay. You don't know how to go back to being the person you used to be, a person who didn't suspect every white person was calling you the N-word behind your back. You'll miss that person like she died, like she was murdered. You never expected that this was going to be your life.

THE DOOR

NATALIE, ANDREA'S MOM, STILL HAD TO GO TO WORK. SHE WAS AN elementary school teacher and she'd been in the process of getting a master's degree, but now she dropped out of school so that she could be more available to her daughter. Truth was, she was afraid. When she left for work in the morning, Andrea would be getting ready for school, but sometimes when she came home in the afternoon she'd find Andrea had gone back to bed.

Andrea had always been a fearless and energetic child, running laps around the house, riding her bike straight off the deck, a kid who catapulted herself through life. But now when Natalie closed the door to leave for work, she worried about the hours she'd be gone, worried about returning home and opening Andrea's bedroom door and finding . . .

She didn't want to think about what she could find. And yet the image kept coming to her with lacerating clarity. Andrea was getting counseling at school, so Natalie focused on doing what she could to boost her daughter's spirits. She got Andrea a Chihuahua puppy so that she would have company during the day. She planned a summer trip to Mexico for just the two of them so that Andrea would have something to look forward to. But it was hard to keep going, keep walking out the door, because she was so angry and sad and tired and there was nothing she could do except hold it together, keep earning the paycheck that supported her family, and try to make sure that her daughter stayed alive.

NASTY

(April 25, 2017)

THE SCHOOL BOARD HELD ITS LAST MEETING OF THE MONTH IN THE Albany High Little Theater, a room that was finally large enough for all the people who wanted to attend. The atmosphere was hostile from the start. Board members sat on the stage at a blue-skirted table while district staff presented a time line both of the Instagram account and of the Nazi salutes and other antisemitic incidents that had occurred in the fall and winter. Audience members quickly lodged objections about things that had been left out, including the *just chillin* Snapchat post from the day of the sit-in, and the fact that a student had been punched in the face and had his nose broken.

Andrea was one of the first to speak. She stood at the podium in a black T-shirt and faded jeans that were ladder-ripped at the thigh.

"So apparently some people need a definition of what a *reaction* is," she said, her voice casual, conversational. "So the boy who got his nose broken was a *reaction* to what happened at this school. Okay?"

There was a smattering of applause. "The civil rights movement is a *reaction* to racism. Reactions are based on what happened. So breaking someone's nose is pretty nasty, right? It hurts, right? So imagine how bad someone would have had to have been hurt to have a reaction that bad."

"Tell it!" someone shouted from the audience.

"I know the pictures that were put up aren't up here because it's pretty nasty and not everyone wants to see everything that's nasty and nitty-gritty," she continued. "There's a reason they don't want to see it. It's disgusting." Her voice broke. "You wouldn't want to see the pictures, you wouldn't want to have them pop into your mind when you're in class and you have to sit with those disgusting people, every day."

Her voice was low and passionate now, shaking with emotion. "So that reaction, I think, was completely justified. Because people have the right to feel their emotions. They have the right to feel"—she took a shaky breath—"the nastiness that's been thrown in their face."

INSIDE THE FIRE

(April 25, 2017)

ONCE THE TIME LINE DISCUSSION WAS OVER, THE SCHOOL BOARD MEMbers got up from the table and sat on the edge of the stage, legs dangling over the edge. If this was supposed to reduce the gulf between them and the public, it wasn't particularly successful. The mood in the room stayed tense as speaker after speaker got up to talk about their own experiences with racism or bullying, either in Albany or in other parts of the country. When a white high school student—the son of a local attorney—stood up to talk about freedom of speech, he was roundly booed.

Then, the parent of one of the sophomores came to the podium. It was Gabriel's father, a slender white man in fashionable glasses and a close-cropped beard. He wanted to speak for "the kids who are part of the Instagram account but they are on a peripheral edge of it," he said. After the events at the mediation and protest, what was supposed to happen next?

"Right now we're looking at kids who are just sort of swinging in the wind," he said. "They're literally terrified to come back to school. They're not in a position to understand what happened with the crowd. I know it wasn't a riot, but they basically—they unleashed on these kids who were not prepared at all for it and are fifteen to sixteen years old and were not prepared to deal with what they faced that day."

The room was very quiet as he spoke, his words coming in hesitant bursts. You could see him struggling to find some way to make the people in the room feel anything other than hatred toward his kid. "I know the symbol for this group was that somebody was texting or snapchatting, that they were not taking it seriously, but I can tell you that many of the kids who were there were there for the best possible reason and felt torn apart by what they contributed to."

He turned to look at the audience of people sitting in the red-cushioned theater seats.

"It's been a hellish month for us as well because we don't know what to do. Are we supposed to move? Is that *it* from this community?" His fingertips came to rest on his chest, as if forming a tent over his heart. "Our friends have poured love on us, and we understand that these actions don't have to define our kids, but—"

An older Black man rose to his feet and turned to the crowd.

"Hate is a learned behavior!" he exclaimed. He had a full white beard and was wearing a black Stetson hat.

"Thank you very much," a woman in the audience called out approvingly.

The older man shook his finger at the dad, who had frozen in place, his fingertips still resting on his chest. "If you want to get to the bottom of this, go home with these kids and you'll find out why they think like they do and why they do the things they do!" he thundered. "You asked this board to put a fire out from *inside* the fire. If you want to start, start at their homes!"

With that, he strode down the aisle of the theater to the exit. The room erupted in applause.

Gabriel's dad tried to go on. "So, as families, we've been dealing with"—he gestured at the man's departing figure—"this voice. I grew up in Canada, and I came to the States and I have not had the context or experience that is necessary and I feel terrible that my son, who I honestly don't think is a racist, is in this situation and I—" He broke off. "I don't want to bare my soul here." He turned to answer a question from someone in the audience.

"Thank you for standing there and saying what you have to say," said this new speaker, a middle-aged Black man with a bald head. "I have one question and I know there might be parents or family members of other children that were involved too. I'd like to know—before we start talking about hate crimes and whatever we're going to categorize this as—Why. Did. They. Do. It? That's all I'd like to know. What was the intention, why they did it?"

That of course wasn't easy to answer.

"I can only speak for my kid. He—in this situation—has some very lazy habits in terms of how he looks at Instagram. Honest to god, he flicks through stuff and he likes everything," Gabriel's dad said. "It's hard to understand, there's a couple of these images that—you can't defend this and he's like, 'I know I can't defend this.' It was a horrible situation and that's the kernel of it." He sighed. "It was a like-for-like situation with a friend. The account was not what it turned into when it started. Every bit of it sounds like rationalization.

I know it's not what people want to hear. I'm glad to actually talk about it."

"Again, young man, I appreciate it," his interlocutor replied. "But when it really comes down to it, it's a situation again, if I see a noose around someone's neck, I just say I like it?"

"No, I—"

"And so what I'm saying is, before we can get to this point that everyone's talking about, where are we at, as neighbors? Where are we at as the Albany family? We're not talking about the United States. This is a small little town. If we can't change this *here*, we can never change anything outside." The man's tone was gentle as he returned to his question. "Why was this done? Why was it *done*? And do you know the *implications* of it being done? That's not for you, father, I hear what you're saying and I respect your position. But as a community we need to know, why did this jump off in the first place? What were they thinking to even start something like that? Once we know that, we can figure out what we need to do to correct something like this."

If the man was asking for a moment of community introspection, an investigation of the ways that Albany itself might need to change, nobody was listening. Instead, some back-and-forth ensued between Gabriel's dad and other people in the room, with a woman in the audience telling him not to "perpetuate fear" by talking about his kid being afraid.

This exchange was interrupted by someone pointing to a girl who had been crouched on the floor at the front of the room, waiting to speak.

It was Billie.

ARE YOU THREATENING ME?

(April 25, 2017)

BILLIE WAS IN A GRAY HOODIE WITH THE HOOD UP, DARK GRAY SWEATS, socks, and shower slides. She stood with one knee bent and shifted her weight from side to side as she addressed Gabriel's dad using a mic someone had handed her.

"I'm the freshman that was targeted. I'm the youngest out of everyone that's been affected right now and *I* am scared to come to school. And *I* am falling behind in school. I'm a 4.0 student. I've never had Ds in my life and that's what I'm getting because of what these kids did to me and my fellow friends."

Gabriel's dad nodded, still standing at the podium.

"I haven't gone to school because I'm too scared to come here. I've been missing classes, I've been *skipping* classes, because I'm too scared to be in them and I can't concentrate. And so although you guys are scared, I think we're scared more, to be here thinking that people are going to be constantly taking pictures of us and posting them up—" She broke off as the white teenager who had spoken earlier about free speech said something to his father, who was sitting next to him. "Can I help you?"

Before the boy could reply, Lewis strode toward him waving

a cautionary finger. "Dude, I'm going to drop you off at Forty-Fourth Street and San Pablo and let you get back home," he said, referencing a street corner in a low-income and historically Black neighborhood. People started to clap.

"Are you threatening me?" the teenager demanded.

"Stop it!" Lewis said. "Stop it! You're insensitive. You're insensitive!"

"*Are* you threatening me?" the boy repeated.

"Are you kidding me, bro?" Billie broke in.

By now the room had erupted into pandemonium. Everyone was shouting at once; some were on their feet. "She had the floor!" Rina's mother shouted. "Stop speaking over her!"

A woman who worked for the district marched up to the free-speech teenager and announced, "I am going to call the police if you don't quiet down."

In the midst of this, Gabriel's dad walked away from the podium, hands in his pockets. Nobody seemed to notice.

At last things quieted enough for Billie to continue.

"He called *that* threatening?" She laughed caustically. "When there are pictures on the Internet with nooses around the neck. Are you *kidding* me? You think that's threatening?" She turned to look at the teenager, who was still in his seat, still talking. "That's bullshit. I'm sorry, but that's bullshit."

TWO MOTHERS

(April 25, 2017)

THE EVENING WASN'T OVER YET. THERE WERE MORE SPEAKERS, MORE speeches, more arguments about who was more hurt and who was more afraid. There was passionate testimony about lynching, about racism, about American history, and about the curriculum at Albany High School. And then, shortly after 11 P.M., as the meeting stretched into its fifth hour, Andrea returned to the podium and asked the speaker who had just started his remarks if she could take the mic.

Then she called to a woman who was about to leave the theater: Greg's mother.

"Before you leave, can I say something really quickly?" She nervously tucked her hair behind her ears, standing with her back slightly arched, her feet firmly planted.

"Okay so I was shopping in Trader Joe's the other day and I thought, it's like weeks past, right? I'm over this. I'm doing a lot better. I'm not thinking about it as much. But I didn't realize that it's like constantly in the back of my brain, constantly affecting me. So I go and you're standing there at Trader Joe's and I know who you are. And I just—"

She gave a heavy sigh.

"—you didn't see me but I broke down. Because I can't be

near you, I can't see you because I'm constantly reminded of what your son and other people's sons have done."

She described going to sit down. Trying not to cry in the middle of Trader Joe's. "I know people like to say 'Get over it, it wasn't that big of a deal' and minimalize what happened. But reactions really tell you how big of a deal it was. Because I would not be reacting this way and no one else would be reacting this way if it wasn't a big deal, if it didn't matter, if we just needed to get over it. And I appreciate you listening."

Greg's mom, Lauren, was standing by the exit, clearly having planned to call it a night. Now someone brought her a mic.

"Thank you. Thank you. For telling me," she said. Her voice was soft, choked with emotion. "I hear you and I apologize. What would you like me to do now?"

"Apologize!" people in the room shouted.

Lauren took a breath.

"I am sorry for what my son did to you, and to all of the others. We are heartbroken. And I am sorry for what we have done to this community. He would like to communicate with people and he would like to talk with you. Are you willing to talk to *him*?"

"Yes," Andrea said.

There was a scattering of applause.

"When can we talk?" Lauren asked, trying to close the deal.

"I don't know," Andrea said, sounding for the first time like the sixteen-year-old girl that she was. "I have to check with my mom."

The room was silent. The few remaining people in the

auditorium looked from one side of the room to the other as if watching a tennis match.

"And I would like to say that I have had an email ready to send to your mother and I've been waiting for the right time," Lauren said. "Because I've been trying to work through people, to understand when we can be part of conversations around the healing. I have tried to work through different conversations with other parents and it has not been open to me."

Andrea's mother, Natalie, got up and walked to the back of the room to stand a few feet away from Lauren. She took the mic.

"So I just want to respond to Greg's mom because we haven't met before and as a parent of Andrea, part of the issue is that there's no expulsion hearing for Greg," she said, explaining that the girls believed Greg to have been a "ring-leader" in making the account. "There's something called stipulation where you could come before the board and basically voluntarily have Greg have the same consequence that Charles and Patrick are having. That would be fair."

Lauren looked over at the school board members and said something about protecting privacy. It was clear that she was uncomfortable having this discussion in a public theater, in front of a camera that was broadcasting the proceedings on live TV.

"Well, we all know who we're talking about at this point," Natalie said.

"And I would have loved some privacy in my classroom when pictures were taken of me and compared to a gorilla," Andrea said and the veneer of calm fell away. "DO I FUCKING LOOK LIKE A GORILLA TO YOU?" she shouted. "*Do* I?

I don't, do I? So my privacy was yanked away from me. So get ready to know what it feels like."

Lauren no longer had a mic, so her response was inaudible. But judging from Andrea's mother's reply, she seems to have said something about wanting to set up a time to talk.

"Well, we *are* talking," Natalie said. "Part of the issue is that the adults whose children were targeted do not feel that her son is receiving anything permanent on his record. We have advocated—I have spoken at every single school board meeting advocating for expulsion of the three boys who started the account."

She handed the mic back to Greg's mother and returned to her seat. Lauren looked around the room. "May I invite a restorative justice program to help us come together? Who can help us?" she said. "I would like some help. I want Greg to talk to his friends and his peers. We want to talk."

ANGRY

(April 26, 2017)

APRIL 26 EMAIL FROM SCHOOL BOARD MEMBER CHARLES BLANCHARD to Superintendent Val Williams:

> I left the board meeting unbelievably angry, as perhaps everyone else in the room did. It was supposed to be a community conversation, but those who spoke chose not to converse. They came to badger, berate, lecture, and harangue . . . I am concerned that adults continue to lay the burden of 500 years of European colonialism on the shoulders of minors. I am concerned that student privacy was not observed by adults. Matters are complicated by intertwined levels of need: personal healing and reconciliation, appropriate disciplinary actions for the specific incidents, deep discussion of the role of public education in structuring a school environment where everyone can succeed, and the social structure of Albany

and other communities. I am confident that we can address the first three. After last night, I lack confidence that we can do so in public meetings.

THE ROLE OF ADULTS

"SO MANY OF THE PARENTS JUST WANTED SO BADLY FOR US TO KNOW that they were sorry," Andrea says now. "And that's not really what I wanted to hear at that time. That's not how I wanted them to react." What she wanted was something more introspective. "It's like, even if you don't think it's okay, you've presented some type of ideals or some type of climate where your *child* feels like that's okay," she explains. So clearly *something* hadn't happened, some educational piece, some conversation.

But every adult in Albany—parent, teacher, administrator, neighbor, community member, or bystander—seemed to have the same goal: to make it crystal clear that what had happened on Instagram had nothing to do with them. *They* weren't like that. Those kids had done it, either because they were bad, racist kids or because they were good-but-misguided kids or because they were just-fooling-around kids or because they were troubled kids or because they were someone else's kids. You could explain it however you wanted to, just as long as you could keep it all at arm's length.

"These boys, yes, are responsible for their actions," observes Rosalind Wiseman, who was unfamiliar with the Albany particulars but has watched similar scenarios play out in cities and towns across the country. "But they're also very much a manifestation of *our* pathology, of *our* sickness, of *our* weaknesses, of *our* lack of civil discourse, of *our* commitment to not seeing the impact of racism in our communities. Really, two things are true: they need to be held responsible for their behavior *and* they also are probably going to get scapegoated, or used by various factions in the community to make statements about whatever people believe. And in the midst of this is real people, young men who are probably confused and conflicted and embarrassed, and angry at each other, and angry at themselves."

FRIENDS

(May 2017)

BY THE BEGINNING OF MAY, FIVE OF THE FOURTEEN INSTAGRAM KIDS were back at school. Two others were facing expulsion. The remaining seven were in a kind of limbo, unwilling to return, but not sure what other options they had.

The boys who had returned steered clear of one another. Most of them hadn't been close friends to begin with, and they weren't about to huddle up now. The only path back into high school society was to sever ties with every other person associated with the account.

"I wanted to be accepted back at school and have people remember I'm an honest person," one of the account followers says. "That was the decision I had to make, where I just had to cut all those guys off."

But cutting off your old friends didn't mean that you were likely to gain new ones. It just meant that you were on your own.

HOW TO BE A PARIAH

WHAT YOU DON'T DO IS CRY, NO MATTER HOW MUCH YOU WANT TO. Because you're a boy, and boys don't cry. Instead, walk through those hallways with your head up, your hood down, your earbuds out of your ears. People will be talking about you, judging you. Act like you don't notice. Not the whispers, not the people who go out of their way to look past you. You're invisible but also larger than life, a giant turd stinking its way down those red-and-white-checked high school hallways.

You'll be afraid most of the time. You'll be pretty sure you're about to get jumped. But don't let it show. Remember, you're a boy.

You can try doing schoolwork. Maybe you'll manage to get through all that junior-year stuff: AP tests, ACTs. Maybe you'll be able to convince yourself it's worth showing up to a school that's declared you to be the highest level of cyber-bully. But chances are you won't feel motivated. You might go to class a quarter of the time. Just try to get Ds instead of Fs so you don't have to go to summer school.

Sometimes you'll go to class, and it will feel unbearable to be in that room. Ask to use the bathroom, and then stay there as long as you can. Go home for lunch so no one can see you sitting by yourself. If you have to sit in the cafeteria, put your headphones in. Try not to think about the friends you used to sit with.

You can deaden the pain with weed, if that's your style. Or by spending money, if you have it. Click, purchase. Click, purchase. Feels good for a minute. Feels okay, anyway.

There will be particularly awful moments. Like when there's a discussion in one of your classes about how people are feeling about what happened. People will talk about the amount of evil you have to have in your heart to have done something like this. You'll sit there listening to the roaring in your ears as the conversation moves around the room. Everyone is supposed to say something and maybe this is your moment to tell them something about how you feel, how sorry you are, how ashamed, but when it comes around to you, you'll just clam up and say, "I don't really have any emotions," like you're exactly the person they think you are.

People will make their opinions about you known. People from other grades, other schools, even. They'll go out of their way to hurt you when you play sports. They'll show up at your job and say things to you when they know you can't respond. They'll make a point of not shaking your hand. They'll make fun of you on social media. They'll shout things at your parents when they see them around town.

Sometimes you'll come home and find your mother crying. You'll know whose fault that is.

Nobody will ever ask you what happened. They'll never say, "Why did you do it?" They'll never even say, "What's *wrong* with you?" If they would, you'd have a chance to tell them that you know how badly you screwed up, but it didn't go down exactly the way they think. That will be the worst part of it, having people think they know everything about you, everything about what happened.

If you were popular before, you have a chance to fix things. People might listen to you when you tell your story, take you seriously when you apologize. But if you weren't popular? Sorry to break it to you, but there isn't much hope for you. If people didn't know who you were before, this is all they're going to know about you now.

Maybe one person will notice that you're suffering and reach out to see if you're okay. One person might tell you that they know you're not a racist or offer to help you catch up with your schoolwork. It won't be a lot, but it will feel like the world. You will be grateful to that person for the rest of your life.

Your close friends will still hang out with you, if you have any. They won't include any photos of you in their posts on social media, of course. You'll need to stay in the background, make sure you don't drag them down with you. Everyone is making a social calculation. You're a liability now.

Stuff the emotions. Stuff them down as far as they'll go. You don't have to deal with them if you can't feel them. You're bleeding, but you don't want to get blood on the furniture, don't want your family stained by your mess, so you have to keep it together. Don't tell anyone how bad it is, certainly not anyone who works for the school—you already know what they think of you. You're a Harmer. If you tell anyone you're having a hard time, they're just going to think to themselves, *Well, what did you expect after what you did?* Whatever you're experiencing, everyone agrees you deserve it.

At the end of the day, lie on your bed and cry. Because boys do cry, sometimes. It's okay, no one has to know. Tell yourself you got through one more day. You're that much closer to being done.

STEREOTYPE THREAT

THE GIRLS WHO HAD BEEN TARGETED WERE STRUGGLING IN SCHOOL. The mental health office kept calling them out of class for counseling, which was great except that missing so much school meant falling even further behind.

Some of them checked out completely, spending their days in the hallways or at home instead of in class.

The others tried to soldier through, but it was hard to focus. Rina remembers telling herself not to let the Instagram account get inside her head, but sometimes the insecurity she'd always carried with her would wiggle to the front of her brain and she'd have to talk herself down.

"There's no reason as to why you should let these boys make you feel this way," she would tell herself. "They're irrelevant. No one likes them anymore. You're good."

But the feelings were always there, the feeling that maybe other people saw her the way the boys who followed the account must, as ugly or stupid. Social psychologists have a name for this phenomenon: stereotype threat. It's what happens when anxiety about confirming a stereotype about your identity—female and Black in this case—makes it harder for you to do well on a task related to that stereotype.

Rina had always worried she wasn't smart enough, even though she had a high GPA. Now that little splinter of self-doubt felt more like a thorn. She began falling behind in math. She needed to do well in the class—she was planning on going to nursing school, so her math and science grades were crucial. But one of the Instagram followers was in that class and so was a guy who'd been friends with all of them even though he didn't follow the account. The two boys had been her study partners before all this happened. Now she couldn't even look at them.

DREAM (1)

THE BOYS WERE CHASING ANDREA THROUGH TOWN. IT WAS NIGHT. SHE was right by the high school and she was trying to get home, trying to get to the place where no one could find her. The boys were in a car, tracking her as she ran. Her legs pumped. Her heart pounded. She was heaving herself through the air, but still she wasn't moving.

She looked around for help, but there was no one there. The streets were deserted.

She would have to hide, that's all. All she needed to do was find something to hide behind—a nook or a crevice big enough for her to fit into. The walls of the school were flat and featureless, so she wedged herself through the storm drain and hid below the street.

Even so, they knew exactly where to find her—Greg and Charles and the others. Their fists were on her, their feet. They were hurting her, stomping her.

That's when she would always wake up.

BILLIE WRITES

IT WAS HARD FOR BILLIE TO GET UP IN THE MORNING, HARD TO GO TO school. She slept through class, if she went at all. Sometimes she went into her older sister's classes and sat on the floor beside her, falling asleep with her face resting on her sister's leg. Other days she went to the mental health office to camp out for the day. She was frightened all the time, though she couldn't say what she was scared of, exactly—it wasn't physical harm as much as it was someone taking pictures of her. Every time a phone was pointed her way, her heart would begin to pound. She felt on display, like a bug under a microscope. Her mind wouldn't stop skittering in circles. *Why is this happening? Are they still here? Are they going to follow me home? Who's going to bully me next? What's the next thing someone's going to come at me for? How the hell did I end up being female, gay, and Black?*

She was mad at herself for everything she was, but especially for being Black. Her mother was a beautiful Black woman, but while she could see her mother's beauty, she couldn't see her own. She sat in her room, writing on her phone, thumbs furiously translating her thoughts into letters, the letters into words, the words into lines.

I wish I was white.
I wish I had blonde hair and icy blue eyes.

I wish to be seen and noticed when I walk around
in the halls,
I wish I was praised,
I wish I was looked up to,
I wish to not face racism,
I wish I was popular,
I wish everything came easy to me.
But this will never happen due to the pigment in
my skin.

She kept thinking about the way people acted toward her at school. She was in an advanced math class, but when they did group tests, the girls in her class were always questioning her answers. Was it because she was Black? Was that why they said she didn't belong in the advanced class, even though she was better at math than they were?

Freshman year of high school had been the hardest of her life, and she couldn't see how it would ever be different. And so she wrote, line after line, page after page, trying to put down in words what it felt like to fear that she would always feel like this, to wonder how she was going to keep moving when she felt so desperately alone.

TRYING TO CHANGE

ONCE SCHOOL ADMINISTRATORS TOLD MURPHY HE'D NEED A BODYGUARD at school, he knew he wasn't going back. They never said he wasn't welcome, but he could read between the lines.

So now what? He'd received enough threats that his parents were worried he'd get attacked if he left the house, but he was going stir-crazy staying home. He took to sneaking out at night to drive around and smoke weed with some neighbor kids who didn't go to Albany High. It didn't take long for his parents to catch on. When his mom found a bag of weed in the pocket of his backpack, Murphy insisted he was just holding it for a friend. She called his bluff by making him do a drug test. Which, naturally, he failed.

"What are you doing with your life?" his parents asked him. "Is this really the life you want to live? You want to go work at a minimum-wage job for the rest of your life?"

No, of course not. He just wasn't sure how to do things differently.

His dad started a tradition of family movie nights where he, Murphy, and Murphy's younger brother would watch films like *Schindler's List* and *Glory*, movies that Murphy's dad hoped might teach them some history about the people they'd been belittling. But Murphy already knew that racism was bad. He just wasn't sure what to *do* with that feeling.

He wanted to prove to the people at school, the friends he'd lost, that he was changing. But how? He talked it over with Steven and they came up with the idea that they could make amends—or at least resurrect their reputations—by volunteering somewhere. Murphy was more concerned about how he was viewed in the community than Steven was, so he was the main driver of the project, sometimes bringing Steven or Patrick or even his mother along for company. He started out at a soup kitchen, and then became a regular at a food bank, sorting donations. He dreaded going at first, but it turned out to be kind of fun. The atmosphere was friendly. The people were nice. The time seemed to speed by. To his surprise, he found he liked it.

"It was kind of an unexpected change over time, because of the people and the morale," he says.

The work was rewarding on its own, but he was still hoping it would help him earn his way back into high school society.

"We were trying to show people we were sorry and this was something that we messed up on and were trying to change," he explains. "But then, no one really cared that we were doing it. They were all just like, 'Oh, good, you *should* be doing that.' Or: 'You're not doing it because you want to, out of the goodness of your heart. You're doing it because you want to win everyone's sympathy back.'"

Which was true, in a way. Still, he felt like his actions should count for something. There had to be some way back to the life he'd known before.

LAWSUIT

(May 1, 2017)

THE FIRST LAWSUIT WAS FILED ON MAY 1 BY FOUR OF THE INSTAGRAM followers—Steven, Patrick, and two other boys named Leighton and Riley—and their parents. Named as defendants were both the Albany Unified School District and Superintendent Val Williams, Principal Jeff Anderson, and Vice Principal Melisa Pfohl, as well as a math teacher who had refused to let Patrick retake a math test that was held while he was suspended. The lawsuit had two main arguments:

1. The Instagram posts were expressive/political speech, which is protected by the First Amendment. So were the likes and comments on those posts.
2. @yungcavage was a private account, created and interacted with outside of school, and so the school district had no authority to punish the students.

The students who had participated in the mediation session also charged that the school had recklessly placed them in harm's way during the sit-in, first by riling up the crowd with the noose email and then by failing to find them a safe way to leave the school.

They asked to be able to return to school, to have their disciplinary records wiped clean, to be able to make up missed schoolwork, and to be awarded unspecified damages.

The story attracted national attention. "Does the First Amendment Protect 'Liking' a Racist Instagram Post?" asked a *Washington Post* headline. "Some Calif. Students Say It Does."

That was the question that got people talking. Did the Instagram kids have a First Amendment right to be racist?

FREE SPEECH/HATE SPEECH

THE LAW IS CLEAR: OFFENSIVE SPEECH CAN'T BE BANNED JUST BECAUSE it's offensive. In decision after decision, the U.S. Supreme Court has ruled that there is no "hate speech" exception to the First Amendment.

"Censoring so-called hate speech . . . runs counter to the long-term interests of the most frequent victims of hate: racial, ethnic, religious and sexual minorities," the American Civil Liberties Union has written. "We should not give the government the power to decide which opinions are hateful, for history has taught us that government is more apt to use this power to prosecute minorities than to protect them."

Banning the kind of speech *you* find offensive, in other words, opens the possibility that someone else will gain the power to restrict the speech *they* find offensive, which could just as easily lead to prohibitions against discussing such topics as feminism, racism, or gender identity. And in fact, this is already happening. In 2022, nineteen states had laws or rules restricting how teachers could talk about racism, American history, or gender identity, a move the free-expression organization PEN America called "a sweeping crusade for content- and viewpoint-based state censorship."

School campuses are thus at the epicenter of a thorny series of questions: How do you allow the free exchange of ideas while still respecting the dignity of human beings? Where is the line between expressing an opinion and bullying? When does tolerance become complicity? When does sensitivity become censorship? And given that there's no universally agreed-upon answer to any of these questions, who gets to decide?

NOW IT WAS ABOUT MONEY

"I'M A BIG CONSTITUTIONAL GUY MYSELF—I LOVE THE FIRST AMENDment," Brutsri says. But in this case, he didn't think the free-speech argument held much weight. "Yes, you have a right to say it, but just because you *can* doesn't mean you *should*," he says. For him, the point was personal responsibility. It irked him that these parents had opted to sue rather than holding their kids accountable for their behavior.

"Be like, 'You have to deal with the consequences,'" he suggests. "Rather than, 'You know what? We're just going to sue our way out of this.'"

The lawsuits felt like a dodge, a way for people who were used to winning to try their hand at winning once more. How could you say you were sorry and then turn around and sue?

"I'm sure they had their reasons for the lawsuits, but in my eyes it was a betrayal," Coach Ray said. "It wasn't about educating and making sure that their children learn the proper lessons. Now it was about money."

NOTHING

(May 5, 2017)

INDEPENDENT STUDY RAN OUT ON MAY 5 AND THE DISTRICT REFUSED to extend it. After weeks of back-and-forth, the district offered to pay for the sophomores to take their classes at Brigham Young University's online high school, where Albany High students sometimes took classes if they had scheduling conflicts. Unlike pricier independent study options, which the district declined to cover, the BYU option had no in-person instruction and required the sophomores to start the entire semester from scratch, tossing out the four months of work they'd already done.

The work was redundant. The days ran together. The depression washed over Eren's head.

"I was not in the right space to do any of this, but that's what was expected of me," he says. "And I just wanted to do nothing."

MORE LAWSUITS

THE SECOND LAWSUIT CAME A LITTLE OVER A WEEK LATER. THIS ONE was filed on behalf of the three sophomores plus Jon, who later switched attorneys. This second suit also included a First Amendment argument, maintaining that while the district might have the right to discipline hateful speech, "liking" a post or following an account was not hateful and was thus protected by the Constitution.

But free-speech issues were not this lawsuit's primary focus. Instead, it was more concerned with the school district's conduct after the account was discovered, arguing that Albany had violated federal educational privacy rules by exposing the students' identities and had violated their due process rights by treating these minimally involved students as if they were responsible for the creation of the account.

The plaintiffs' lawyers argued that by lumping the lesser-involved students together with the account creator, failing to protect their identities, and allowing them to be publicly shamed and threatened, the district had made it impossible for the students to return to school, thus depriving them of their right to education.

The school district, the complaint alleged, "would rather see students get socially ostracized to the point of effective expulsion and even physically beaten before sharing the truth about the student plaintiffs' lack of involvement."

The lawsuit asked the district to expunge the students' disciplinary records and cover the cost of an education "comparable to Albany High School" that included "interaction with human instructors during class."

They hadn't wanted to sue, Gabriel's mother says. But in the end, they felt like they were out of options. A school counselor advised her, she says, that unless Gabriel was already popular, there was no way he could reintegrate back into the high school. Since news of the account had spread throughout the region, he was likely to face similar repercussions at any nearby public school. Most private schools wouldn't take him, both because of the scandal and because it was midsemester. The one exception was Tilden Prep, a tiny college-prep academy that offered individualized and in-person instruction. But the school came with a hefty price tag—more than Gabriel's parents had in savings, even after emptying out Gabriel's college fund. In the end, suing the school district was the only option that seemed like it might get Gabriel through high school without burying them in debt.

"Just pay for the school. That's all I wanted," Gabriel's mother says. "Just see us through this thing you created."

By the end of June, Murphy and Charles would both file lawsuits of their own, bringing the total of litigating students to ten.

Four of the Instagram followers didn't sue at all. Wyatt's family didn't, and neither did Greg's. But no one would remember that later.

WE DON'T HAVE MUCH TO LOSE

CHARLES SAYS THAT ONCE THE OTHER LAWSUITS WERE UNDERWAY, HE and his mom just decided to hop on the train. (His stepfather, Alexander, advised against it.) They wouldn't have to pay the attorney unless they won, so the only risk was the filing fees.

"We just thought, *Okay, we don't really have much to lose,*" Charles says.

But there was something to gain: money.

"We just want compensation for the stress and the everything," he explained. He had been sitting at home for months now, and his teachers hadn't provided him with any classwork. It felt like his school had completely abandoned him.

But wasn't that stress self-inflicted, given that he'd made the account?

It wasn't that he didn't think he did anything wrong, he said. "But I think the way [the school district] handled it was very bad and we should be compensated for their lack of knowledge on how to handle the situation. I think I do deserve some sort of punishment, and that's totally fine if the expulsion stays on my record. So morally, it's like if they handled it properly, I wouldn't feel entitled to anything."

Charles couldn't really point to something in particular that the school district had mishandled in his case. He just knew that being hated by the entire city took a big toll on his mental health.

“I was severely messed up after that,” he says. “It’s like, no one really cares because they just think that I deserve it, which I think is unfair.”

CAN WE SUE TOO?

ALMOST AS SOON AS THE ACCOUNT-FOLLOWERS' LAWSUITS WERE FILED, parents of the account's targets began investigating whether they could sue as well. But it wasn't easy to find an attorney. Coach Ray was part of the group that approached various law firms. He says no one they talked to was interested in taking the case, not if the plan was to sue the families of the Instagram kids. The families just didn't have enough assets to make it worthwhile.

The attorneys would be interested if there was a case to be made against the school district, which had the resources to pay out big settlements.

"But to go after the parents?" Coach Ray says. "They felt like it was nothing monetarily."

EXPULSIONS

(May–August 2017)

ON MAY 26, TWO MONTHS AFTER THE ACCOUNT'S DISCOVERY, JUDGE James Donato issued a temporary restraining order halting Patrick's expulsion hearing, saying that for a rising senior to be wrongfully expelled would "cause irreparable harm to his college admission prospects." The question of whether the school could legally expel students for commenting on an Instagram post, Donato said, would have to be settled in the course of litigation.

The expulsion hearing for Charles began less than a week later, and lasted until June 20. Two days after the whole thing was over, Charles was officially expelled.

IN HIS ROOM

BY NOW CHARLES HAD BEEN OUT OF SCHOOL FOR THREE MONTHS. HE had finally been approved for online school through Brigham Young University in mid-May, which the district was paying for, but he couldn't make himself do the work. He couldn't make himself do much of anything. Before the account was discovered, he had been awarded a scholarship for a summer program in France, but now he just couldn't imagine himself going. He told himself it was because he needed to stay close to home so he could meet with lawyers about his lawsuit, but in truth it just seemed too difficult. He could barely work up the energy to leave his room, much less get on a flight to Paris.

Most of his friendships had ended, including the ones with Greg, Wyatt, and Otis. Steven—the genius of their group—had moved to China for an internship with a software company. That left Patrick, Jon, and Murphy. Sometimes the four of them went out to get food or walk around one of the nearby cities, but Charles spent the majority of his time in his room by himself, playing video games, bingeing on *Family Guy* and *Breaking Bad* and random cartoons, emerging only to eat.

Over the summer, he appealed his expulsion to the Alameda County Board of Education. But in August, his expulsion was upheld.

STILL FRIENDS

FOR A WHILE MURPHY PRETENDED TO HAVE CUT CHARLES OUT OF HIS life. "I hate that guy," he'd tell anyone who asked. "He's a racist."

But eventually he realized that he wasn't going to be able to rejoin high school society no matter what he said. So why keep up the pretense? Let people judge him for staying friends with Charles. He didn't care.

"It's not just Charles's fault," he explains. "It was also all of our faults. We can't just let Charles take the blame for all of it, because we—I guess you could also say we did instigate it almost, or keep it going by liking the pictures and being like, 'Oh, that is funny,' or things like that. So it's not just Charles's fault. Everyone contributed to it equally."

RUMORS

RUMORS WERE FLYING FAST AND FURIOUS AROUND ALBANY. THEY appeared in letters to the school board and in impassioned statements during televised school board meetings. They were posted on Facebook and Nextdoor, passed from person to person. People were sure they knew what had really happened and who was really involved, based on things they heard from their children, or their friends' children, or their children's friends.

After the lawsuits were filed, the hostility only intensified. A woman posted on Nextdoor asking if someone could send her a private message with the Instagram kids' names and addresses, so she could make donations on their behalf to the NAACP, ACLU, and Southern Poverty Law Center and "make sure they get thank you letters."

A flame war broke out on the thread, with some arguing that the original poster had crossed a line by requesting the names of minors so that the families could be shamed, and others saying that shaming was the only way for bullying to be stopped "when the parents at home are bullies and support bullying."

A few people spoke up to remind posters that they didn't actually know anything about the families of the Instagram followers, who were watching the rising temperatures of these neighborhood conversations with alarm. But those posts didn't seem to convince anybody.

"I'm not generally a proponent of vigilante justice," wrote one poster, "but to hell with it: ride these aholes out on a rail."

EGGED

(June 3, 2017)

THE THUMPS BEGAN HITTING GREG'S HOUSE A LITTLE BEFORE MIDNIGHT on a Saturday night. *Thump. Thump. Thump.* When his mother, Lauren, went to investigate, she saw liquid leaking through the bottom of the front door. They'd been egged.

It was when they went out to investigate that they saw the writing. Someone had spray-painted the word *Racist* on the hood of the family's white Rav4.

Lauren called the police, who came out to take a report of the damage. After that, she and her husband moved the car off the street and covered it so the neighbors wouldn't ask questions. Then she called the high school. Called the superintendent. Sent an email to the other involved families. She wanted people to know what was happening. When they said they were afraid, they weren't "perpetuating fear," like the woman at the school board meeting had said. There was actually something to be afraid of.

MOST HATED

GREG WAS THE ONE EVERYONE KEPT FOCUSING ON, PARENTS AND STUdents alike. Many believed that he had been the real mastermind behind the account and had gotten away scot-free. In this version of events, which both Charles and Greg dispute, Greg was "the popular kid who was egging on his minions," as Ana's father put it.

Charles emphatically denies that Greg was at the helm of the account, and so do the other inner-circle account followers. Greg didn't want to be interviewed for this book, but he did agree to respond to some of the statements made about him. He agrees that he had a fair amount of social power and "some not-so-nice tendencies" when it came to using put-downs to jockey for status. But while he was the one who first suggested that Charles make the account, he denies that he was a primary driver of the posts once it was up and running.

"I wasn't the gatekeeper for the memes within the group," he says.

Even so, he was the person the account's targets seemed most angry at, the one people collected anecdotes and rumors about, the first name to be mentioned when the account was discussed. The hair-touching incident with Andrea was one explanation—it was the one incident that had taken place in the real world, rather than being confined to social media, and he was at the center of it. But that didn't quite explain why he seemed to symbolize the whole account. Charles thinks that people focused on Greg, rather than on him, because Greg was well-known and popular at school, whereas he and the rest of his circle weren't. The involvement of a kid like Greg was simply a bigger deal than the involvement of a social nobody. Greg was also the only one of the three main participants who was white.

"I don't mean to stereotype you, but you're just some white kid that gets whatever he wants," Ana said, addressing an imaginary Greg as if he were standing in front of her. "You have hella white privilege. You get away with hella shit, because you're a charming, white, young boy."

After Greg's mother's plea for help at the April 25 school board meeting, Albany school officials had introduced both Greg's parents and Andrea's mother to a restorative justice facilitator named Kyle McClerkins, with the thought that McClerkins might facilitate a session between the two young people. Greg's parents were eager to move forward and so McClerkins met with Greg a few times to help prepare him for what they hoped would be an eventual meeting with Andrea. (In the end, Andrea declined to meet. She felt like it was something Greg's parents were pushing, not something Greg himself wanted to make happen.)

McClerkins, who is Black, was good at opening up conversations about race—he did it all the time in his job as a restorative justice facilitator in the Oakland schools, where racial animosity often leaked into conflicts between students from different backgrounds.

He'd ask Greg questions like *What does the word* race *mean to you? How much of your life is impacted by race? Do you ever feel like your race has more social advantages than others? How are you going to make things right? What are you doing to learn more and make the situation better?*

He remembers Greg being engaged in those conversations. He remembers Greg reading books about Black history and volunteering at the Boys and Girls Club in Oakland and going out of his way to reach out to people who were angry at him about the account and listen to what they had to say. In his view, the community's focus on punishment wasn't likely to bring anyone the satisfaction they were hoping for.

"People don't seem to understand that he's already been punished, whether he did it, or he didn't, or it was a mistake. He's been punished. He continues to be punished," McClerkins says. "He's a teenager that cannot walk down the street without somebody saying something. He's a teenager who can't go to parties like he was because a fight might jump off. He is a teenager who has to continuously watch his back all the time now. And I'm not putting race in it—he's a teenager, a human, who was displaced from his school. He is a teenager who has things posted about him. He's a teenager that adults pretty much will say something about when they see him. He's a teenager who has lost his friends and his peers who he used to hang around with. He has to live through all of this. At the end of the day, you have to live through it every single day, knowing that you are probably one of the most hated people in the community because X, Y, and Z. And most people are like, 'He needs to be punished.' Well, I mean, damn. How much do you have to punish a person?"

McClerkins was still working with Greg when he got a

call from Superintendent Val Williams informing him that some of the Instagram families were suing. At that point, he decided to step aside so as not to be pulled into the litigation. The situation in Albany, he felt, "wasn't conducive to me for taking a restorative approach."

A DAY AT THE BOARDWALK

THE SCHOOL YEAR WAS WINDING DOWN. FINALS WERE COMING AT THEM like a freight train. The girls tried to focus on their work, but most of them weren't having much success. Rina, the junior class president, did so poorly in math that she had to retake it over the summer. Ana had summer school ahead of her too, finishing up the online history class she was taking to make up for the one she'd had to drop.

Someone from the Albany's Black Parent Association had organized a retreat day at the Santa Cruz Beach Boardwalk amusement park for the girls who had been impacted and a few of their friends. Free wristbands for all of them. It was a fun day, but Rina felt tension beneath the surface. Andrea didn't want to talk about the account, and neither did Ana. But Rina wanted to talk about it, and so did Lolia and Tiana and Sita.

"I don't know, I just feel like there's so many different perspectives," Rina says. There were two different friend groups involved—Ana, Andrea, and Kerry were one group, and Lolia, Tiana, and Sita were another. Rina was friends with everyone, which made her uniquely sensitive to the undercurrent of tension. In retrospect, the day in Santa Cruz was a missed opportunity.

"I just wish we had talked about it more," she says. She

means the Instagram account and how to respond to it going forward. "It would have been a little better."

Maybe if they'd talked about it, they'd have understood each other's future choices. But instead, they just climbed into the brightly colored cars of the Giant Dipper roller coaster and white-knuckled their way up and down its rickety hills.

A MEETING IN THE PARK

ANA DIDN'T TELL ANYONE WHEN SHE WENT TO MEET WITH CHARLES. He'd texted her soon after the account was discovered and said he wanted to talk. She'd sent back a scorching response. But the summer after junior year she reached out and told him she was ready.

"I just didn't want to tell my friends because I knew they were going to be like, 'Bitch, what did you say? Did you go off?'" she says now. "It's not like that for me. I'm trying to forgive people."

They sat at a picnic table at Memorial Park, beside the giant stone fireplace that had inexplicably been erected there in 1933. Ana told Charles how betrayed she and her friends had felt—she tended to use the pronoun "we" rather than "I." Charles explained as best he could how the account had come to be, how he had meant it to be a gross kind of joke. He told her he was sorry for making it, sorry for the impact it had had on her.

After that, they just caught up on their lives. How they were feeling. How school was going. What they were doing over the summer. Even after everything that had happened, they still had the same ability to talk openly with each other. Charles told her about being stuck in his room all the time, how he basically never went out.

"Don't feel sorry for me," he said.

"I don't," Ana retorted.

That made him laugh. "Okay, good."

Ana hadn't felt much sympathy for any of the Instagram kids, but now she was struck by how much Charles's life had been affected by the account's discovery, not in the same way hers had been, but in ways that were more lasting and serious than she had expected.

"Everyone hated him," she says. "If everyone hated me, I would be like, *fuck*. No one likes you. Can't even have your face seen around here, that's how bad it is."

It wasn't like they were going to be friends again now. But both of them seemed to find some solace in the meeting. A place to leave things that didn't hurt to think about.

"Everybody does stuff for a reason," Ana says. "I don't want to just be like, 'You're a terrible person. You lose.'"

THE *TINKER* TEST

(July 27, 2017)

SHORTLY AFTER 10 A.M. ON A THURSDAY IN LATE JULY, THREE ATTORNEYS for the students who were suing the school district and two attorneys who were defending the school district and its employees appeared at the Phillip Burton Federal Building and U.S. Courthouse in San Francisco to argue a motion over some of the First Amendment claims in the lawsuits. Presiding over the case was Judge James Donato, a white man with dark eyes and expressive eyebrows who wasted little time with preliminaries. As soon as he got everyone's names on the record, he invited the attorneys for the litigating students to make their case. Why, he wanted to know, wouldn't the high school have the right to discipline the students who had created, followed, or liked the posts on the @yungcavage account?

The question was one that has bedeviled school districts since 1969, when the U.S. Supreme Court issued a decision in *Tinker v. Des Moines Independent Community School District.* That case involved a high school student named Mary Beth Tinker who was disciplined, along with two other students, for wearing a black armband to school to protest the Vietnam

War. Two lower courts upheld her suspension, but the Supreme Court ruled that the school had acted improperly.

"It can hardly be argued that either students or teachers shed their constitutional rights to freedom of speech or expression at the schoolhouse gate," Supreme Court justice Abe Fortas wrote in the decision. Instead, the court held, school officials must prove that a student's conduct would foreseeably lead to a substantial disruption of school operations. These conditions have become known as "the *Tinker* test."

One aspect of the *Tinker* test is the question of whether the speech that's being disciplined has enough of a connection—or *nexus* in legal speak—to the school to fall within the school's jurisdiction. In the digital age, the line between things that happen at school and things that happen off campus can be difficult to determine. That was the first question the judge wanted the lawyers to address: Was there enough of a nexus between the Instagram account and the school?

Alan Beck, who represented Charles, Steven, and several other plaintiffs, took the first stab at answering.

"This is a private Instagram page that was done completely out of school," he said. "And there was no intent on my clients' part for this Instagram page to reach school. And they intentionally made it private so that no one else outside the small circle of friends could access it."

Judge Donato interrupted. "Invitation only, right?"

"Correct, Your Honor," Beck replied.

"He invited thirteen other students to participate," the judge continued, referring to Charles.

"Correct."

"He put a high degree of faith in privacy on the Internet," Judge Donato remarked wryly.

Katherine Alberts, who represented Albany Unified, argued that the connection between the school and the account was obvious. "These are students sharing pictures and comments about other students with a group of students," she said. "I think the best nexus factor is the fact that it reached campus, it did get there," she said, adding that if you talk about other students in a derogatory manner, somebody was likely to feel uncomfortable and tell other people.

Judge Donato didn't like this second line of reasoning and he said so. Let's say these students had formed an off-campus study group with online postings that was devoted to studying racist and antisemitic texts, he suggested. If they didn't mention the names of any students or teachers, but were "simply a group of students off campus, on their own time, studying things that most people would find offensive," wouldn't she agree that the school had no ability to discipline them? Even if another student found out about it and mentioned it at school?

"You would have to look at whether or not there would be a substantial disruption," Alberts said. And anyway, she added, that wasn't the situation. "They *are* talking about other students. These are not political discussions about racism in theory. They are racist posts directed at other students."

Donato turned to the plaintiffs' attorney. "I do think that makes a difference, Mr. Beck, in terms of nexus," he said.

Having declared himself satisfied for the moment that there was "sufficient nexus," Donato turned his attention to a second question: Did the school have the right to discipline all fourteen students?

"There was one poster," he said. "That's it. Everybody else was a bystander, literally. They liked or may have added a comment." He noted that at least one of the plaintiffs didn't interact with the account at all. "Now all of them are being lumped together for discipline. And I have some qualms about that."

His qualm was this: According to the standard established by the *Tinker* case, a school can only discipline student speech if that speech would have a foreseeable and substantial disruptive effect. While that standard could be met for the original poster, he was having trouble seeing how it applied to people who liked or commented. Those were different actions from creating and posting a meme, and it was harder to prove that a like or a comment caused substantial disruption on its own.

"I do not see how they fall within the disciplinary powers of the school," Donato said. "They have a perfect right to be an observer and express a comment."

He offered another hypothetical scenario. "Let's say this happened on campus, and one student was yelling racial epithets at another student, and fifty students walked up and watched. And some of those students voiced vague but positive words of support like, *yeah*, *right on*, *good point*," he said. "You think the school district, within the parameters of *Tinker*, could discipline the students who just gave the vague words of support?"

"Yes," Alberts said. "Because they're helping cause the disruption and interfering with the rights of that student who's being bullied."

"That's not the *Tinker* test," Judge Donato countered, citing two circuit court cases that said specifically that offensive speech alone did not interfere with the rights of other students. The speech had to actually *cause* a disruption. So, did the follows, likes, and comments cause *more* disruption than the posts would have done on their own?

Alberts argued that they did, at least in the view of the students who were targeted. "The fact that all of these other students were liking these comments, the fact that they were following and hadn't told on them, they saw that as this *group* was bullying them," she argued. "The students who came to the administration were not just saying, Oh, it's just this guy. They were talking about the entire group."

"Let me jump in," Donato said. "I appreciate how the individuals portrayed in the pictures would feel degraded, offended, maybe fearful. I appreciate all of that. And I accept that. That is not, though, the *Tinker* test."

In fact, he said, he was "genuinely mystified" about the school district's decision to discipline one of the plaintiffs, an account follower who did not like or comment on a single post. "That is a far net to cast for First Amendment purposes," he said.

Alberts countered that a follower who didn't comment or like a post should still have come forward and reported the account. "Can you be a bystander?" she asked. "Should you be an upstander?"

"You know the law of California is you, as an adult, can sit idly by while you watch someone get murdered and you have no obligation to volunteer," Judge Donato said, referring to the state law that says that you cannot be prosecuted or sued for failing to rescue or assist someone who is in danger.

"Schools are different environments," Alberts said.

"Not on that issue," Donato said. "Students are not charged with being snitches. That's not school policy. It shouldn't be if it is. You cannot have a culture where students are expected to be snitches and turn people in at the risk of being disciplined if the school second-guesses their decision not to. That can't be right."

The hearing was adjourned at 10:57 A.M. Judge Donato wouldn't issue a ruling until November.

RIGHTS

The right to make mistakes.
        The right to fix them.
        The right to be treated with dignity.
        The right to apologize.
        The right to have a future.
        The right to be a child.

The right to be a child.
        The right to be left alone.
        The right to an education.
        The right to be treated with dignity.
        The right to have a future.
        The right not to forgive.

CHARLOTTESVILLE

ON AUGUST 11 AND 12, 2017, ABOUT SIX HUNDRED WHITE NATIONALISTS gathered in Charlottesville, Virginia, armed with sticks, shields, handguns, and long guns, and carrying Nazi and Confederate flags. The organizers called their rally Unite the Right, and it was the largest and most violent gathering of far-right and extremist groups in decades, with dozens of neo-Nazi and white supremacist organizations represented. They had come to protest the planned removal of a statue of Confederate general Robert E. Lee, and they carried tiki torches and chanted slogans like "White lives matter" and "Jews will not replace us." (Many in the white power movement believe that Jews are behind a plan to "replace" people of European descent with nonwhite immigrants.)

At 1:42 P.M. on the second day of the protest, a twenty-year-old neo-Nazi named James Fields Jr. drove his Dodge Challenger into a crowd of peaceful counterdemonstrators, injuring thirty-five people and killing thirty-two-year-old Heather Heyer, a paralegal. Fields, who was eventually sentenced to life in prison without the possibility of parole plus 419 years, had posted a meme on Instagram a few months earlier of a car driving into a crowd of people. The caption said: *You have the right to protest but Im late for work.*

After Heyer's murder, President Donald Trump downplayed

the violence by blaming "both sides." In the next few days, traffic to the white nationalist website Stormfront would more than triple, reaching three hundred thousand daily page views.

Brutsri watched the whole thing unfold from his home in Albany.

"I was like, *This is* real *real*," he says.

It was depressing, to be honest. Growing up, he'd always thought about racism as something you learned about in history class, accompanied by grainy black-and-white footage from some segregated lunch counter of long ago.

"Racism to me was people saying, 'We're not going to serve you hot coffee because you're brown,'" he says. "And now, to me, it's like, 'Oh, we're going to shoot you because you're brown.'"

He saw the world differently now. He advocated against gun control, because he wanted to be able to protect himself against violent white supremacists.

"It's crazy to see it come back," he says. "I grew up when all of that was in the past."

PART 11

SCIENCE

THE NEXT LEVEL

(September 18, 2019)

"I HONESTLY GET A LITTLE UNCOMFORTABLE TALKING ABOUT THIS SUBject with all these people around me," Jon said. Charles's old friend, the onetime punching bag of their group, was sitting at a metal table at an Oakland Starbucks. It was a chilly fall Wednesday, the sky blinking between sun and shadow. School had just gotten out, which meant that the streets and café were filled with middle-schoolers, many of whom were Black. Jon, who is white, was in a white T-shirt and khakis, his dark bangs falling over his eyes in a ragged fringe. More than two years had passed since the discovery of the @yungcavage account and he was in college now, although the semester had yet to begin.

As uncomfortable as he was, he still didn't shy away from saying what was on his mind.

"I am, in part—*significantly* in part—responsible," he said of the @yungcavage account. "Me and Patrick were the people that elevated it from that level to the next level. And mostly me, honestly. Mostly me."

That level was the racist jokes, the use of the N-word. Not to refer to Black people, mostly, but as a way of insulting each other or simply for the thrill of speaking the forbidden syllables.

"When we'd be at the mall or watching a movie, Charles would say it much louder than he probably should have and Patrick would follow suit," he said. "And I would tell them to stop. 'What the hell are you doing? You're going to get our asses beat up one of these days.'"

The next level?

He grinned awkwardly.

"I'm trying to figure out how to say this in the least offensive way possible," he said. "It really is kind of reprehensible stuff."

GOOGLING

(2016)

"IT WAS ALL BORN OUT OF CURIOSITY," JON SAID. "I LIKE SCIENCE. I read about science every day. I'm a math major in college. It's what I would like to do for the rest of my life."

He didn't remember now exactly why he'd started googling race back in high school, but he thinks it was because he was white and all of his friends were Asian. He wanted to know why they looked so different from him. His investigation led him to some unexpected places.

"Online you can find websites that rank different races according to different metrics," he explained. "Like income, scores on psychometric tests, various physical attributes." He trailed off, as if hoping to soften the impact of what he was about to say. "With that information, a kid can do a lot of damage. He can start making assumptions about people based on this information. I did that and I told my friends about it and they started doing it."

For most people in their friend group, it was just something to joke about—"edgy" humor. Jon didn't think they took him seriously.

"I would research a lot about this because I thought it was really interesting," Jon explained. "And then I would share this information with my friends, and they would do something with it that I wouldn't consider good. Making jokes. Making memes. Saying things in public that they probably shouldn't say. And because they seemed to be entertained by the information that I'd share with them, that I found online, I continued to do it."

In Jon's telling, he had come across a knowledge so powerful, so explosive, that the media had tried to suppress it. His error, he felt, was not in *believing* this information, but in allowing others to use it improperly.

"It's science," he said. "Scientists from very prestigious universities, they've said they do believe these sorts of things and I don't even like to use the word *believe*, because you don't *believe* science. There's the facts. There is a logical process that led to these facts being produced."

And what were these "facts"?

"I think it's been very well established in scientific literature that there are differences in average cognitive ability," he explained. "You know, honestly, you don't really need to be a scientist to see that. Just observe in our day-to-day lives."

I DON'T HAVE AN AGENDA

"OBVIOUSLY CERTAIN GROUPS OF PEOPLE ARE BETTER AT RUNNING," Jon said. "I mean, that's obvious. It sounds like some really mean shit to say, but I think that's really just the way it is. I'm telling you, I don't have an agenda—I really don't. If I met a Black person in the dining hall one day, sat down, and had a conversation with the guy and found out he was a nice person, I would have no problem whatsoever being friends with this person. I don't allow this to influence my behavior. There are a lot of people who live totally regular lives who believe exactly the same things I do."

Jon didn't approve of what Charles and Patrick had done with the account, he emphasized. He'd never been part of the social media piece of this. Not because he thought it was wrong to make those jokes, but because doing so on Instagram was way too public.

"It's not good fun, but bad fun," he explained. "But bad fun, if you want to make it private, there's nothing too wrong about it."

Jon said that his interest in the topic of racial difference wasn't born out of "genuine racism." These days, it wasn't something he cared or thought about much. So did he think the word *racist* applied to him?

He paused to think.

"Not that word, probably a different word," he said. "I don't think that I'm racist because I don't view any group of people as better than any other. What basis would I have for that? I'm not religious or anything. I don't subscribe to any ideology. The only thing I believe is there are certain differences in certain traits. That one group of people is superior, if you want to use that word, on the average, in respect to one trait."

The trait, if it isn't obvious, is intelligence—or what Jon termed "average cognitive ability." Jon and his friends had always been in the top math classes at school. It was easy for them to conclude they were more intelligent than other people. But Jon insisted that he wasn't swayed by this.

"I don't think that I'm all that great," he said. "I mean, I've got crippling OCD that I've had since I was a six-year-old. Crippling. When I was a child, I would spend hours and hours standing over by the faucet washing my hands with scalding hot water. I could not help myself. I still have this problem to this day. I am by no means superior. Trust me. People with OCD have all sorts of cognitive deficits. Problems with memory, they have spatial problems. Not using this to make myself feel better. I'm really not."

Instead, what made Jon feel special was his belief that he had accessed a secret knowledge, something the people around him didn't know or didn't want to believe.

The word that he said describes him is "realist."

It's an innocent-sounding word. But there's a history behind it. More history, in fact, than science.

SCIENTIFIC RACISM

RACE REALISM IS ONE OF THE TERMS FOR THE FAKE SCIENCE THAT JON had discovered. Other terms are *scientific racism*, *biological racism*, and *human biodiversity*, or *HBD*, a once-neutral term that has been co-opted by some proponents of racialist ideas. To the casual googler, the websites that promote these ideas can indeed look a lot like science. While some websites are clearly created by white supremacist groups, many are designed to hide their origins by looking as if they are created by legitimate scientists or come from peer-reviewed journals. They use scientific language and even have scientific adherents, the most prominent of whom was James Watson, half of the Nobel Prize–winning team that deciphered the double-helix structure of the DNA molecule. (Watson, though undoubtedly brilliant, had a long history of making bigoted and scientifically questionable statements.)

Yet the vast majority of geneticists say that the notion that race is a predictor of intelligence is a complete distortion of their research. In 2014, more than 140 of the nation's most prestigious population geneticists signed a letter that said, "There is no support from the field of population genetics" for the idea that "recent natural selection has led to worldwide differences in I.Q. test results, political institutions and economic development." In 2018, the American Society of Human Genetics

(ASHG) issued a statement that stated unequivocally: "Any attempt to use genetics to rank populations demonstrates a fundamental misunderstanding of genetics."

Even so, ideas linking race and intelligence remain stubbornly popular. The people who promote them tend to portray themselves as the few brave voices willing to speak the explosive and politically incorrect truth. Sociologist Dr. Reanne Frank has dubbed this narrative "the forbidden knowledge discourse." It's a clever rhetorical device if you want to explain why your ideas have been rejected by most scientists—it's not that your science is bad, it's that your ideas are too hot to handle.

The irony, of course, is that "race realism" is nothing new. One of the first people to divide humans into "races" was Carl Linnaeus, sometimes called the "Father of Taxonomy," who invented the two-part naming system we use to classify all life-forms. Writing in the mid-1700s, when people didn't know much about human difference, Linnaeus suggested that there were four races of people from four different continents. *Homo sapiens americanus*, as he labeled Native Americans, was "red, ill-tempered, subjugated." *Homo sapiens europaeus*, as he labeled Europeans, was "white, serious, strong," and so on. Four colors of people, with white people at the top, and Black people at the bottom. (Linnaeus also believed there was a fifth race of "monstrous" humans that included dwarfs who lived in the Alps and giants who lived in Patagonia.) Linnaeus's ranking system was undoubtedly influenced by the fact that his native Switzerland was at that moment heavily invested in the transatlantic slave trade. But his categories, and his ideas about the "nature" of each group of people, have lived on long after the abolition of race-based slavery. In fact, they bear an uncanny resemblance to the claims of today's "race realists."

"It's basically just taking genetics to rebrand what is really an idea from the eighteenth century," explains Dr. Ann Morning, a sociologist who studies the intersection of race and science. "Since the 1700s we've used whatever our shiniest, sexiest science was at the time to show that the racial categories were real in some biological sense."

Evolution, blood groups, the measurement of skulls, IQ tests, genetics—each of these scientific breakthroughs was almost immediately used by someone to bolster the argument that people can be divided into racial groups and then ranked, with white people always landing at the top.

What makes people susceptible to this kind of thinking, Morning says, is the fact that we talk about race all the time as if it were a genuine scientific concept.

"In this country, we're bombarded all the time with messages suggesting to us not only that racial categories are real and authoritative categories but also that they're linked to our bodies, to our abilities, our physical tendencies," she explains. Race is constantly being discussed in contexts that seem scientific and official—medical forms, DNA tests, government applications. Statistics about poverty, education, crime, and employment are all divided by race. When we look around, we see people clustering by race—in friend groups, in careers, in neighborhoods—all of which reinforces the idea that race is real.

"We all know there's no place on the genome which is the race locus, nothing like that," Morning says. "But nonetheless, a lot of times when scientists are just doing their work and trying to come up with divisions or clusters of types in the human species, pretty regularly they fall back on a racial kind of shorthand."

In this context, telling people that race is a socially constructed category can feel like asking them to deny the evidence of their own eyes. People from Norway and people from Nigeria look totally different—so they *must* be different races.

"But in applying that logic, we could also say that people from Japan and India look totally different, but we tend to think of them as being part of the same race," Morning observes. "I can tell the difference between Norwegians and Italians and again, we think of them as being part of the same race. So we have to do this harder work of getting people to realize that what seems to be just their eyes relaying some objective truth to them, that those perceptions are always filtered through this cultural lens, this cultural filter that we are brought up to have in our brains."

It wasn't that long ago that biological race was taught in science class. Up until World War II, many U.S. textbooks talked about the superiority of the white race as if it were an established fact, and promoted eugenics—the idea that "defective" humans should be prevented from reproducing—as an example of forward-thinking social policy. After fascism was defeated in Europe and the horrors of the Nazi regime were exposed, these ideas were taken out of textbooks and for a while they were actively refuted. But in the 1960s, race nearly disappeared from science textbooks. The political upheavals of the civil rights movement made the topic too "controversial."

But when race isn't discussed in science class, people tend to fill in the blanks with conclusions of their own, conclusions that don't reflect the complexity of genetic science. Education researcher Dr. Brian Donovan has looked at the beliefs of high school students in schools very much like Albany High School: affluent, majority white, but still relatively diverse. About a fifth of the students at these schools believe what Jon believes—that there are genetic differences between the races that determine people's intelligence and other abilities. That belief is shared by about the same percentage of U.S. adults.

Here's what science actually knows about racial difference:

- Any two humans share 99.9 percent of their DNA.
- The physical or phenotypic differences that we associate with "race"—skin color, eyelid form, hair texture, nose and mouth shape—don't indicate significant genetic differences between human populations. The gene variants associated with both dark and light skin color are found in every major human population, for example.
- Within the tiny sliver of DNA that varies between individual humans, the vast majority—about 95.7 percent—of human variation occurs between people who are *within* each of the populations.
- Genetic differences between groups of people from different regions of the world don't explain why members of those groups do better or worse on tests of athletic or intellectual ability.

One reason that people can be susceptible to false ideas about biological race is that in high school science classes, genetics is often taught in its most simplified form, where a single set of gene variants, or alleles, govern a particular trait like eye color. Left out of the equation is the role of the environment, which can influence how genes behave.

"It's inappropriate to think of a gene without thinking of the environment—the two are fundamentally interlinked," explains Donovan, an education researcher who studies the way science is taught. "Evolution is all about selective pressures in the environment. It could be the social environment, or the physical environment, or it could be the cultural environment."

Donovan has tested student beliefs about race and genetics following a lesson on sickle cell disease. He taught two different lessons to two groups of students and then surveyed each group about their understanding of race. The students who were taught that the disease is more prevalent among Black people were more likely to say in the subsequent survey that race is a biological fact. The students who were taught, more accurately, that the sickle cell trait is more common among people of all skin-tones whose ancestors are from parts of the world with high levels of malaria, including west-central Africa, India, the Arabian Peninsula, and parts of the Mediterranean, were more likely to understand that race is a social construct.

A social construct is something that we have made real because of what we believe and how we behave. There is no science behind race. But there is plenty of history. And that history continues to impact people's lives, day after day, year after year, century after century.

DNA, IQ, AND THE NFL

ABOUT HALF OF A PERSON'S COGNITIVE ABILITY COMES FROM THEIR DNA. But there is no single set of alleles that govern intelligence. More than five hundred different genes have been linked to intellectual performance so far, with tens of thousands of possible variations. And while there is plenty of genetic variation among individual humans, none of the genetic variants correlated with cognitive ability have been found to vary significantly between global populations. In other words, there is no evidence that groups of people from different parts of the world have inherited more or less capacity for intelligence.

At the same time, a wide spectrum of environmental factors plays a role in shaping cognitive ability. Health, nutrition, standard of living, and education all influence cognitive ability, which explains a phenomenon called the Flynn effect.

In the mid-1980s, political scientist James Flynn observed that IQ scores had risen steadily throughout the twentieth century, a trend that's now been observed in populations throughout the world. That wasn't because people suddenly became more intelligent; it's because people started getting better nutrition, health care, and education. Humans are also getting better at athletics, performing feats that would have been unimaginable a century ago. That's not because of a change in human genetics; it's because of training, diet, equipment, and overall know-how. While people like James Watson tend to say that certain regions of the world are poor because their populations have a lower IQ than wealthier regions, it's far more likely that it is the *poverty* that is lowering IQ scores and not the other way around.

But discredited ideas about race and intelligence are everywhere, often lurking just below the surface. In August 2021, for example, a *Washington Post* investigation found that the National Football League was using a practice called "race norming" to deny the injury claims of Black football players with the severe concussion-related brain damage known as chronic traumatic encephalopathy (CTE), or to pay them less than white players with the same injury.

The rationale was that Black players had *started* with a lower level of cognitive function and thus weren't as severely impaired as they would be if they were white. This assumption was then embedded in a computer model that determined the fates of hundreds of professional athletes who had been injured on the job. According to attorneys who sued the NFL on behalf of some twenty thousand Black football players, race-norming meant that white players qualified for monetary settlements at two or three times the rate of their Black counterparts, despite the fact that 60 percent of living retired players and 70 percent of current players are Black. In October 2021, the NFL settled the lawsuit for $1 billion and agreed to end the practice. Under the terms of the agreement, the league agreed to rescore the test results of those players whose claims were denied to determine if they should have qualified for compensation.

THE ZONE OF BOTH

JON DOESN'T THINK THE OTHERS IN HIS GROUP PAID MUCH ATTENTION to his ideas about race, with one exception. "If root beliefs were transmitted to anybody, it was probably Patrick," he says. "I spent the most time with him, generally. I also spent the most time with him talking about this stuff." The class presentation that Patrick made about college admissions seems to be a direct result of the stuff Jon had found online. So does a post on the @yungcavage account that paired a 2016 *BuzzFeed* headline about Black inventors—"Things the World Wouldn't Have If Black People Didn't Exist"—with a KKK hood, a photo of men dressed in orange prison garb, and a statistic about the average IQ in the United States being ninety-eight.

Some of the others in the friend group remember Jon talking about race and genetics, although they didn't track it too closely. He was always offering them fun facts from his trips down Wikipedia rabbit holes, and this didn't seem any different.

"He would always say that's why certain people are better at certain things," Murphy recalls. "That's why you don't see the U.S.A. coming in top in running. We're still fast and things like that, but some people are just born with it."

He trails off uncertainly, not sure now if he's saying something that's based in fact, or just something that Jon used to tell them.

"It'd kind of go in one ear, out the other ear sometimes, because it's Jon," he explains. "We pick on him a bit. We use him as the butt of the joke."

So that was the paradox. In their friend group, Jon was both a wise man and a fool. Which meant that his assertions about race lived in a kind of twilight realm where they were not exactly absorbed but not exactly rejected either. It was a familiar territory, this semi-lit world of half beliefs. Racist jokes lived here, simultaneously funny and not funny, meant and not meant. So did the harassment of lower-status guys in the group.

Call it the Zone of Both. You could feel safe there, because you never had to commit to feeling strongly about anything. And if you didn't feel strongly about anything, nobody could turn your feelings into a joke.

PART 12

EVERY DAY ANOTHER DAY

JUDGMENT BOMB

ANDREA WAS TRYING TO REJOIN THE SOCIAL WORLD, BUT IT WAS HARD. She felt like she was labeled now as a difficult person, particularly by the people who thought the Instagram kids had been treated unfairly. In their eyes, she was the pursed-lipped social justice warrior, a ticking judgment bomb. None of them could see the person she actually was, an anxious and depressed seventeen-year-old girl who was working her hardest just to get through the day. A girl who was going to have to see some of the people who had followed the account in her daily passage through the school's corridors.

"Just working on not being fazed by them being there was hard," she says. Keeping her hands from clenching into fists. Keeping her breath slow and even.

And yet, as much as she tried to seem normal, she still felt like an outcast. "People had already decided what I was like or how I would react or what type of opinions I had because I was offended by people offending me," she says. "They would assume that I wasn't going to be cool or fun or a ball of joy."

Once she went to a party with her best friend, Lydia. Lydia had just started going out with Rosie, and the two of them disappeared somewhere, leaving Andrea by herself.

There she was, in a room full of people she'd known her entire life, and nobody had anything to say to her.

"I hate this," she thought. So she drank too much and was too blatantly honest with people she didn't like, cementing her reputation as someone who was "difficult."

NOT OKAY

I'm not okay
with racists.
I'm not okay with people
who are okay with racists.
I'm not okay with people
who are okay with people
who are okay with racists.
I'm not okay with people who are
okay with people who are
okay with people who are
okay with racists.
I'm not okay
with people.
I'm not okay.

SOLANO STROLL

(September 10, 2017)

THE SOLANO AVENUE STROLL IS A STREET FAIR HELD ON THE SECOND Sunday in September. A Berkeley-Albany tradition since 1974, it has food booths and performers and handcrafts and mechanical rides and a parade.

Patrick, Charles, and Jon went together in the afternoon. They were walking down Solano, caught up in their own banter, when they passed a couple of Black boys from Albany High. Their eyes met. The boys were younger than them, just fourteen and fifteen, but bigger—one of them was well over six feet tall.

"What the fuck are you laughing at?" the taller boy said.

He and his friend began to follow them. When Patrick, Charles, and Jon turned around, the taller boy wrapped his arm around Patrick's neck and choke-slammed him to the ground. Patrick tried to get up, and the boy punched him on the back of the head.

Just then, a passerby yelled for them to stop. The two boys walked away, shouting "Racist!"

Two police officers who had been patrolling the street arrived about ten minutes later to take a report. The passerby, a white woman in her early forties, stayed to give a statement.

She could identify the boys if she saw them again, she said. She was sure of it.

An hour or so later, the same two officers ran into two teens who fit the description provided by Jon, Charles, and Patrick. According to his police report, Officer Andrew Jones was acquainted with the boys and had a good rapport with them, and the boys spoke candidly to him about what had happened. The taller one explained that he knew Patrick, Charles, and Jon were responsible for the racist Instagram account, and so when he saw Patrick laughing, he was sure that Patrick was laughing at *him*.

Since Patrick had no lasting injuries, the whole matter was dropped and the boys went on their way. But word of the attack spread quickly among the families of the Instagram followers. Like the vandalism of Greg's family's car and Murphy's broken nose, like the threats they had all received in person and on social media, it added to the sense that none of them were safe.

There was another outcome as well.

About forty-five minutes after Patrick was punched, the woman who had broken up the altercation flagged down two other police officers who were patrolling the street fair.

"Those are the boys that beat up the kid," she said, pointing out two Black teenagers.

Except they weren't. They were just two random kids who happened to be Black.

The police detained them until Patrick and the others could come by and confirm that it was the wrong kids. Their names were redacted in the police report, so it isn't clear how old they were or whether they lived in Albany. Still, it seems likely that if you could find them, they would still remember that Sunday afternoon when they went to the Solano Stroll and found themselves inexplicably detained by the police and accused of beating someone up.

TO SUE OR NOT TO SUE

NATALIE, ANDREA'S MOM, WANTED HER TO SUE THE BOYS. GET HERSELF some justice. Andrea hated the idea.

"No, no, no, no, no," she said. "This is not going to be a continuous way that I spend my ever-so-fleeting time."

Natalie persisted. "Honey, there are times when you let things go for your own mental health or peace of mind, but this is not one of them," she said. "This time, we're going to fight."

She picked up Andrea from school and took her to meet the lawyer. Just entertain the idea, she said.

A small and sturdy Black woman with a soft voice and a wide smile, Elizabeth Riles was an employment attorney who specialized in workplace discrimination and personal injury. Andrea and her mom met with her at Riles's office on a boutique-lined street in Oakland, upstairs from a kung fu studio.

Riles talked about the approach she would take. The laws she would sue under. She had a precise way of speaking and an air of calm confidence, but Andrea remained unconvinced.

"Stop talking to me about it," she told her mom. "You don't get to make me do it. I'm not going to."

#GOALS

BILLIE SPENT THE SUMMER IN AN INTENSIVE FIVE-DAYS-A-WEEK THERapy program before returning to school in the fall. The program had been great for her, but she still hated high school.

It's not getting better, she thought. *I don't fit in at the school. I never will. I just need to get out.*

But how? She wanted to go to nursing school—she needed that high school diploma. Her counselor provided the answer. Billie had taken a medical terminology class at Berkeley City College her freshman year and received an outstanding grade. If she kept taking college classes over the summer and during the year, she could get the credits she needed to graduate a year early.

Now she had a goal:

Take the extra classes.

Graduate early.

Go to college.

Get as far away from all of this as possible.

GET TO A BETTER PLACE

EREN WAS TAKING CLASSES AT TILDEN PREP, THE TINY COLLEGE-PREP academy that several of the account followers now attended. He was still having trouble focusing, and he hated himself for it. The school was expensive and his family wasn't rich. Every day he didn't do his schoolwork felt like money down the drain. Six months had passed since the discovery of the account, but he was still trying to finish up the online work from repeating half of his sophomore year. Now he had junior-year schoolwork to do as well. He'd actually enjoyed school before all this happened, but these days he was just going through the motions. Still, he tried to make himself claw through the miasma of his depression and find some motivation. If he could just get through high school, then he could leave town and start again. That was the only goal that kept him going.

"To get through it," he says. "To get free."

His friend Lucy had already moved away. By the start of senior year, he would do the same. There was nothing left for him in Albany.

BACKWOODS BACKLASH

LEIGHTON, ONE OF THE ACCOUNT FOLLOWERS, FELT HE'D RECOVERED enough to host a party. "I was at the point where I was socially acceptable again," he says. Not even his closest friends would post a picture with him on social media, but at least no one was trying to beat him up.

The party's theme was "backwoods hicks and country hicks." It seemed neutral enough to the mostly white crowd that was organizing the party—in their eyes, the theme was trading on stereotypes about white people, which seemed like fair game. But to some of the people who'd been impacted by the account, the party had an ominous, Confederate-flag-waving feel to it. Most of them made a point of not attending. The one exception was Ana, who put on a cropped flannel top and a pair of acid-washed Daisy Dukes and went to the party.

The backlash was fast and furious.

"Hella people were posting shit on Instagram like, 'You went to Leighton's party and you didn't go to mess shit up and fuck with it? Why would you even go?' Blah, blah, blah," she recalls.

She tried to talk to the other girls, to explain the toll the @yungcavage account had taken on her. More than half a year had gone by. She just wanted to go to a party and get drunk with her friends and have it be no big deal. Was that so terrible?

"I'm so over this," she said. "I'm just so done. I don't care about anything at this point. Can you blame me?"

Ana knew people had a certain expectation of her, both because of the video she'd made and because her father, Lewis, was the de facto spokesperson for the parents of the people targeted by the account. But she still wanted to find her own path, and that path didn't involve feeling angry all the time.

"I feel like everyone was just wanting me to react to it in a certain way," she says. "And then I didn't. Why do I have to? If I'm going to be hella mad, the only person that's going to be hurting is me."

It was the same feeling she'd had about being biracial, that she was never going to fit into Albany's neat little categories. "There's just going to always be some way someone is going to want me to be, because of the color of my skin. You're trying to put me in a box," she says. "Just let me do what I want to do."

TORN

AS THE SPLIT BETWEEN THE TWO GROUPS OF GIRLS INTENSIFIED, RINA felt pulled in half. There were always new situations to assess, new choices to make, and plenty of disagreement about how to respond.

One of Ana's close friends was now dating an Instagram follower named Otis. Otis seemed like the best of the bunch—he hadn't commented on any of the racist posts and had written personal apology letters to the girls who were targeted.

"He was the only one who physically wrote handwritten cards for us, like really long cards for each of us," Rina says. "When Ana and Andrea started getting better friends with him again, I kind of said, okay, if they're getting better friends I guess I'll support them because they're my best friends. But then Lolia and Tiana were like no, none of them. None of them."

So which was the right way to go?

Rina had always been the person whom everybody liked and who liked everybody. But she still felt deeply mistrustful of anyone who had had anything to do with the Instagram account, and that distrust couldn't just be wished away. As she tried to navigate her way through the high school's social landscape, she felt like someone trying to sit on a bench with nails jutting out of the seat. Even if she could manage to find a place to settle, she'd have to twist her body up to do it.

"I was in the middle," she says. So when it came to the boys who had followed the Instagram account she came up with a policy: "If I had to talk to them, it would be short and it would not be one-on-one."

THE EQUATION

FOR PEOPLE ON THE SIDELINES, THERE WAS A CALCULATION TO BE made when deciding how to treat the people who had followed the Instagram account. One part of the equation was your opinion about what they had done. A second factor was how much you believed they'd changed. A third was the social cost of being categorized as their friend.

In Rosie's circle, people looked down on anyone who befriended one of the six account followers who had returned to school for senior year. "They viewed it as ignorant white kids hanging out with people who were part of the Instagram account because it didn't personally affect them," she says. Which made sense to her. For her own part, she couldn't talk to any of those boys without thinking of the pictures she'd seen on Eren's phone.

"I was always nice to them and I think I also felt bad for them," she says. "With this mixture of being really uncomfortable and also feeling really sorry for them. They should have known better. There's no excuse. It was such a dichotomy of feelings and I didn't know what to do with myself aside from to be nice but to distance myself."

A LITTLE BIT OF HEALING

WYATT WAS IN KERRY'S AP ART HISTORY CLASS. IT WAS A TOUGH CLASS for keeping your distance from someone because there were so many group projects and field trips and reasons to meet up outside of class. Kerry found herself sitting around a table with Wyatt at a café a few times, and then he started giving her and another girl a ride to their group's café meetings.

At first it was just small talk, nothing important. But then one day he asked about Andrea.

Kerry remembered how much he'd liked her, how cute it had been. "You should apologize to her," she suggested.

Wyatt sent Andrea a Snap that said something along the lines of *Hey*.

Hey, Andrea replied. *Want to get lunch someday?*

She didn't feel like holding on to the hatred anymore. She felt like she understood Wyatt, maybe better than he understood himself.

"Most boys like to not acknowledge that they're sensitive people and their emotions really affect them, but that is literally what being human is," she says. "And I feel like he didn't really want to acknowledge that his friends hurt his feelings consistently, so he was willing to be part of and go along with what they were saying to get in the in-crowd. So that he wasn't getting ripped at as much. He was willing to do anything."

Not long after that first lunch, the two of them showed up at the Thai restaurant that Kerry's parents owned, where she often worked on weekends and after school. Kerry ate lunch with them, and then they all went back to school to watch a soccer game.

"It was really comfortable," Andrea remembers. "We started hanging out again and I was like, this is super easy and it still feels good."

She and Kerry talked about it afterward.

"That was not so bad," Andrea said. "He's not evil."

"That was a little bit of healing for me," she says, "because I was like, *Okay, I didn't lose anyone that I was already friends with.*"

SUMMARY JUDGMENT

(November 29, 2017)

ON NOVEMBER 29, 2017, JUDGE DONATO ISSUED A DECISION ON THE First Amendment claims from all the various overlapping lawsuits. After sorting through the different levels of participation, he came to the conclusion that six of the ten plaintiffs had been properly disciplined by the school and four had been improperly disciplined.

Overall, the school district had aced the *Tinker* test. The account was definitely within the school's jurisdiction, Donato ruled, since both the followers and the targeted students and coach were from Albany High School and some of the pictures were either taken at school or referred to events that had taken place at school. In addition, the creator of the account could not reasonably expect that it would remain private since he invited people he didn't really know to follow the account. Finally, Donato said, the account caused a substantial disruption at the school from the moment it was discovered.

Given these facts, he wrote, any plaintiff who liked or commented on a harassing post "meaningfully contributed to the disruptions at AHS by embracing [Charles's] posts in this fashion."

"Students have the right to be free of online posts that

denigrate their race, ethnicity or physical appearance or threaten violence," he continued. "They have an equivalent right to enjoy an education in a civil, secure, and safe school environment." Charles, Patrick, Steven, and three other account followers "impermissibly interfered with those rights" either by creating the harassing posts or by liking them or commenting on them in an approving fashion. That gave the school the right to discipline them either by expulsion, in Charles's case, or suspension, in the case of the others.

The exceptions were the four students who did not indicate approval via a "like" or a comment on any content that targeted specific people. Leighton, Riley, and Eren had commented, but their comments didn't show support for any harassing post. Jon didn't seem to have interacted with the account at all.

"Although some of these plaintiffs' conduct may have been experienced as hurtful and unsettling by classmates," the judge explained, "the court cannot say that their involvement affirmatively infringed the rights of other students to be secure and to be let alone."

Judge Donato also weighed in on Murphy's second suspension, the one he'd gotten after Lolia asked him to send her more evidence of his friends' racist behavior. The school district hadn't even tried to defend this suspension, and Donato ruled that while the first suspension was justified, this second one wasn't.

Darryl Yorkey, the attorney for Charles, Steven, and Patrick as well as several others, promised to continue litigating. The school district had mostly won this first round, but the legal battle was far from over.

STUCK

(December 2017)

WHEN ELIZA CAME HOME FOR CHRISTMAS BREAK, SHE WAS ALARMED by what she saw. Charles had opted to get his GED rather than try to finish high school, but once he'd passed the exams he didn't have much to do. Nine months after the discovery of the account, he still spent most of his time in his room, emerging occasionally to bicker with their stepfather.

"What are your plans?" Eliza asked him.

Charles admitted that he didn't really have any.

"Come live with me," she said. She was working as a schoolteacher in Florida and she offered to cover his expenses until he got a job. It would be a fresh start, she said. A way to put a few thousand miles between him and the place where everything went wrong.

But Charles didn't want to leave Albany. His few remaining friends were there, and he hated the idea of leaving them.

Eliza marveled at the power these social relationships still had for him.

"There's a bigger world out there," she told him. "You are so stuck in this small world that is not good for you right now and you're not happy in. You have to be able to take that risk and let go and experience something else."

It was Alexander who forced the issue. He gave Charles an ultimatum: *Get a job and pay rent or you're out of here.*

Fine, Charles said, because what choice did he have? By the middle of January he was on a flight to Florida.

PART 13

ALMOST OUT THE DOOR

AIRDROP

AND STILL, SHE WAS NOT OKAY.

Sometimes Andrea imagined printing out hundreds of copies of the posts from the account. She'd take the stack in hand and climb the red staircase that led up to the top of the main building. Four floors below, students would be milling through the atrium, staring at their phones, joking with their friends, wrapped up in their normal lives.

Andrea would raise the stack over her head and send the pages fluttering down. *Gorilla . . . noose . . . KKK Starter pack . . . nappy-ass piece of shit . . .*

Maybe then they'd understand why she couldn't move on.

A BOY WITH A GUN

(January 2018)

BRUTSRI WAS FINE, ABSOLUTELY FINE, UNTIL SUDDENLY HE WASN'T.

"Something kind of broke down within me—like this wall of emotions hitting me," he says. He couldn't exactly explain how it happened. He hadn't planned on letting the Instagram account affect him. "But then, I guess later on it made me feel really self-conscious about the color of my skin and it's just one of those things where you start to question a lot of things about yourself and it starts to degrade who you are as a person."

He remembered all the times someone had said something about his skin color. The times he'd been called the N-word. The time a stranger had come up to his cousin in the Albany library and tossed him a map, saying, "Here's India. Start walking."

In December, close to nine months after the discovery of the account, his girlfriend dumped him. Then his grades began to slip. He got a D in math, which meant he no longer qualified for admission to any University of California campus. He felt like he couldn't do anything right.

"I always felt like I owed something to my country for giving my parents the opportunity they have here," he says.

"I always wanted to serve my country." He wanted to work in federal law enforcement, perhaps in counterterrorism, but now all of that seemed distant, impossible.

"I felt like I wasn't good enough. I felt like my skin color was a shitty thing," he says. "And it was like, *Wow, I hate myself.*"

January came. His parents had bought him a silver 2005 Toyota Highlander for his sixteenth birthday. Now Brutsri began taking it out late at night and driving up twisty unlit roads to Lake Anza in the Berkeley Hills. The lake was small, more like a pond really, and it was tucked into a vast regional park where coyotes, bobcats, and mountain lions roamed. When he was younger he used to go there with his friends, string a hammock between two trees, revel in the silence. There were river otters at the lake that few people knew about, and if you sat there quietly, you could watch them dip and frolic, shaking the water from their whiskers.

But now he stayed in the parking lot, sitting in his car with the windows rolled up. He had a silver airsoft gun, a replica of a CZ 75 semi-automatic pistol. He imagined calling the police to report a man with a gun. When they came, he'd run toward them waving the silver pistol. He knew they'd have no choice.

"No matter what," he says, "you see a gun, you shoot."

The parking area was always deserted. Tall trees framed a black sky speckled with a scattering of stars. He sat in the darkness in his silver car with his silver gun and cried and cried and cried.

"Is it now?" he asked himself. "Is it now? Do I do it now?"

The gun in the center console. The phone in one hand.

Praying for a park ranger to happen by, because a park ranger would be armed.

And then, eventually, he'd be so exhausted from crying that he'd turn the key in the ignition and drive home. "Maybe next time," he'd tell himself.

Months later, he got called into the office at school. His parents were cleaning his room and they'd found his suicide note. But by then, the danger had passed. After driving to Lake Anza a handful of times, he'd told a few friends what was going on with him and had gone to see a counselor at school. Slowly, he began to feel less alone, and to see that the things that had felt so catastrophic were just one piece of his story. He became more of an activist, focusing on an organization he had helped found called SPEAK, in which high school students gave presentations about social issues like sexism and racism to upper-elementary and middle-school students in the hope that these students might reach high school better prepared to combat bigotry. Eventually he was appointed to one of the two student seats on the Albany school board, where he worked to hire more counselors for the high school so that kids like him could get the help they needed.

He applied to an out-of-state school for college that not only let him in but also gave him a hefty scholarship. In the fall of his first year there, he met a girl in his chemistry class whom he charmed by opening a coconut with his bare hands and kissed for the first time at a haunted house.

"The biggest lesson I took away from this was the worst moments ended and I've had the best time," he says now. "So hopefully, other kids going through the same thing know that my life has gotten exponentially better."

WORK

CHARLES ARRIVED IN FLORIDA ON A FRIDAY AND HAD THE WEEKEND TO settle in. But on Monday, Eliza had to go to work. Charles seemed like a ghost to her, quiet and withdrawn. She worried about leaving him alone.

"Come to school with me and see my students," she said. "I don't want you to just be home and do nothing."

But Eliza's boyfriend, Matt, had another idea. Why didn't Charles walk down to the local strip mall and start applying for jobs?

So that's what Charles did. The day was warm and breezy. He went into a grocery store and asked for an application. Stuck it in his backpack. Then he went into a Subway.

"Are you hiring?"

"You can apply online," the lady behind the counter said. Charles was already turning around when the manager came out. As soon as he spoke, Charles knew he was Korean. "He just reminded me so much of my uncles and my grandparents in Korea," he says.

The manager must have recognized something in Charles as well, because his very first question was "Are you Korean?"

He handed Charles an application. Before Charles had even finished filling it out, the manager was asking if he could start that day.

When Eliza got home from school, Charles wasn't there. Worried, she texted him, then called when he didn't answer. It went straight to voicemail. Eventually he called her back.

"What do you want?" he said, sounding bothered. "I'm at work!"

KLAW

THEY CALLED THEMSELVES KLAW, FROM THE FIRST INITIAL OF EACH OF their names—Kerry, Lydia, Andrea, and Wyatt. Other people called them that too, because they were always together, at lunchtime and break, after school, on the weekend.

It was fun having a boy in their group. Wyatt had boundless energy and was game for anything. They went adventuring all over the Bay Area, the four of them packed into Wyatt's four-door sedan or Lydia's black Prius. They went to Stinson Beach. They climbed Mt. Tamalpais. They went to Barney's burgers and binged on curly fries and milkshakes. Once they hiked out to a waterfall in Marin. The water was freezing, so none of them got in except Wyatt. It wasn't until they were hiking back that they saw the sign warning people not to swim because of bacteria in the water. So then they were driving to Walgreens and Wyatt was dousing himself with rubbing alcohol and they were laughing their asses off.

"He was just funny to be around," Andrea says. "You know?"

CONSIDERING

BY MARCH, CHARLES WAS WORKING FULL-TIME AND ATTENDING COMmunity college. A year had passed since the discovery of the account. The fog was lifting. Colors began to flood the landscape. *Oh,* this *is what I'm supposed to feel like,* he thought. And then, remembering how he'd felt before, "My god, I don't ever want to ever feel like that again."

He wasn't paying rent, so he didn't have a room—he slept on the couch at first, and later, when Eliza and her four roommates moved to a different house, he set up a bed in a nook in the dining room. It was less privacy than he was accustomed to, but he got used to it fast. He loved the bustle and activity.

"The first few months he was here, he was quiet and sad, didn't have a lot of opinions about anything, didn't open up about anything," Eliza says. "And by the end, he was the favorite person in the house."

Eliza and her roommates were all teachers, and they knew Charles's backstory. All of them were interested in social justice, and so Charles found himself engaging in conversations he'd never had before, about race and privilege and identity.

It happened almost by osmosis—that sense that there was a different way to be in the world. "I had so many role models and just great people to look up to and strive to be like," he says.

He could see that the teachers were all stressed out and

overworked, so he made himself useful, going grocery shopping and running errands for them. Eliza's housemates took to inviting him to go with them when they wanted to grab something to eat. And as it became clear that no one was judging him, Charles began to open up about the @yungcavage account.

"I think it was really liberating for him to be around people who know everything about him and they're like, 'We still accept you,'" Eliza says.

Not only did they accept him, but they wanted him to talk about it. Eliza's boyfriend, Matt, was particularly good at asking questions that invited introspection, like "Have you ever considered that maybe you seek attention in unhealthy places?"

Eliza was thinking about that too. She'd seen plenty of bullying in the school where she taught, and she'd noticed that the dynamic seemed to be more about power than anything else. "Powerless people bully because they want to have power over other people," she says. And in the years that their family had been rocked by one crisis after another, Charles had been completely powerless.

"Since he didn't have any information, things just happened to him," she says. "He didn't really have any power over what happened in our family."

EDUCATING

"I'M DOING CHARITY WORK HERE," ANDREA TOLD THE BLACK GIRLS WHO criticized her for being friends with Wyatt. "I'm trying to educate a white male. You know how hard that is?"

That wasn't the whole story, of course. Wyatt was her friend. But Andrea, Lydia, and Kerry also saw him as someone who needed to become better informed.

"We spent a lot of time talking to Wyatt about issues and trying to educate him," Kerry remembers. "He was really great about it. He took in the information and he was trying to understand."

So the three girls talked to him about the world as they understood it, particularly about racism, but also about sexism and homophobia. Wyatt was already compassionate and kind, they thought; he just needed more knowledge.

"It felt like we were changing someone's opinion," Andrea says. "Or the way they saw things."

STATUTE OF LIMITATIONS

ANDREA'S MOTHER KEPT BRINGING UP THE LAWSUIT IDEA. THE ONE-year anniversary of the account's discovery was coming up. They were running out of time to sue.

"You'll have no options after that," she told Andrea. "You're limiting a plethora of opportunities for yourself if you don't do anything."

The word *limiting* hit Andrea like a truck.

Because she did feel limited. She hadn't applied to any four-year colleges. She hadn't even taken the SAT. But those boys, they were going to college, weren't they? They were going to go on with their lives.

"I already felt limited in certain aspects by my social class," she says. "How I felt like I had to stay and take care of my sister and be there with my family."

She took the lawsuit question to Lydia, whom she still considered her "logical half."

"Why would you drag all that up again?" Lydia asked.

She didn't see how Andrea could win a lawsuit, but more than that, she didn't see why Andrea would want to spend more time thinking about something that made her so unhappy.

Andrea felt crushed by Lydia's response. It was hard to argue with her reasoning, but at the same time, Andrea wondered if her friend could really understand her situation.

Lydia lived in an adjacent town, a wealthy enclave of just over five thousand people. Did she really know what it was like to feel *limited*?

Of course Andrea didn't want any of this to be part of her life for one second longer than it needed to be. But at the same time, she wanted some kind of satisfaction, some sense that the boys who had done this were being made to pay. And money—you could measure money.

"I can't limit myself just because I feel limited," she decided.

In March 2018, Andrea's attorney filed a complaint in Alameda County Superior Court against Greg, Charles, Patrick, and their parents for battery (in the touching of her hair), violation of her civil rights, intentional infliction of emotional distress, negligent infliction of emotional distress, and invasion of privacy.

Even if she lost, Andrea decided, even if she settled for peanuts, it was still worth giving it a try. This way she could at least say that she fought on her own behalf.

KILL OUR DEMONS

CHARLES BOUGHT AN OLD CAR, A RUNDOWN 2000 HONDA CRV STICK shift that he had to teach himself how to drive. It wasn't registered or insured because it couldn't pass a safety check, and it had no air conditioning. To stay cool on the way to work he drove shirtless, with the windows rolled down as far as they would go, which wasn't actually very far. He loved that drive, loved the long bright vistas of the ocean as he motored along the coast.

As he drove, he listened to the Kendrick Lamar songs he'd listened to a thousand times before. The songs had always slapped. But now, for the first time, he began to listen to the words.

Molly, one of Eliza's housemates, was really into rap. She encouraged Charles to analyze the songs he was playing, to think about the meaning of the lyrics. What was Kendrick saying about the Black experience in his song "Alright"? What was he saying about America in "XXX"?

Molly, who was white, played him the song "Boogieman" by Childish Gambino and asked Charles what he thought.

"I was too afraid to tell her because I didn't want to get it wrong and be offensive," he remembers. But finally, with some prodding, he gave his interpretation.

"He's talking about police. And the main line in the chorus

is that 'with a gun in your hand I'm the boogieman.' So what I've interpreted from that is he's talking about when there's a cop, and when he has a gun in his hand, that the Black person is like the boogieman—super scary or whatever."

Listening to music became their own special ritual.

"It was this elaborate thing that we'd do," Charles says. He remembers sitting in one of their other roommates' rooms to listen to *KOD*, the new album by J. Cole. Molly in a beanbag chair in the corner. Charles on the floor, leaning against the bed.

On the official album trailer, J. Cole had said "KOD" had three meanings. The last was "Kill Our Demons."

"'Kill Our Demons' is, like, finding that shit, whether it be from traumatic childhood experiences, whether it be from a lack of attention, confidence issues, insecurities," Cole explained. "Whatever it is, we gotta be honest with ourselves. Look in the mirror or look inside and ask ourselves questions like 'Yo, what's really eating me? What's causing me to run to this thing as an escape?' And once I find the root of that, let me look it in his face and see what it really is."

Molly was Charles's friend, but because she was five years older, she was also his teacher. So were the rappers whose songs he was listening to.

"I just appreciate their culture—just a lot more," Charles says. "It's made me appreciate that a lot more and know why what I did was so bad."

PAYOUT (1)

IN APRIL, THE SCHOOL DISTRICT ANNOUNCED IT HAD REACHED SETTLEment agreements with seven of the ten Instagram followers who had sued.

Murphy got enough to cover his tuition at Tilden Prep and pay for counseling and the medical expenses for his broken nose, plus a small settlement for his own personal use.

The three sophomores each received $73,353.90, after attorney fees and court costs were subtracted, which the settlement agreement noted was not enough to fully cover the cost of tuition at Tilden Prep or—for two of the three families—of moving to other Northern California cities where they could attend public school.

The three account followers whose First Amendment rights the court said had been violated by the district because they had never indicated any approval of the harassing posts each received $80,000, not including the money for their attorneys. Since all three were back at Albany High School, none of that money was earmarked for tuition or other expenses.

The settlements would be paid by the district's insurance. "No District funds will be impacted or used for the settlements," explained the AUSD website, as if anticipating the outrage that was coming. But for most people, the district's budget wasn't the issue. The issue was that the account followers had received settlements at all.

Clearly the district's attorneys had calculated that continuing to fight the lawsuits was a losing proposition. But explaining that to the community was going to be tough.

SALT IN A WOUND

(April 24, 2018)

THE ALBANY SCHOOL BOARD MEETING WAS FULLER THAN USUAL, although not nearly as full as it had been a year earlier. Some two dozen members of the public filled the seats in the pea-green room at city hall. Darryl Yorkey, the white attorney who represented many of the account followers, sat in the back, his wraparound sunglasses resting on his head. Andrea's mother, Natalie, sat near the front of the room with Ana's, Billie's, and Rina's mothers. Their faces were drawn, their eyes tired, their mouths set.

When it was time for them to address the board, the mothers huddled together at the podium, as if sheltering from the wind. Natalie was already in tears. She wore a black leather jacket over a striped turtleneck, her long blond hair spread over her shoulders and her arms folded across her chest.

"How could you not even have said *no*?" she demanded. "How could you not have fought settling?"

She described the posts—the noose, the gorilla, the KKK starter pack.

"What you have done has been like putting salt in a wound. And our girls still have to go to school because they want to graduate. They have to go to school and hear these boys talk about how they're going to have a victory party?"

"*Oooooh, we got paid!*" Ana's mother said, imitating the boys.

"Because you gave it to them," Billie's mother said.

"You can give money, but you didn't have to give *that* kind of money," Rina's mother added.

Afterward, Ana's mother, Sheila, was still trying to make sense of it. She understood Murphy getting money for his broken nose, she said. She understood that the district had screwed up. What she couldn't understand was why those families thought *their* children's suffering was worth more than *her* child's suffering.

"What's really hard for us to swallow is these people who are okay with suing the district because they feel their kids were bullied and harassed and made to feel uncomfortable," she said. "Do you have any idea what your child's comments did to *my* child? But it doesn't matter to you, because it wasn't *your* child."

She'd pleaded with Ana to sue, she said. They'd met with an attorney. But Ana hadn't wanted to. She was tired of the whole thing.

So now it was up to Andrea.

"Please god, let her get paid," Sheila said. "It's not about the money. It's about them understanding that they caused pain."

WINDFALL

FOR THE STUDENTS WHO HAD RETURNED TO ALBANY HIGH SCHOOL, THE settlements were a windfall. Their families didn't have private school tuition to pay, so the money was simply absorbed into bank accounts that were already well stocked. It didn't create new opportunities or ease hardships or even provide for unexpected luxuries, other than maybe bumping the car chosen as one of the boys' graduation gifts from used to new.

For many students, that new car—a Subaru—came to symbolize everything that had happened: the self-perpetuating unfairness of it all. For the rest of the school year, that one car would be an all-wheel-drive thorn in the sides of the people who had been pictured on the account.

"Just pulling up to school in his new car with the money he got—*really?* That's too much," Ana says. "You really just said 'Fuck you' to all of us."

The apologies offered. The contrition expressed. All of that seemed hollow now.

"If you were willing to gain eighty thousand dollars from an experience like that, then you didn't learn from that," Andrea says. "You didn't feel any type of sorry about that, because you ended up profiting from it."

As time passed, rumors awarded big paychecks and new cars to all the account followers, even ones who hadn't sued or whose settlements had gone to pay for private school tuition rather than into their pockets. But the truth was more mundane: In an affluent community like Albany, a lot of high school seniors get new cars.

Still, some cars are more than just a car. Not just a way of getting from here to there, but a symbol of all the roads that are open to you.

"The racist kids got thousands of dollars, almost paying off their tuition fees," one of the account's targets said. "I couldn't even fucking *go* to college because of the tuition fees."

A LETTER FROM MS. CURRY

THE TENSEST CLASSROOM IN ALL OF ALBANY HIGH SCHOOL WAS MS. Curry's third-period Women's Literature class, which contained one student who had followed the account and five students who were directly impacted by it, including Tiana, Rina, Andrea, and a girl who had been mocked on the account but had remained friends with some of the boys who had followed it. More than once, the tension had erupted into full-blown conflagrations. Ms. Curry, who was white, didn't think she had handled this well, although she still wasn't sure how she could have handled it better. She was used to talking about race and gender with her students—that was a hallmark of her teaching—but she wasn't used to feeling like she couldn't stop them from wounding each other.

Now, as the year staggered to a close, she sat down to write a letter to her seniors. She wanted to talk to them about mistakes, about the uncomfortable twinge or ache she felt when she felt she had done something wrong as a teacher. Guilt was motivating, she wrote, "a call to reflect and act towards change." And change, she said, is the only thing that life guarantees us.

> **So don't shy from your guilt, rage, or despair.**
> **They are some of the most important emotions**

that prompt you to shape the change you encounter. To collaborate in powerful revisions of the world you see.

Shame, however, is a heavier burden. Shame paralyzes change. Shame doesn't focus my thoughts on relevant mistakes but instead pushes a misguided belief that "*I am a bad person.*"

Shame's falsehood will gnaw at you. It will obstruct your ability to act and grow. Don't believe the lie. When shame threatens to overwhelm, seek out your family and friends. Find the love that nurtures your growth.

Love, you see, is the most important emotion.

She concluded her letter with three simple reminders:

You are not perfect, but you are good. Read the word and the world. Learning is contemplation over time.

With love always,
Meghann Curry

NO THIRD CHANCES

(August 2018)

IT WAS THE END OF THE SUMMER, NOT LONG BEFORE THEY WERE ALL going to go their separate ways. Wyatt was telling the other members of KLAW about hanging out with some guys from school and how ignorant they were. One of them, he said, would even use the N-word. (Wyatt doesn't remember this conversation.)

Andrea, Kerry, and Lydia couldn't believe what they were hearing.

"Why would you put yourself in that position again?" they wanted to know. "Why would you want to be friends with someone like that again?"

Wyatt protested that he wasn't close with that guy in particular; he just was friends with other guys in that group. Not the ignorant ones.

"But you're still putting yourself around those guys," the three girls countered. It seemed to them that he was doing the exact same thing he'd done before—being part of a group of friends for the sake of closeness without caring about their morals.

Wyatt accused them of being controlling, of having an Us vs. Them mentality.

"You don't get to decide who my friends are," he said.

"We shouldn't *have* to," Andrea retorted.

In the moment, Andrea didn't let on how annoyed she was. But she talked about it with Lydia later. "It's like there's no learning going on," she said. "It's past being hurtful."

They distanced themselves from him after that. When her birthday rolled around, Lydia didn't invite Wyatt.

"It was a second chance and we weren't going to give a third one," Kerry says.

Kerry wanted to be supportive of her friends, but she could see both sides. There weren't a lot of woke guys at the high school for Wyatt to hang out with, after all.

"Those were his only other friends besides us," she says. "And I don't know, maybe it was because he was friends with three girls and those were his guy friends that he needed to have in his life." After Kerry saw that Wyatt had unfollowed her on social media, she reached out to him to ask if something was wrong.

"I just don't think we should be friends anymore," he said.

"I was like, 'Okay, I wish you the best at college,'" Kerry recalls. "'You do you.'"

PART 14

RECKONING

GOOD GUY, BAD GUY

(2020)

CHARLES HAD MOVED BACK TO THE BAY AREA IN 2019. HE'D MISSED having friends his own age, going to parties, having the regular experience of being eighteen. He ended up moving in with Steven, who had lived in China for a while and then returned to the United States and gotten a job as a software engineer despite never having gone to college. Charles slept on a mattress on the floor in a nook next to the kitchen that was separated from the living room by a fold-out screen. He took community college classes and worked at a sporting goods store. He also had a girlfriend, his first real relationship, a woman he had met through Patrick.

Meanwhile, the lawsuits continued. In 2020, Steven received a $125,000 settlement from the Albany Unified School District after the trial court concluded that Superintendent Val Williams and Principal Jeff Anderson had placed him in danger of assault "with deliberate indifference" to his safety on the day of the sit-in. That left Charles and Patrick as the only remaining people suing the district. Charles, his mother, and Patrick were also the last remaining defendants in Andrea's lawsuits against people connected to the account. (Greg, Greg's parents, and Patrick's parents had already settled.)

Charles sat down for deposition after deposition, not really clear about which case he was being interviewed for.

"I definitely, objectively think, *Okay, I'm in the wrong and Andrea's in the right*," he said. "She didn't really do anything wrong."

Even so, he allowed the lawsuits to keep going, fighting on two fronts, as plaintiff and as defendant.

TWEET ME THE RECEIPTS

(Summer 2020)

ON MAY 25, 2020, AS THE COUNTRY ENTERED ITS THIRD MONTH OF COVID-19 lockdown, a seventeen-year-old girl named Darnella Frazier used her phone to film the murder of a forty-six-year-old Black man named George Floyd by Minneapolis police officers, one of whom knelt on his neck for more than nine minutes even as Floyd lapsed into unconsciousness and bystanders pleaded for someone to help him. The video quickly went viral. In the days that followed, protesters filled the streets in cities from coast to coast.

On June 3, Disney Channel actress and YouTuber Skai Jackson invited her 558,000 Twitter followers to expose their racist peers and classmates.

"If you know a racist, don't be shy! Tweet me the receipts," she posted on Twitter. She issued the same invitation on Instagram, singling out middle school, high school, and college students who had made racist social media posts in response to Floyd's murder.

Once these students were exposed, social media users would mete out the punishment: doxing them, sending them hate messages, reporting them to their job or school. On Twitter and Instagram, people talked freely about "cyberbullying" and "ruining lives." Most of their targets were people who had posted something overtly racist, particularly people who had defended the police officers who killed Floyd or had even rejoiced over his death. Some, however, had made more generic statements, like "Not all cops are bad." A few just had the misfortune to have the same name as someone who had done something racist.

"Please do not comment on his page anymore," Jackson wrote at one point, trying to walk back what she had unleashed. "Someone sent me the wrong Dylan. He is not the one who made the racist song, just to clear that up."

Seeing her opportunity, Tiana took to Twitter. She posted a 27-tweet thread about her experience in Albany:

> How the @CityofAlbanyCA, educators, administrators, school body, and @albanypolice dropped the ball and allowed me and my friends to be bullied and excluded.

Her thread, which has since been deleted, included names and photos of the Instagram followers. Now it was time for Twitter to do its thing. Get the account followers kicked out of college. Make them lose their jobs. Make them suffer.

Skai Jackson didn't pick up the thread, but another online activist did. She posted screenshots of Tiana's post on her own Instagram account, along with the names of the colleges several of the account followers attended.

The platform where it all started was now poised to be the instrument of revenge. This irony meant nothing to the algorithm, of course. It was designed to do one thing and one thing only: increase engagement by increasing conflict.

Outrage, shame, envy, hate—all of it earns money for social media companies and provides them with useful information. The more those companies learn about people's allegiances, the more precisely they can target them with ads. And because our brains are wired to get an intoxicating jolt of pleasure from shaming or insulting a foe, we are all too happy to give the algorithm exactly what it's looking for.

Over the next few days, Tiana's post began to attract attention.

NOTHING TO LOSE

(Summer 2020)

CHARLES WAS ON HIS BREAK AT WORK WHEN A FRIEND SENT HIM TIANA'S post. He had known it might happen, but he felt a wave of nausea when it did. He reminded himself that it wasn't a secret. Anyone who knew him already knew what he'd done.

"Ever since I started making new friends and meeting new people when I moved to Florida, I bring it up so they know," he explains. "If they find out about it down the line, it'll feel like I was trying to hide it. Which I'm not. I like letting people know that this is a mistake that I made, that I've learned from."

Later, he texted with Murphy, Jon, and Patrick. They each acted as if annoyance was the only thing they felt about the post, because anger was the one emotion that you didn't have to be ashamed of feeling. But privately they were each playing out scenarios in their heads, reckoning up what they still had to lose. Charles was still in community college, but what if he finally got into a four-year? Could they get him kicked out? What if they came after his job?

He texted Ana, letting her know he was open to talking with anyone who wanted to. But he knew that he couldn't do that with everyone. And when he thought about it, he couldn't even really feel that mad. Because Black lives *did* matter, and overall he was glad people were using social media to get the word out.

"It's cool to see so many people coming together to support this message," he said. "I don't know what the turning point was. I mean it was obviously someone's death, but how many deaths had to happen?"

He tried to focus on that, rather than his own future. Because he suspected this was what it was going to be like forever. "I don't think it's ever going to go away because it's related to such a big and controversial topic," he says. "I feel like I'm going to have to deal with it for the rest of my life."

DREAM (2)

(Summer 2020)

ANDREA HAD BEEN DRIVING THROUGH ALBANY WITH HER BOYFRIEND the previous week when she saw Charles on the street by the middle school. Right away, the nightmares started up again. A dream in which Charles was demanding to know why she was suing him. A dream in which friends of hers were hanging out with him.

"We see you staring at us," the friends said. "Do you have something to say?"

She did have something to say. But in those dreams the words scattered like a flock of birds, leaving her mute.

So when she saw Tiana's Twitter post, she felt an odd kind of relief. Tiana always seemed to her to have it all together.

Oh my god! Andrea thought. *You still care about that? It's not weird to still care about that?*

IN A CIRCLE

(Summer 2020)

RACIST DISGUSTING PRIVILEGED PIECE OF SHIT, THE INSTAGRAM MESSAGE said.

Murphy had been watching Tiana's posts on Twitter and Instagram, so he knew why he was getting flamed.

His first reaction was irritation: *Come on, really? This is coming back up again? Didn't we settle this?*

But something else had happened that had overridden that thought. It was George Floyd's death, the protests, the conversation. It made him rethink what had happened in Albany. What he'd done.

"A picture of a girl with a noose around her neck? Like, that's pretty fucked up," he said.

He'd been reading the things people were posting on social media, and then he'd started googling, going down news and history rabbit holes to figure out who these names were that people kept mentioning, trying to get both sides of the story. In general he didn't really keep up with the news, because he'd always figured it really didn't affect him. But now he was thinking, *Isn't that what privilege is, knowing that the news doesn't affect you the way it affects other people?* Just because *he* wasn't suffering didn't mean he shouldn't be paying attention, because maybe there was something he could do to help someone else. But then again, who was he to think he had anything to offer anyone? He was a guy who had laughed at someone having a noose around her neck.

"I was an ignorant, cocky sixteen-year-old, like just continuing to play it off almost like it was a joke," he said. "But it's not a joke. Slavery and racism has been going on for such a long time, and for us to kind of throw it under the rug like it was a joke, like it doesn't mean anything or like, 'get over it,' was insensitive and a little immoral and inhumane."

For the first time since the account was discovered, he allowed himself to sit with that feeling. Instead of rationalizing it away, instead of hurrying to atone, instead of trying to prove that he wasn't a bad guy, he simply let the feeling wash over him.

"It made me sad. It made me feel not as good about myself," he said. "Just knowing I didn't do something right and I've got to change."

Back in 2017, his parents had told him that this would be with him forever. At the time he'd thought, *Okay, Boomer.* But here it was, still part of his life.

"If Skai Jackson ever said my name, I feel like I would never be able to get a job," he said. "These are the kind of worries I've been having, and it sucks. But then again, it's like I have no one to blame for my actions except for myself. Like, I'm the one who kinda did it. But I was just sixteen. Like, I didn't know what the heck I was doing."

One bad action, he thought, shouldn't define who you are. Everyone was more complicated than that. People could change. You could learn about racism. Unless people were just going to label you, just constantly push you down as *racist, racist, racist,* without giving you a chance to do better.

He broke off, having spoken for a long time without taking a breath.

"I don't know. I feel like I'm just kind of like in a circle," he said. "I'm kind of lost."

PAYOUT (2)

(Fall 2020)

BY NOVEMBER 2020, PATRICK AND CHARLES WERE THE ONLY REMAINING defendants in Andrea's lawsuit. Charles's mother had recently settled and was eager for him to settle as well. A trial date had been set for November 30. By now, three years and eight months had passed since the account was first discovered.

Charles wanted to settle, but he was having trouble coming to terms with the fact that he'd have to hand over money out of his own pocket. He was still working a retail job, still going to community college. He hadn't gotten any money from his own lawsuit, which his lawyer continued to appeal. (In December 2022, the United States Court of Appeals for the Ninth Circuit rejected Charles's and Patrick's First Amendment claims against the high school, saying that they had been properly disciplined.) Funds were tight.

"It's hard," he said. "It's not like I don't want them to get something out of it. It's just I don't want them to take it from *me*."

On Monday, November 30, the date set for trial, the lawyers for both sides appeared in a virtual courtroom before Judge Paul Herbert. COVID-19 restrictions were still in effect, so the trial would have to happen online.

"I assume this is a jury trial, correct?" the judge asked, shuffling through the courtroom calendar.

"Yes, your honor," Riles said. "But I have some information. The parties have reached a settlement actually, just this weekend."

Under the terms of the settlement, Charles would pay Andrea $15,000. Patrick would pay her $10,000. Added together with the $18,000 received from the two boys' parents, that was $43,000, plus the undisclosed settlement from Greg and his family. After attorney fees were subtracted, the total didn't quite reach the hoped-for $80,000 benchmark, but it was still a nice chunk of change.

So had justice finally been served?

That was hard for anyone to say. How do you quantify the loss of your senior year in high school? How do you quantify the person you are now compared to who you would have been before?

"You have to figure out how to exist and be in this world after being targeted like that," Riles says. "It's hard to put a number on that."

But, she added, having taken a stand had its own worth.

"You're able to have a voice, have a chance to say 'This was wrong and it wasn't okay,'" she says. "There's a value in that. Regardless of what the ultimate outcome is. There's a value in that for people."

Afterward, Andrea sounded more relieved than jubilant. "I'm very glad that this chapter is over in my life," she said.

Now she had a little money, a little freedom. She'd gotten into Howard University in Washington, D.C., the year before, but because of the pandemic she'd had to take her classes virtually. She could go back to school in January or she could do something different.

"I've been battling with myself about whether I should play it safe or travel and take bigger leaps that have been presenting themselves to me," she said. "This is just kind of affirming to me that I should keep taking leaps. Because it's working."

PART 15

MAKING IT THROUGH

WHAT TIME DOES

It doesn't heal all wounds
It doesn't erase the pain
What time does is
add
new pages
to your story
so when you scan the past
there's something else to read.

WINDOWS AND DOORS

IT WASN'T EASY, IT DIDN'T HAPPEN IN A STRAIGHT LINE, BUT IN THE end each of them found a path through it. On the other side, life was waiting for them.

Rina studied health sciences in college. After she got some tutoring and did some extra studying, she overcame her self-doubt and realized that she was actually perfectly good at math—good enough to run statistical models as part of a study of sickle cell disease and be accepted into a public health master's program at one of the top universities in the country.

Ana played soccer for a community college team in the Bay Area and then went to Boston to play for a college there. But eventually she decided to take her life in a different direction. A cross-cultural psychology class had made her think she'd like to be a therapist. Mentoring a middle-schooler, a Black girl going to a majority-white school, convinced her she might be good at it. As she transferred to a four-year university to study psychology, she had the sense that doors were opening, and beyond those doors were more doors—doors and doors and doors, refracting and multiplying as if seen through a kaleidoscope.

Billie met her goal of graduating a year early and started community college, planning to transfer to a four-year university as a junior. On Friday nights, she took a four-hour dissection class, working on real cadavers. It was exquisite, she said. It was divine. Observing her enthusiasm, her professor set her a series of challenges.

"If you can do this, you can be a surgeon," she said, assigning Billie the brachial plexus, a network of nerves in the shoulder.

It was just Billie and the body, alone in a room. The nerves ran from the brain through the chest, to the shoulder, and down the arm to the hand. Billie worked for hours, sweat running off her face. She found the roots, the trunks, the branches, the subclavian artery. She tied them off and tagged them. She did everything right.

By the fall of 2021, she was at a University of California campus on the pre-med track.

But wait, Billie—before you go? Remember the lonely girl sitting in her room, writing poems on her phone? If you could travel back in time to talk to her, is there anything you would say?

Billie rolls her eyes at the question. She's never going to think of herself as a font of wisdom and she's not the type to sugarcoat the truth. She can't tell her past self that it's all going to be okay, because it hadn't been. It had been hard as hell. It might always be hard. All she can tell her is that this particular hard thing will pass.

So picture her now, materializing in front of her freshman self. She's got two nose rings, a perfectly oval face, and expressive eyes behind square black frames. She looks beautiful. She looks strong.

"Oh my god," says ninth-grade Billie. "Your hair is purple!" Because it is, in fact, an electric shade of violet.

Time travel isn't easy to do. Future Billie is already

wavering, molecules peeling off and flying back to the present. She won't have time to tell her past self about graduating early or dissecting cadavers. She only has enough time to tell her one thing. She deliberates, but just for a moment.

"Love your skin color no matter what dumb fuckers say about it!" she calls through the void. "Just love it and embrace it!"

And then she's gone.

A FORK IN THE ROAD

BY THE TIME EREN WAS A FRESHMAN IN COLLEGE, HE COULD TALK about what had happened to the new friends he'd grown close to. There was power in owning his story, as messy as it was.

"I recognize that I fucked up. I also recognize that the person I was sophomore year and the person I am right now are two very different people," he says. "I'm glad that everything turned out the way that it did and that I'm the way that I am now."

Which led to a perplexing question. If he could do what Billie did, go back in time and speak to his fifteen-year-old self, what would he say?

"It would be easy enough to go back and say 'Unfollow the account,'" Eren says. "But I wonder if that would be the right thing to do, honestly."

Two forking paths. Two possible destinies. One path dodges the bullet. Never goes through any of this. Who would that guy end up being?

"Had I just continued that trajectory at Albany—how I would be as a person—I think I would be worse off," Eren says. "I would probably be less introspective, less critical. I would think less. Because I question things now in a way that I don't think I could have before, had I not gone through the experience like this."

And so here he was. A guy who still sometimes panicked if someone wanted to look at his phone. A guy who struggled with depression and anxiety. A dancer who was just starting to feel like he might be able to dance again for the first time since his sophomore year of high school.

This was the person he'd choose to be. He knows who he is. He knows what he did. And he knows what he'll never do again. Maybe there would have been another way to get here. But this is the path he took.

THE LEAP

AFTER SETTLING HER LAWSUIT, ANDREA MOVED TO SAN MARCOS LA Laguna, in the southwestern highlands of Guatemala, to study meditation, metaphysics, and yoga at a retreat center by Lake Atitlán. Once, when she was there, she dreamed that she was back in Albany, walking on the street by the library. In the dream, she panicked, feeling exposed and vulnerable.

"Why am I here?" she asked herself. "I hate this place."

But then, instead of cowering in the storm drain like in the other dreams, she jumped, and in jumping, she flew. She knew then that she was dreaming, and that in her dreams she could go anywhere she wanted.

Lake Atitlán is bright blue with flashes of green like the fire inside an opal. It's fifty square miles of rippling water rimmed by green, cone-shaped volcanoes. There's a video of Andrea standing on a platform some fifty feet above it. Her hair is short. Her body is muscular in a brown one-piece bathing suit. She breaks into a run. Five long strides and then she leaps into the air, holding her arms by her sides as she knifes downward.

When she hits the water, she sends up a fountain of white and turquoise spray and disappears. For a moment there is nothing but ripples and foam. Then she surfaces and rolls onto her back, whooping with delight. The afternoon breeze that the indigenous Maya call Xocomil, "the wind that carries away sin," ripples over the water. The camera pans across the lake. When it turns back to Andrea, she is breaststroking away, a solitary figure in that vast expanse of blue, going forward, never looking back.

SOME NUMBERS: ONLINE AND REAL-WORLD HATE AMONG YOUNG PEOPLE

Portion of students ages twelve to eighteen who saw hate words or symbols written in their schools during the 2018–19 school year: 1 in 4

Percentage of youths and young adults ages fifteen to thirty-six who have personally been targeted by online hate: 23

Percentage of youths and young adults ages fifteen to thirty-six who have personally created online hate materials: 19.8

Percentage of U.S. young people ages fifteen to twenty-five who have encountered hate online: 73.2

Percentage of those young people who encountered that hate accidentally, without seeking it out: 84.9

Percentage of that hate that focuses on race or ethnicity: 49.6

Number of U.S. students who were bullied because of some aspect of their identity during the 2018–19 school year: 1.3 million

Percentage of those students who were targeted because of their race: 48

Number of times per day that the average Black teenager encounters racial discrimination either online, offline, individually, vicariously, or through teasing: 5

A NOTE ON SOURCING

WHEN I STARTED REPORTING THIS STORY, I WAS HOPING TO GET ONE or two people on each side to work with me. In the end, I was able to speak with the vast majority of the people directly involved with these events. Everybody who participated understood the nature of this project, which was to tell a complicated story from multiple perspectives.

Taken together, these many interviews provided me with a remarkable level of clarity about the events surrounding the creation, discovery, and aftermath of the @yungcavage Instagram account. Many people spoke without reservation or restriction, spending hours in conversation with me over more than three years and sharing troves of photos, videos, screenshots, text threads, and personal writings. Some shared information but did not want to be quoted, while others agreed to be quoted but did not want to be identified. A few agreed to speak for fact-checking purposes only or otherwise limited the nature of their participation. Given the devastating nature of these events and their lasting impact on those involved, I did my best to accommodate each of these requests as long as I felt I could do so without violating journalistic standards of ethics.

Unless otherwise noted, the quotes and information in this book came from my own interviews with the participants and my firsthand observations, as well as court documents, sworn declarations, police reports, text messages, diaries, photographs, videos, social media posts, letters, emails, public testimony, and the like. Wherever possible, each person's account was cross-verified against other firsthand accounts or contemporaneous evidence. Where two recollections contradict each other, both are included unless one recollection could be definitively confirmed.

Information that came from academic and other outside sources is credited in the endnotes.

ACKNOWLEDGMENTS

THANKS, FIRST AND FOREMOST, TO EVERYONE WHO AGREED TO SPEAK to me about their experiences in Albany while these events unfolded. Some of you were quoted, some were not, but each of you helped shape my understanding of what happened. I will be forever grateful to you for trusting me with your stories and for believing that something positive could come out of so much pain.

My thinking about justice in relation to these events was shaped by the conversations I had with many in the restorative justice community, particularly Aishatu Yusuf, Ashlee George, Kyle McClerkins, and Barbara Coloroso. Thank you all for being willing to talk through the complexity of seeking justice in an unjust world. Boundless gratitude and love to the members of the Oakland Citizen's Circle and Restore Oakland's weekly Community Building Circle, whose hard-won insights about shame, accountability, and justice have deepened my understanding of these topics in countless ways. *The Little Book of Race and Restorative Justice* by Fania E. Davis lived on my desk while I was writing and provided an essential framework for my thinking.

Thanks to all the researchers and experts who took the time to help me find the information I needed, verify the accuracy of my explanations, and explain the complexities of their work, particularly Rosalind Wiseman, Brian Donovan, Ann Morning, Alan Goodman, Brian Friedberg, James Hawdon, and Lindsay Schubiner.

Thanks also to the many current and former teachers and administrators from Albany High School who sat down with me to explain both what happened in 2017 and 2018 and what has happened since. I was struck over and over by the dedication and commitment of these educators and their desire to do right by their students. I'm grateful to each of you for being willing to revisit some of the most painful moments of your careers and for your sober reflections on the complicated dynamics at play.

Thanks to Alan Beck, Cate Beekman, Elizabeth Riles, Joe Salama, and Darryl Yorkey for keeping me abreast of legal developments and providing insight into the thinking behind your respective cases.

A heartfelt shout-out to Alisha Niehaus Berger, Deborah Davis, Marcus Ewert, Nidhi Chanani, and Susie Ghahremani, who read early sections of this manuscript and provided essential feedback and support. Deepest gratitude to Brandy Colbert, Lynn Brown, and Grace Li for giving this manuscript the benefit of your perceptive analysis and feedback. Much appreciation to the Wellstone Center in the Redwoods for providing a place for me to write.

Thanks to Rob Liguori for fact-checking key chapters with his usual meticulousness and weighing in on the tying of knots. A vigorous round of applause for Henry Sene Yee for once again designing the book cover of my dreams. Joy Peskin and Erin Murphy were guiding lights during the tumultuous ups and downs of the writing and reporting process. I would never have made it through without your wisdom, support, and guidance. Thank you both for your abiding belief in the power of books to change the world.

I am blessed to have an amazing team at Farrar Straus and Giroux working to create meaningful books and get them in the hands of readers. Thanks to all of you for your keen eyes and hard work, particularly Allyson Floridia, Hannah Miller, and Mary Van Akin.

Thanks, most of all, to Milo, my music, media, and slang consultant, and Cliff, the other half of my brain. How lucky I am to have you both.

ENDNOTES

EPIGRAPHS

"Being called all manner of things": Tracy K. Smith, excerpt from "We Feel Now a Largeness Coming On," in *Such Color: New and Selected Poems.* Copyright © 2021 by Tracy K. Smith. Reprinted with the permission of The Permissions Company, LLC on behalf of Graywolf Press, Minneapolis, Minnesota, https://www.graywolfpress.org.

"How do we hold people accountable": bell hooks, in conversation with Maya Angelou, *Shambhala Sun*, January 1998, http://www.hartford-hwp.com/archives/45a/249.html.

AUTHOR'S NOTE

A report by the Southern Poverty Law Center documented 3,265 such incidents: Southern Poverty Law Center, "Hate at School," May 2, 2019, https://www.splcenter.org/sites/default/files/tt_2019_hate_at_school_report_final_0.pdf.

PART 1: BEFORE

SMALLBANY

Black students are about one third less likely to graduate from a public four-year university: CJ Libassi, "The Neglected College Race Gap: Racial Disparities Among College Completers," The Center for American Progress, May 23, 2018, https://www.americanprogress.org/wp-content/uploads/2018/05/CollegeCompletions-Brief1.pdf.

SOME THINGS THAT HAPPEN WHEN YOU'RE BLACK IN A MOSTLY WHITE SCHOOL

These anecdotes are taken from the author's interviews with Black Albany High School students as well as from the @BlackatAlbany Instagram account.

WHAT A NOOSE SAYS

at least 4,384 Black people were lynched: Equal Justice Initiative, *Lynching in America: Confronting the Legacy of Racial Terror*, 3rd ed., 2017, https://lynchinginamerica.eji.org/report.

for being too successful: One example among many is the lynching of Frazier Baker, who was murdered along with his infant daughter in Lake City, South Carolina, in 1898 after being appointed postmaster. See Equal Justice Initiative, *Lynching in America: Confronting the Legacy of Racial Terror*, 3rd ed., 2017, https://lynchinginamerica.eji.org/report; see also Brandy Colbert, *Black Birds in the Sky* (New York: Balzer + Bray, 2021).

or too outspoken: Equal Justice Initiative, "Mary Turner, Pregnant, Lynched in Georgia for Publicly Criticizing Husband's Lynching," A History of Racial Injustice, https://calendar.eji.org/racial-injustice/may/19.

for owning property that white people wanted: Martha Park, "The Economics of Lynching in Memphis," MLK50, August 6, 2018, https://mlk50.com/2018/08/06/the-economics-of-lynching-in-memphis; Lynching Sites Project of Memphis, "The People's Grocery Lynchings," https://lynchingsitesmem

.org/lynching/peoples-grocery-lynchings-thomas-moss-will-stewart-calvin-mcdowell.

for attempting to collect their wages or other debts: Sydney Trent, "In Texas, a Struggle to Memorialize a Brutal Lynching as Resistance Grows to Teaching Historical Racism," *The Washington Post*, June 3, 2021, https://www.washingtonpost.com/history/2021/06/03/sherman-riot-texas-lynching-marker.

for asking for food: Martha Park, "The Economics of Lynching in Memphis," MLK50, August 6, 2018, https://mlk50.com/2018/08/06/the-economics-of-lynching-in-memphis.

often public occasions. Equal Justice Initiative, "Public Spectacle Lynchings," https://eji.org/news/history-racial-injustice-public-spectacle-lynchings.

advertised in advance: Roberta Smith, "Critic's Notebook; An Ugly Legacy Lives On, Its Glare Unsoftened by Age," *The New York Times*, January 13, 2000, https://www.nytimes.com/2000/01/13/books/critic-s-notebook-an-ugly-legacy-lives-on-its-glare-unsoftened-by-age.html.

"a black man, woman or child was murdered nearly once a week": Stewart E. Tolnay and E. M. Beck, *A Festival of Violence: An Analysis of Southern Lynchings, 1882–1930* (Champaign: University of Illinois Press, 1995), ix.

menace and intimidate: *Klan Warns Negro Voters*, Miami, Florida, May 3, 1939, photograph, Library of Congress, https://www.loc.gov/item/2005676212. The photo caption reads: "Masked Ku Klux Klan member riding in a car, holding noose outside window during a parade through an African American neighborhood of Miami on the night before a primary election."

PART 2: THE ACCOUNT

THE RULES OF INSTAGRAM

In April 2017, Instagram was reporting 700 million active users: Statista Research Department, "Number of Daily Active Instagram Users from October 2016 to September 2017," https://www.statista.com/statistics/657823/number-of-daily-active-instagram-users.

By June 2018, that figure had reached 1 billion: Josh Constine, "Instagram Hits 1 Billion Monthly Users, Up from 800M in September," *TechCrunch*, June 20, 2018, https://techcrunch.com/2018/06/20/instagram-1-billion-users/.

the app's estimated worth was over $100 billion: Emily McCormick, "Instagram Is Estimated to Be Worth More Than $100 Billion," *Bloomberg News*, June 25, 2018, https://www.bloomberg.com/news/articles/2018–06–25/value-of-facebook-s-instagram-estimated-to-top-100-billion#xj4y7vzkg.

Instagram had earmarked: Sheera Frenkel, Ryan Mac, and Mike Isaac, "Instagram Struggles with Fears of Losing Its 'Pipeline': Young Users," *The New York Times*, October 16, 2021, https://www.nytimes.com/2021/10/16/technology/instagram-teens.html.

FOLLOWERS

"model minority myth": Jennifer L. Young, Grace Li, Laura Golojuch, and Haedong Kim, "Asian Americans' Emerging Racial Identities and Reactions to Racial Tension in the United States," *Emerging Adulthood* (April 2022) 10(2): 342–353, https://doi.org/10.1177/21676968211051163.

PART 3: REVEALED

NOTHING'S GOING TO HAPPEN

blistering editorial: Ya Davis, "Cyberbullying Reemerges: Where Are You?," *The Cougar*, February 6, 2015.

as Ted Barone, who was then the school principal, admitted: Ted Barone, "Gender-Discrimination Through Cyberbullying—AHS Administration Response," *The Cougar*, February 6, 2015.

PART 4: UNDISCUSSED

THINGS THEY DIDN'T TALK ABOUT (2)

Izumizaki had been arrested the previous week: Matthias Gafne, "Albany: Police Conclude Investigation in Teacher James Izumizaki's Molestation Case," *The Mercury News*, March 13, 2013, https://www.mercurynews.com/2013/03/13/albany-police-conclude-investigation-in-teacher-james-izumizakis-molestation-case.

PART 5: INVESTIGATION

WHAT A GORILLA SAYS

Europeans told about Africans as far back as the 1600s: Wulf D. Hund, Charles W. Mills, and Silvia Sebastiani (eds.), *Simianization: Apes, Gender, Class, and Race* (Zürich: Lit Verlag, 2015).

a savage brute: Brent Staples, "The Racist Trope That Won't Die," *The New York Times*, June 17, 2018, https://www.nytimes.com/2018/06/17/opinion/roseanne-racism-blacks-apes.html.

"The whole argument in defense of slavery": Frederick Douglass, "The Claims of the Negro, Ethnologically Considered," in Nicholas Buccola (ed.), *The Essential Douglass: Selected Writings and Speeches* (Indianapolis: Hackett, 2016), 84.

stereotypes persist: Hannah Eko, "As a Black Woman, I'm Tired of Having to Prove My Womanhood," *BuzzFeed News*, February 27, 2018, https://www.buzzfeednews.com/article/hannaheko/aint-i-a-woman.

misogynoir: Moya Bailey and Trudy, "On Misogynoir: Citation, Erasure, and Plagiarism," *Feminist Media Studies* (2018) 18(4): 762–768, https://doi.org/10.1080/14680777.2018.1447395.

dating apps: Thomas McMullan, "Are the Algorithms That Power Dating Apps Racially Biased?," *Wired*, February 17, 2019, https://www.wired.co.uk/article/racial-bias-dating-apps; Sarah Adeyinka-Skold, "Dating in the Digital Age: Race, Gender, and Inequality" (PhD diss., University of Pennsylvania, 2020), Publicly Accessible Penn Dissertations, 3816, https://repository.upenn.edu/edissertations/3816.

less likely to be treated for pain: Vanessa Fabien, "My Body, My Pain: Listen to Me and All Black Women," *The Root*, April 16, 2017, https://www.theroot.com/my-body-my-pain-listen-to-me-and-all-black-women-1794332651.

adultification: The Georgetown Law Center on Poverty and Inequality, "Listening to Black Women and Girls: Lived Experiences of Adultification Bias," The Annie E. Casey Foundation, May 15, 2019, https://www.aecf.org/resources/listening-to-black-women-and-girls; Rebecca Epstein, Jamilia Blake, and Thalia González, "Girlhood Interrupted: The Erasure of Black Girls' Childhood," SSRN, June 27, 2017, https://ssrn.com/abstract=3000695.

PART 6: LAUGHING

FUNNY

Rosalind Wiseman: Interview with the author, April 30, 2021.

HOW DOES A JOKE BECOME FUNNY?

"The constant exchange": Jillian Guffy, "What Does It All Meme?," *The Cougar*, June 9, 2017.

POE'S LAW

Lindsay Schubiner: Interview with the author, June 11, 2020.

"non-ironic Nazism masquerading as ironic Nazism": Luke O'Brien, "The Making of an American Nazi," *The Atlantic*, December 2017, https://www.theatlantic.com/magazine/archive/2017/12/the-making-of-an-american-nazi/544119.

"The tone of the site": Ashley Feinberg, "This Is the Daily Stormer's Playbook," *Huffington Post*, December 13, 2017, https://www.huffpost.com/entry/daily-stormer-nazi-style-guide_n_5a2ece19e4b0ce3b344492f2.

far-right meme farms: Stephanie Mencimer, "'The Left Can't Meme': How Right-Wing Groups Are Training the Next Generation of Social Media Warriors," *Mother Jones*, April 2, 2019, https://www.motherjones.com/politics/2019/04/right-wing-groups-are-training-young-conservatives-to-win-the-next-meme-war.

originated on a tiny number of right-wing forums: Savvas Zannettou, Tristan Caulfield, Jeremy Blackburn, Emiliano De Cristofaro, Michael Sirivianos, et al., "On the Origins of Memes by Means of Fringe Web Communities," arXiv:1805.12512 [cs.SI], September 22, 2018, https://doi.org/10.48550/arXiv.1805.12512.

Brian Friedberg: Interview with the author, May 6, 2021.

The app iFunny: Ryan Broderick, "iFunny Has Become a Hub for White Nationalism," *BuzzFeed News*, August 15, 2019, https://www.buzzfeednews.com/article/ryanhatesthis/the-meme-app-ifunny-is-a-huge-hub-for-white-nationalists.

millions of views on TikTok: Ciarán O'Connor, *Hatescape: An In-Depth Analysis of Extremism and Hate Speech on TikTok* (Institute for Strategic Dialogue, 2021), https://www.politico.eu/wp-content/uploads/2021/08/24/ISD-TikTok-Hatescape-Report-August-2021.pdf.

had run into extremist content online: James Hawdon, "Perpetrators and Victims of Online Extremism: Status and Vulnerability," presented at *Les jeunes et l'incitation à la haine sur Internet: victimes, témoins, agresseurs? Comparaisons internationales*, Nice, France, January 24, 2017; Matthew Costello and James Hawdon, "Who Are the Online Extremists Among Us? Sociodemographic Characteristics, Social Networking, and Online Experiences of Those Who Produce Online Hate Materials," *Violence and Gender* (2018) 5(1): 55–60.

"saw hate words or symbols written in their schools": U.S. Government Accountability Office, *K-12 Education: Students' Experiences with Bullying, Hate Speech, Hate Crimes, and Victimization in Schools*, GAO-22–104341, November 24, 2021, https://www.gao.gov/products/gao-22–104341.

The algorithmic filter bubbles that shape all of our online experiences: Matthew Costello and James Hawdon, "Hate Speech in Online Spaces," in A. Bossler and T. Holt (eds.), *The Palgrave*

Handbook of International Cybercrime and Cyberdeviance (New York: Palgrave, 2020), 1397–1416, https://doi.org/10.1007/978-3-319-78440-3_60.

The more you interact with it, the more normal it begins to feel: "Deconstructing Online Hate," MediaSmarts, Centre for Digital and Media Literacy, https://mediasmarts.ca/online-hate/deconstructing-online-hate.

PART 7: JUSTICE

FOUR KINDS OF JUSTICE

A good discussion of the difference between punitive or "retributive" justice, restorative justice, and transformative justice can be found in a March 10, 2011, blog post by Howard Zehr at the Zehr Institute for Restorative Justice, https://emu.edu/now/restorative-justice/2011/03/10/restorative-or-transformative-justice.

THE MATRIX IS A GUIDE

A 2021 study by the American Institutes for Research: Christina LiCalsi, David Osher, and Paul Bailey, *An Empirical Examination of the Effects of Suspension and Suspension Severity on Behavioral and Academic Outcomes* (American Institutes for Research, 2021), https://www.air.org/sites/default/files/2021-08/NYC-Suspension-Effects-Behavioral-Academic-Outcomes-August-2021.pdf.

TARNISHED

"These guys deserve to be expelled": Email from former board member with the subject heading "They Must Be Expelled," April 1, 2017.

IT LIVES IN THE BODY

"hate crimes have a more destructive impact": Jessica Henderson Daniel, "Statement of APA President in Response to Shooting at Pittsburgh Synagogue," press release, American Psychological Association, October 28, 2018, https://www.apa.org/news/press/releases/2018/10/pittsburgh-shooting.

A comparison of hate crime victims: Paul Iganski, *Hate Crime and the City* (Bristol: The Policy Press, 2008), 12, 13, 82, 83.

people in Sacramento, California: Gregory M. Herek, J. Roy Gillis, and Jeanine C. Cogan, "Psychological Sequelae of Hate-Crime Victimization Among Lesbian, Gay, and Bisexual Adults," *Journal of Consulting and Clinical Psychology* (1999) 67(6): 945–951, https://doi.org/10.1037/0022-006X.67.6.945.

higher blood pressures: Nancy Krieger and Stephen Sidney, "Racial Discrimination and Blood Pressure: The CARDIA Study of Young Black and White Adults," *American Journal of Public Health* (1996) 86(10): 1370–1378, https://pubmed.ncbi.nlm.nih.gov/8876504.

shorter life spans: David H. Chae, Yijie Wang, Connor D. Martz, Natalie Slopen, Tiffany Yip, et al., "Racial Discrimination and Telomere Shortening Among African Americans: The Coronary Artery Risk Development in Young Adults (CARDIA) Study," *Health Psychology* (2020) 39(3): 209–219, https://doi.org/10.1037/hea0000832; Vickie M. Mays, Susan D. Cochran, and Namdi W. Barnes, "Race, Race-Based Discrimination, and Health Outcomes Among African Americans," *Annual Review of Psychology* (2007) 58: 201–225, https://www.ncbi.nlm.nih.gov/pmc/articles/PMC4181672.

premature aging at the cellular level: Mary-Francis Winters, *Black Fatigue: How Racism Erodes the Mind, Body, and Spirit* (Oakland, CA: Berrett-Koehler, 2020), 74.

give birth prematurely: Paola Scommegna, "High Premature Birth Rates Among U.S. Black Women May Reflect the Stress of Racism and Health and Economic Factors," Population Reference Bureau, January 21, 2021, https://www.prb.org/resources/high-premature-birth-rates-among-u-s-black-women-may-reflect-the-stress-of-racism-and-health-and-economic-factors/#:~:text=Just%20over%2014%25%20of%20Black,who%20calls%20them%20%E2%80%9Calarming.%E2%80%9D.

feeling excluded or rejected: Elitsa Dermendzhiyska, "Rejection Kills," *Aeon*, April 30, 2019, https://aeon.co/essays/health-warning-social-rejection-doesnt-only-hurt-it-kills.

Older Black women who contend with racism: Patricia Coogan, Karin Schon, Shanshan Li, Yvette Cozier, Traci Bethea, et al., "Experiences of Racism and Subjective Cognitive Function in African American Women," *Alzheimer's and Dementia: Diagnosis, Assessment and Disease Monitoring* (2020) 12(1): e12067, https://doi.org/10.1002/dad2.12067.

linked the health effects of racism to the impact of shame: Sally S. Dickerson, Tara L. Gruenewald, and Margaret E. Kemeny, "When the Social Self Is Threatened: Shame, Physiology, and Health," *Journal of Personality* (2004) 72(6): 1191–1216, https://doi.org/10.1111/j.1467–6494.2004.00295.x.

focused on feelings of powerlessness: Eve Ekman, "Power Sickness," *Greater Good Magazine*, December 1, 2007, https://greatergood.berkeley.edu/article/item/power_sickness.

the way feeling powerless affects baboons: Mark Shwartz, "Robert Sapolsky Discusses Physiological Effects of Stress," *Stanford*

News, March 7, 2007, https://news.stanford.edu/news/2007/march7/sapolskysr-030707.html.

THE BYSTANDER EFFECT

a thirty-seven-year-old man died on a grassy traffic island: Heather Knight, "'Guy Lay Dead Here and No One Noticed': What Happened to Supposedly Compassionate San Francisco?," *San Francisco Chronicle*, February 23, 2021, https://www.sfchronicle.com/bayarea/heatherknight/article/Guy-lay-dead-there-and-no-one-noticed-What-15974081.php.

the bystander effect: Ruud Hortensius and Beatrice de Gelder, "From Empathy to Apathy: The Bystander Effect Revisited," *Current Directions in Psychological Science* (2018) 27(4): 249–256, https://doi.org/10.1177/0963721417749653.

"diffusion of responsibility": Bibb Latane and John M. Darley, "Group Inhibition of Bystander Intervention in Emergencies," *Journal of Personality and Social Psychology* (1968) 10(3): 215–221, https://doi.org/10.1037/h0026570.

people are more likely to intervene if: Peter Fischer, Joachim I. Krueger, Tobias Greitemeyer, Claudia Vogrincic, Andreas Kastenmüller, et al., "The Bystander-Effect: A Meta-Analytic Review on Bystander Intervention in Dangerous and Non-Dangerous Emergencies," *Psychological Bulletin* (2011) 137(4): 517–537, https://doi.org/10.1037/a0023304.

particularly prone to the bystander effect: Hana Machackova, Lenka Dedkova, and Katerina Mezulanikova, "Brief Report: The Bystander Effect in Cyberbullying Incidents," *Journal of Adolescence* (2015) 43(1): 96–99, https://doi.org/10.1016/j.adolescence.2015.05.010; Sarah E. Jones, "Examining Cyberbullying Bystander Behavior Using a Multiple Goals Perspective" (master's thesis,

University of Kentucky, 2014), Theses and Dissertations—Communication, https://uknowledge.uky.edu/comm_etds/22.

Rosalind Wiseman: Interview with the author, April 30, 2021.

PUNISHMENT AND ACCOUNTABILITY

Ashlee George: Interview with the author, July 9, 2020.

Aishatu Yusuf: Interview with the author, October 26, 2020. To read the full conversation with Aishatu Yusuf, please visit accountablebook.com/yusuf-interview.

PART 8: SEEDS OF DESTRUCTION

SHAME

"It's holding something we've done": Brené Brown, "Shame vs. Guilt," January 15, 2013, https://brenebrown.com/articles/2013/01/15/shame-v-guilt.

inherently bad for society: Kate Klonick, "Re-Shaming the Debate: Social Norms, Shame, and Regulation in an Internet Age," *Maryland Law Review* (2016) 75(4), http://dx.doi.org/10.2139/ssrn.2638693.

"There is no rhyme or limit to the terms the public may impose": James Q. Whitman, "What Is Wrong with Inflicting Shame Sanctions?" *The Yale Law Journal* (1998) 107(4): 1055–92, https://doi.org/10.2307/797205.

University of Chicago law professor Eric Posner: Eric A. Posner, *Law and Social Norms* (Cambridge: Harvard University Press, 2000).

people are more likely to turn around their behavior: John Braithwaite, Valerie Braithwaite, and Eliza Ahmed,

"Reintegrative Shaming" in Stuart Henry and Mark M. Lanier (eds.), *The Essential Criminology Reader* (Boulder: Westview Press, 2005), 286–295; Eliza Ahmed, Nathan Harris, John Braithwaite, and Valerie Braithwaite, *Shame Management Through Reintegration* (Melbourne: Cambridge University Press, 2001), 230–235, 236–239, 256, 317–318.

"Calling out happens": Loretta J. Ross, "Speaking Up Without Tearing Down," *Teaching Tolerance* (Spring 2019) 61: 19–22, https://www.learningforjustice.org/magazine/spring-2019/speaking-up-without-tearing-down; Jessica Bennett, "What If Instead of Calling People Out, We Called Them In?," *The New York Times*, November 19, 2020, https://www.nytimes.com/2020/11/19/style/loretta-ross-smith-college-cancel-culture.html.

PART 10: WHY CAN'T YOU JUST GET OVER IT?

THE ROLE OF ADULTS

Rosalind Wiseman: Interview with the author, April 30, 2021.

LAWSUIT

Washington Post *headline*: Derek Hawkins, "Does the First Amendment Protect 'Liking' a Racist Instagram Post? Some Calif. Students Say It Does," *The Washington Post*, May 5, 2017, https://www.washingtonpost.com/news/morning-mix/wp/2017/05/05/does-the-first-amendment-protect-liking-a-racist-instagram-post-some-disciplined-calif-students-are-suing-to-find-out/?outputType=amp.

FREE SPEECH/HATE SPEECH

"Censoring so-called hate speech": American Civil Liberties Union, "Freedom of Expression: ACLU Position Paper," https://www.aclu.org/other/freedom-expression-aclu-position-paper.

In 2022, nineteen states had laws or rules: Olivia B. Waxman, "Anti-'Critical Race Theory' Laws Are Working. Teachers Are Thinking Twice About How They Talk About Race," *Time*, June 30, 2022, https://time.com/6192708/critical-race-theory-teachers-racism/. See also Cathryn Strout and Thomas Wilburn, "CRT Map: Efforts to Restrict Teaching Racism and Bias Have Multipled Across the U.S.," *Chalkbeat*, February 1, 2022, https://www.chalkbeat.org/22525983/map-critical-race-theory-legislation-teaching-racism.

"a sweeping crusade for content- and viewpoint-based state censorship": PEN America, "Educational Gag Orders: Legislative Restrictions on the Freedom to Read, Learn, and Teach," https://pen.org/wp-content/uploads/2022/02/PEN_EducationalGagOrders_01–18–22-compressed.pdf.

MOST HATED

Kyle McClerkins: Interview with the author, October 27, 2020.

THE *TINKER* TEST

the U.S. Supreme Court issued a decision: *Tinker v. Des Moines Independent Community School District*, 393 U.S. 503 (1969), https://supreme.justia.com/cases/federal/us/393/503.

CHARLOTTESVILLE

On August 11 and 12: Debbie Lord, "What Happened at Charlottesville: Looking Back on the Rally That Ended in Death," *Atlanta Journal-Constitution*, August 10, 2018, https://www.ajc.com/news/national/what-happened-charlottesville-looking-back-the-anniversary-the-deadly-rally/fPpnLrbAtbxSwNI9BEy93K; "Two Years Ago, They

Marched in Charlottesville. Where Are They Now?," Anti-Defamation League Blog, August 8, 2019, https://www.adl.org/blog/two-years-ago-they-marched-in-charlottesville-where-are-they-now.

Many in the white power movement believe: Anti-Defamation League, "'The Great Replacement': An Explainer," April 19, 2022, https://www.adl.org/resources/backgrounders/the-great-replacement-an-explainer; Eli Saslow, *Rising Out of Hatred: The Awakening of a Former White Nationalist* (New York: Knopf Doubleday, 2018), 33.

sentenced to life in prison: Laurel Wamsley and Bobby Allyn, "Neo-Nazi Who Killed Charlottesville Protester Is Sentenced to Life in Prison," NPR.org, June 28, 2019, https://www.npr.org/2019/06/28/736915323/neo-nazi-who-killed-charlottesville-protester-is-sentenced-to-life-in-prison.

had posted a meme: Jazmine Ulloa, "A Grisly Blueprint of Terror," *Boston Globe*, November 1, 2021.

traffic to the white nationalist website Stormfront: Eli Saslow, *Rising Out of Hatred: The Awakening of a Former White Nationalist* (New York: Knopf Doubleday, 2018), 282.

PART 11: SCIENCE

SCIENTIFIC RACISM

a once-neutral term that has been co-opted: Aaron Panofsky, Kushan Dasgupta, and Nicole Iturriaga, "How White Nationalists Mobilize Genetics: From Genetic Ancestry and Human Biodiversity to Counterscience and Metapolitics," *American Journal of Physical Anthropology* (2021) 175(2): 387–398, https://pubmed.ncbi.nlm.nih.gov/32986847.

James Watson: Amy Harmon, "James Watson Had a Chance to Salvage His Reputation on Race. He Made Things Worse," *The New York Times*, January 1, 2019, https://www.nytimes.com/2019/01/01/science/watson-dna-genetics-race.html.

bigoted and scientifically questionable statements: Josh Gabbatiss, "James Watson: The Most Controversial Statements Made by the Father of DNA," *Independent*, January 13, 2019, https://www.independent.co.uk/news/science/james-watson-racism-sexism-dna-race-intelligence-genetics-double-helix-a8725556.html.

most prestigious population geneticists: Graham Coop, Michael B. Eisen, Rasmus Nielsen, Molly Przeworski, Noah Rosenberg, et al., "Letters: 'A Troublesome Inheritance,'" *The New York Times Book Review*, August 8, 2014, https://cehg.stanford.edu/letter-from-population-geneticists; "ASHG Denounces Attempts to Link Genetics and Racial Supremacy," *American Journal of Human Genetics* (2018) 103(5): 636, https://doi.org/10.1016/j.ajhg.2018.10.011.

"the forbidden knowledge discourse": Reanne Frank, "Forbidden or Forsaken? The (Mis)Use of a Forbidden Knowledge Argument in Research on Race, DNA, and Disease," in Keith Wailoo, Alondra Nelson, and Catherine Lee (eds.), *Genetics and the Unsettled Past: The Collision of DNA, Race, and History* (New Brunswick, NJ: Rutgers University Press, 2012), 315–324, https://doi.org/10.36019/9780813553368–020.

One of the first people to divide humans: Isabelle Charmantier, "Linneaus and Race," The Linnean Society of London, September 3, 2020, https://www.linnean.org/learning/who-was-linnaeus/linnaeus-and-race; Brittany Kenyon-Flatt, "How Scientific Taxonomy Constructed the Myth of Race," *Sapiens*, March 19, 2021, https://www.sapiens.org/biology/race-scientific-taxonomy.

Switzerland was at that moment: Noele Illien, "Banking and Slavery: Switzerland Examines Its Colonial Conscience," *The Guardian*, November 19, 2020, https://www.theguardian.com/world/2020/nov/19/banking-slavery-switzerland-examines-its-colonial-conscience.

Ann Morning: Interview with the author, January 16, 2020.

each of these scientific breakthroughs: Ann Morning, "Scientific Racism Redux? The Many Lives of a Troublesome Idea: A Troublesome Inheritance Indeed," *Du Bois Review: Social Science Research on Race* (2015) 2(1): 187–199, https://doi.org/10.1017/S1742058X1500003X.

we talk about race all the time: Ann Morning, *The Nature of Race: How Scientists Think and Teach About Human Difference* (Berkeley: University of California Press, 2011).

biological race was taught in science class: Michael Schulson, "Should 'Race' Be Taught in High School Biology?," *Undark*, September 12, 2018, https://undark.org/2018/09/12/biology-textbooks-race-high-school.

Brian Donovan: Interview with the author, June 12, 2020.

Any two humans share 99.9 percent of their DNA: "Genetics vs. Genomics Fact Sheet," National Human Genome Research Institute, https://www.genome.gov/about-genomics/fact-sheets/Genetics-vs-Genomics.

dark and light skin color: Ed Yong, "The Ancient Origins of Both Light and Dark Skin," *The Atlantic*, October 12, 2017, https://www.theatlantic.com/science/archive/2017/10/a-brief-history-of-the-genes-that-color-our-skin/542694; Nicholas G. Crawford, Derek E. Kelly, Matthew E. B. Hansen, Marcia H. Beltrame, Shoahua Fan, et al., "Loci Associated with Skin Pigmentation

Identified in African Populations," *Science* (2017) 358(6365): 1–25, https://doi.org/10.1126/science.aan8433.

Within the tiny sliver of DNA: Noah A. Rosenberg, "A Population-Genetic Perspective on the Similarities and Differences Among Worldwide Human Populations," *Human Biology* (2011) 83(6): 659–684, https://doi.org/10.3378/027.083.0601.

Genetic differences between groups of people: Adam Rutherford, *How to Argue with a Racist: What Our Genes Do (and Don't) Say About Human Difference* (New York: The Experiment, 2020).

Donovan has tested student beliefs: Brian Donovan, "Framing the Genetics Curriculum for Social Justice: An Experimental Exploration of How the Biology Curriculum Influences Beliefs About Racial Difference," *Science Education* (2016) 100(3), https://doi.org/10.1002/sce.21221.

DNA, IQ, AND THE NFL

About half of a person's cognitive ability: Valerie S. Knopik, Jenae M. Neiderhiser, John C. DeFries, and Robert Plomin, *Behavioral Genetics*, 7th ed. (New York: Worth, 2017); Adam Rutherford, *How to Argue with a Racist: What Our Genes Do (and Don't) Say About Human Difference* (New York: The Experiment, 2020), 169ff.

More than five hundred different genes: Ian J. Deary, W. Johnson, and L. M. Houlihan, "Genetic Foundations of Human Intelligence," *Human Genetics* (2009) 126(1): 215–232, https://doi.org/10.1007/s00439-009-0655-4.

the Flynn effect: Adam Rutherford, *How to Argue with a Racist: What Our Genes Do (and Don't) Say About Human Difference* (New York: The Experiment 2020), 163–164.

a Washington Post *investigation found*: Will Hobson, "How 'Race-Norming' Was Built into the NFL Concussion Settlement," *The Washington Post*, August 2, 2021, https://www.washingtonpost.com/sports/2021/08/02/race-norming-nfl-concussion-settlement; Will Hobson, "'Race-Norming' Kept Former NFL Players from Dementia Diagnoses. Their Families Want Answers," *The Washington Post*, September 29, 2021, https://www.washingtonpost.com/sports/2021/09/29/nfl-concussion-settlement-race-norming; Will Hobson, "NFL, Former Players Agree to Remove 'Race-Norming' from Concussion Settlement Evaluations," *The Washington Post*, October 20, 2021, https://www.washingtonpost.com/sports/2021/10/20/nfl-players-race-norming-concussions.

PART 13: ALMOST OUT THE DOOR

KILL OUR DEMONS

J. Cole had said "KOD" had three meanings: Latifah Muhammad, "J. Cole Debuts 'KOD' Trailer, Explains Meaning of Album Title," *Vibe*, April 19, 2019, https://www.vibe.com/music/music-news/j-cole-album-trailer-k-o-d-meaning-580858.

PART 14: RECKONING

TWEET ME THE RECEIPTS

increase engagement by increasing conflict: Cathy O'Neil, *The Shame Machine: Who Profits in the New Age of Humiliation* (New York: Crown, 2022), 95–101; Steve Rathje, Jay J. Van Bavel, and Sander van der Linden, "Out-Group Animosity Drives Engagement on Social Media," *Proceedings of the National Academy of Sciences of the United States of America* (2021) 118(26): e2024292118, https://www.pnas.org/doi/10.1073/pnas.2024292118#con1.

PART 15: MAKING IT THROUGH

SOME NUMBERS: ONLINE AND REAL-WORLD HATE AMONG YOUNG PEOPLE

who saw hate words or symbols: U.S. Government Accountability Office, *K-12 Education: Students' Experiences with Bullying, Hate Speech, Hate Crimes, and Victimization in Schools*, GAO-22–104341P, November 24, 2021, https://www.gao.gov/products/gao-22–104341.

who have personally been targeted by online hate: Matthew Costello and James Hawdon, "Hate Speech in Online Spaces," in A. Bossler and T. Holt (eds.), *The Palgrave Handbook of International Cybercrime and Cyberdeviance* (New York: Palgrave, 2020), 1397–1416, https://doi.org/10.1007/978-3-319-78440-3_60.

who have personally created online hate: Matthew Costello and James Hawdon, "Who Are the Online Extremists Among Us? Sociodemographic Characteristics, Social Networking, and Online Experiences of Those Who Produce Online Hate Materials," *Violence and Gender* (2018) 5(1): 55–60, https://www.liebertpub.com/doi/abs/10.1089/vio.2017.0048.

who have encountered online hate / who encountered that hate accidentally / that focuses on race or ethnicity: Ashley Reichelmann, James Hawdon, Matt Costello, John Ryan, Catherine Blaya, et al., "Hate Knows No Boundaries: Online Hate in Six Nations," *Deviant Behavior* (2020), 42(9): 1–12, https://doi.org/10.1080/01639625.2020.1722337.

who were bullied because of some aspect of their identity / were targeted because of their race: U.S. Government Accountability Office, *K–12 Education: Students' Experiences with Bullying, Hate Speech, Hate Crimes, and Victimization in Schools*,

GAO-22–104341, November 24, 2021, https://www.gao.gov/products/gao-22–104341.

the average Black teenager encounters racial discrimination: Devin English, Sharon F. Lambert, Brendesha M. Tynes, Lisa Bowleg, Maria Cecilia Zea, et al., "Daily Multidimensional Racial Discrimination Among Black US American Adolescents," *Journal of Applied Developmental Psychology* (2020) 66: 101068, https://doi.org/10.1016/j.appdev.2019.101068.